DIALOGUE WITH HEIDEGGER

Studies in Continental Thought

John Sallis, EDITOR

Dialogue with Heidegger

Greek Philosophy

Jean Beaufret

Translated by Mark Sinclair

Indiana University Press

BLOOMINGTON AND INDIANAPOLIS

This book is a publication of

Indiana University Press
601 North Morton Street
Bloomington, IN 47404-3797 USA

http://iupress.indiana.edu

Telephone orders   800-842-6796
Fax orders   812-855-7931
Orders by e-mail   iuporder@indiana.edu

The paper used in this publication meets the minimum requirements of American
National Standard for Information Sciences—Permanence of Paper for Printed Library
Materials, ANSI Z39.48-1984.

Manufactured in the United States of America

Library of Congress Cataloging-in-Publication Data

Beaufret, Jean.
[Dialogue avec Heidegger. English]
Dialogue with Heidegger : Greek philosophy / Jean Beaufret ;
translated by Mark Sinclair.
p. cm. — (Studies in Continental thought)
Includes bibliographical references and index.
ISBN 0-253-34730-0 (cloth : alk. paper)
1. Heidegger, Martin, 1889–1976. 2. Philosophy—History. I. Title. II. Series.
B3279.H49B3713 2006
193—dc22
2005034521

1 2 3 4 5   11 10 09 08 07 06

Contents

Translator's Introduction

Jean Beaufret is perhaps best known for having posed the questions to which Martin Heidegger responds in December 1946 in a letter addressed to the Frenchman that will achieve world renown as the "Letter on Humanism." Yet these questions, which were hastily written in a Parisian café so as to be delivered by a friend ready to leave for Freiburg, constitute but one early and improvised moment of a profound philosophical engagement with Heidegger's thinking that endured until Beaufret's death, six years after that of Heidegger, in 1982. This engagement came to its fullest fruition with the publication of the four volumes of Beaufret's *Dialogue avec Heidegger*, the first of which is translated here.[1]

Born in la Creuse in 1907, Beaufret was accepted into the Ecole Normale Supérieure in 1928 upon completing his preparatory classes (*khagne*) at the lycée Louis-le-Grand in Paris. After his military service and a year in Berlin in 1930–31, he passed the *agrégation*, the national competitive examination, in philosophy in 1933 and taught in Guéret, Auxerre, and Alexandria before the war. During the war he was taken prisoner in the "debacle" of 1940, only to escape and resume teaching in Grenoble and then in Lyon. Notwithstanding a role in the Resistance, Beaufret spent the rest of the war studying phenomenology. It was in 1940 that he decided, after a discussion with Maurice Merleau-Ponty, to study Husserl and then Heidegger, rather than to develop his previous studies of German Idealism and Marx; and as he would recount later, the day of the first Allied landings in Normandy was the day that he felt he had come to understand something of Heidegger's *Sein und Zeit*.

Some months before formulating his questions for Heidegger, in September 1946, Beaufret had paid his first visit to Heidegger in Todt-nauberg. The Frenchman described himself as having found everything he was looking for in the author of *Sein und Zeit*, while Heidegger was struck by the frankness and freedom of Beaufret. Heidegger was also impressed by two of Beaufret's articles concerning Heidegger's work that had been published in 1945 in the Lyon-based journal *Confluences*. These two articles had appeared as the third and fourth of a series of six entitled "On Existentialism," which offered accounts of the thought of Kierkegaard and Sartre, in addition to that of Heidegger, and of the relationship between existentialism and Marxism. The possibility of a synthesis of Sartrean existentialism and Marxism was, in fact, the most immediate of Beaufret's concerns in this period, and yet the two articles that Heidegger had consulted allowed him to remark, as he would later often do, that the Frenchman had "read him well." A close personal and philosophical friendship subsequently developed between them.

Heidegger evidently perceived in Beaufret the possibility of the dialogue with French philosophy for which he had been searching before the war. The need for this dialogue had only become more pressing with the French Military Government's decision in October 1945 to bar Heidegger from teaching, and as he wrote in response to Beaufret's first letter in November of the same year: "Profound thought requires, in addition to writing and reading, the *sunousia* of discussion and of the work that is teaching and being taught."[2] Beaufret was perhaps an ideal French representative in such a discussion or dialogue. Not only was he a reader of exceptional acuity, but he also occupied a position of no small influence within the tumult of postwar Parisian intellectual life: teaching at the Ecole Normale Supérieure from 1946 to 1962, he enjoyed the friendship of, among others, Jean Hyppolite, Maurice Merleau-Ponty, Louis Althusser, and Jacques Lacan. Beaufret used this influence to facilitate the reception of Heidegger's later work in France. In 1955, with Kostas Axelos, he organized the conference "What Is Philosophy?" at Cerisy, Normandy, in which Heidegger was welcomed by the leading lights of French philosophy. During this time, at Heidegger's behest, Beaufret also arranged for him to meet the poet René Char and the painter Georges Braque. In time, he even acted as a spokesman for Heidegger; it was Beaufret who read, for example, "The End of Philosophy and the Task of Thinking" in his own translation to the surely bemused delegates of a UNESCO conference on Kierkegaard in Paris.

The publication of Beaufret's 1947 article "Heidegger and the Problem of Truth"³ indicated that he had decided to set himself to the long task of studying Heidegger seriously. At a certain remove from both existentialism and Marxism, he would henceforth dedicate his philosophical work to studying the history of philosophy with the aim of elucidating Heidegger's still misunderstood questioning of being. Such a decision, "perilously original at the time," was one for which his "university career very happily paid the price" (*Dialogue* IV, p. 81). Beaufret never submitted a doctoral thesis, apparently much to Heidegger's chagrin, but he was above all, and by all accounts, a pedagogue of remarkable talent.⁴ His teaching after the war in Paris at the E.N.S., the lycée Henri IV, and the lycée Condorcet, which was seldom concerned directly with Heidegger but rather with the history of philosophy from a Heideggerian perspective, left its mark on a generation of students that included Jean-François Courtine, François Fédier, Dominique Janicaud, Jean-Luc Marion, and Emmanuel Martineau, to name but a few. It was with many of these students that Beaufret organized much of the translation and dissemination of Heidegger's work in France. Without Beaufret, then, the peculiar history of Heidegger in France would not be what we know it to be today. What is more, without understanding his work and its influence, it is impossible to comprehend the nature of the controversy that arose in France in 1987 with the translation of Victor Farias's *Heidegger and Nazism*,⁵ a text which challenged Heidegger's account — one that Beaufret had accepted — of his own activities in the 1930s.

The approach to Heidegger's thinking inherent in Beaufret's teaching is manifest in the four volumes of the *Dialogue*, which bear the titles *Philosophie grecque* (*Greek Philosophy*, 1973), *Philosophie moderne* (*Modern Philosophy*, 1973), *Approche de Heidegger* (*Approach to Heidegger*, 1974), and *Le chemin de Heidegger* (*Heidegger's Path*, 1985). Only in the third volume does Beaufret turn explicitly to the work and texts of Heidegger. In the first two he is concerned instead to read the history of philosophy from the perspectives opened up by Heidegger's questioning of being. In this way the essays that constitute the volumes of the *Dialogue* seek to enact an original repetition of Heidegger's thinking, one that issues from another language and culture. The erudition of this repetition is often brilliant, replete as the essays are with references to poets and artists such as Baudelaire and Braque, to philosophers such as Comte and Pascal, and to scholars such as Pierre Aubenque and Etienne Gilson. Allied to its polemical force and poetic resolution, the erudition of the *Dialogue* allows it to stand both as an essential supplement to Heidegger's work and as a vital study of the history of philosophy in its own right.

x

The entirety of the first volume of the *Dialogue* is translated here, whose foreword consists of a letter that Beaufret wrote to Heidegger for his eightieth birthday in 1969. The letter offers a belated response to a short text that Heidegger had published in 1937, *Wege zur Aussprache*,[6] which attempted to instigate a dialogue between French and German philosophy. This letter is followed by six essays written between 1956 and 1973:

"The Birth of Philosophy" — Serving as an introduction to the volume, this essay seeks to apprehend the specificity of philosophy, and of the Greek thinking that precedes the advent of philosophy proper in the work of Plato, as a questioning of being. It thus takes up Heidegger's attempts to provide a 'birth certificate' of philosophy in showing how its concepts do not have their 'place of birth', as Kant metaphorically supposed, in an a-historical human faculty, but rather in ancient Greece, and in the mode of questioning that was instituted there. The essay was first published by the Presses du Massif Central in 1968 and subsequently in *Modern Miscellany: Festschrift for Eugène Vinaver* in 1969 (ed. T. E. Lawrenson, F. E. Sutcliffe, and G. F. A. Gadoffre [Manchester: Manchester University Press and New York: Barnes & Noble]).

"Heraclitus and Parmenides" — Without once referring explicitly to Heidegger, this essay develops the latter's attempts to overturn the still prevalent account of Parmenides and Heraclitus as articulating opposing concepts of being and movement in the early stages of Greek thinking. On this traditional account Parmenides would deny movement with his doctrine of being, whereas Heraclitus would deny being with a doctrine of becoming. Beaufret shows, on the one hand, that if the words 'everything flows' are to be attributed to Heraclitus, then these words have to be understood in the context of his thinking of *fire* and *phusis* (nature) as the heart and the possibility of all polemic or contrariety, and thus of all movement. On the other hand, the essay argues that Parmenides does not yet condemn the world of movement as a world of pure illusion. If the apparent world seems to bear no discredit in the second half of the Poem, after having been counter-posed to the truth of being in the first half, then this is because truth is not yet a world apart from the empirical world, as Plato will have it, but rather the horizon of being in and through which things are in movement. An early version of the essay was published in *Botteghe Obscure*, Rome, no. 25, 1960.

"Reading Parmenides" — This reading of Parmenides' Poem was presented to the actors of the Groupe de théâtre antique de la Sorbonne in March 1967, twelve years after the publication of Beaufret's study *Le poème de Parmenides* by the Presses Universitaires de France. The reading presents a more extended version of the argument concerning the Poem articulated in "Heraclitus and Parmenides." In its introduction Beaufret presents an illuminating survey of the different interpretations offered in the late nineteenth and twentieth centuries concerning the Poem, showing how Heidegger's interpretation, already signaled in a footnote to *Sein und Zeit*, departs from that of Karl Reinhardt.

"Zeno"—A first version of this short article appeared in *Les philosophes célèbres* (Paris: Mazenod, 1956), a volume edited by Maurice Merleau-Ponty; in it Beaufret situates Zeno's arguments concerning movement within the history of Greek thinking. Developing the ideas of Auguste Diès and Theodor Gomperz, Beaufret argues that Zeno is less a faithful defender of the Parmenidian thesis concerning the nonbeing of movement, as he is held to be in Plato's *Parmenides*, than he is the master of a dialectical technique that could turn against the thesis of 'immobilism' itself. Zeno would be but a skeptic, if not a sophist, who shows only that the adversaries of Parmenides are equally incapable as he is of accounting for the fact of movement.

"A Note on Plato and Aristotle"—Perhaps Beaufret's tongue was firmly in his cheek when he gave such a title to an extended essay that attempts to ascertain, first, the transformation that Plato's *eidetic* determination of being effects on earlier Greek thinking, and, second, the nature of Aristotle's challenge to Plato's philosophy. The 'note' opposes any interpretation of Aristotle's thinking as resulting from a penchant for the concrete and the empirical; Aristotle does not simply assert the primacy of 'concrete things' in relation to their *eidos*, for his conception of the 'subject' (*to hupokeimenon*), with which he attempts to rein in Platonism, is a thinking within which resonates the difference between beings and being. In this way Beaufret counters the arguments of France's greatest twentieth-century scholar of medieval philosophy, Etienne Gilson, according to which the work of Saint Thomas would represent philosophical progress in relation to Aristotle insofar as it articulates a veritable thinking of the being or existence of things.

"*Energeia* and *Actus*"—This essay offers an extended historical reflection that develops Heidegger's argument according to which the translation of the Greek *energeia* by the Latin *actus* is nothing less than an event in which "with one blow the Greek world was toppled."[7]

The translation or transmission of the Greek by the Latin involves the interpretation of Aristotle as a thinker of the *causa efficiens* (efficient causality), and thus the essay also develops Heidegger's claim that "Aristotle's doctrine does not know the cause that this name designates, any more than it employs a corresponding Greek term."[8] Beaufret shows that both medieval philosophy and students of it such as Gilson distance themselves unknowingly from the Greek beginnings of philosophy as a result of the transformation that *energeia* has endured in any Latinate thinking of actuality.

To these essays that constitute the first volume of the *Dialogue*, I have added two essays from the fourth volume that was edited by Claude Roëls and published posthumously in 1985. Both essays merited inclusion in this translation since they quite seamlessly extend Beaufret's reading of Aristotle. These are the following:

"The Enigma of Z" — First published in 1976 in *Savoir, faire, espérer: les limites de la raison* (Brussels: Publications des Facultés Universitaires Saint-Louis), this essay engages with Rudolf Boehm's innovative reading of Aristotle's *Metaphysics* in *Das Grundlegende und das Wesentliche* (The Hague: Martinus Nijhoff, 1965).[9] Boehm attempts to dismantle centuries of scholarship by arguing that Book Z, properly understood, presents an account of the radical insufficiency of the 'subject', *to hupokeimenon,* as a determination of being as *ousia.* This argument hinges on a revision of Z's third chapter, wherein Aristotle has traditionally been understood to assert the primacy of the 'subject' for ontological inquiry, subdividing it in terms of matter, form, and the combination of the two: for Boehm, it is not the 'subject' that is subdivided in this way, but rather *ousia* itself, and recognizing this would allow us to take much more seriously than we have heretofore Aristotle's subsequent statement concerning the insufficiency of the 'subject' as a determination of *ousia.* In examining these arguments Beaufret has two main concerns: first, to underline that if *Metaphysics* Z renders problematic the assertion of the 'subject' as *ousia* in the primary sense in the *Categories,* then this problem is a function of the difference between the categorical and the techno-poetic determination of being. It might be said, following a recent Anglophone commentator, that the problem is a function of *Aristotle's Two Systems,*[10] but Beaufret shows that it relates to the radically *unsystematic* nature of his thinking. Second, Beaufret counter-poses Boehm's arguments concerning *to hupokeimenon* to those of Heidegger, which, in stressing the verbal sense of the Greek participle form, seek to show that it does not simply denominate an ontic 'core' of beings. The essay demonstrates how both approaches, each in its own way, allow us to apprehend more in the work of Aristotle than an ancient 'metaphysics of subjectivity'.

"Aristotle and Tragedy" — Originally delivered at a conference on Aristotle organized by UNESCO in Paris in 1978, this brief essay announces a double-headed thesis concerning the account of tragedy in the *Poetics:* on the one hand, the account of tragedy according to the idea of the 'purging' of emotions derives from Euripidean tragedy, oriented as the latter is toward producing affects in the spectator; on the other hand, Aristotle goes back from Euripides to Sophocles and Aeschylus in stating that "the principle and the soul, as it were, of tragedy is myth." Myth would be more proper to the tragedies of Sophocles and Aeschylus than those of Euripides, since the latter has already begun to transform Greek myths, and Beaufret concludes in reflecting on the essence of Greek myth itself.

Without wanting to transform the translation into a critical edition, I have furnished many of the bibliographical references which are lacking in Beaufret's original text. Throughout the translation my occasional notes are indicated by the abbreviation T.N., whereas those of Roëls in the last two essays are indicated by E.N. In all of the essays, many of which were presented orally, I have sought to maintain, within the limits of the less precise syntactical rigors of the English language, something of the singularity of Beaufret's French prose, which is the work of a great stylist for some, but, and as the author himself remarks in good cheer within "Reading Parmenides," precious and otiose for others.

I would like to thank those who, in some form or another, have had a hand in this translation: Mike Garfield and Ullrich Haase at Manchester Metropolitan University and Julien Abriel in Paris. For having supported the project when it was but a vague idea, I am indebted to Miguel de Beistegui, Françoise Dastur, and, finally, Dominique Janicaud, whose philosophical generosity will always remain as an example for me.

Abbreviations

HZW	*Holzwege,* Frankfurt am Main: Klostermann, 1950
ID	*Identität und Differenz,* Pfullingen: Neske, 1957
KM	*Kant und das Problem der Metaphysik,* Klostermann, 1951
N I & *N* II	*Nietzsche* (2 vols.), Neske, 1961
PL	*Platons Lehre von der Wahrheit, mit einem Brief über den 'Humanismus',* Bern: Francke, 1947
SG	*Der Satz vom Grund,* Neske, 1957
SZ	*Sein und Zeit,* Tübingen: Niemeyer, 1927
US	*Unterwegs zur Sprache,* Neske, 1959
VA	*Vorträge und Aufsätze,* Neske, 1954
WD	*Was heisst Denken?,* Niemeyer, 1954
WM	*Was ist Metaphysik?,* Klostermann, 1949
ZSD	*Zur Sache des Denkens,* Niemeyer, 1969

Letter to Martin Heidegger for His Eightieth Birthday
The 26th September 1969

A little over thirty years ago—it was two years before the Second World War—a few pages of yours appeared within a volume of essays. They are still unknown today, although they are mentioned in William J. Richardson's bibliography.[1] The same year of 1937 you were invited to Paris by the organizers of the congress that gathered there in the spring to commemorate the third centenary of the *Discourse of Method,* and again in September by the French Society of Philosophy. But, in Germany, if Professor Heidegger continued in his profession, the writer, already for some years, had entered into an almost complete silence. It was to last ten years.

Your pages of 1937 had for a title *Wege zur Aussprache.* The 'debate' for which you were searching paths was the debate between the two neighboring German and French peoples. It was, therefore, a question of a letter that was addressed to both peoples at once. This letter has remained without a response. My letter of today would like to be a first attempt at a response, the response of a Frenchman to what you were saying in 1937.

When we met for the first time at Todtnauberg in September 1946, I was unaware of the existence of *Wege zur Aussprache.* At that time a knowledge of it would not have granted me anything essential. It was only in 1959 that I asked to read these old pages, but my question still remained external to them. I had no other goal than to be better informed, as one says, about a time when you were only a name for me.

xvii

You write in *Wege zur Aussprache,* however, that the singularity of "one of the most German of the thinkers of Germany," namely Leibniz, consists in having been "ceaselessly led in his work of thinking by his debate with Descartes." It is in relation to this debate which Leibniz will never abandon that you defined for the Germans and the French the double 'condition' of a reciprocal understanding, and that is to say, of an authentic debate, in the following terms: "Der lange Wille zum Aufeinanderhören und der verhaltene Mut zur eigenen Bestimmung," the patient will to listen to one another and the resolute and contained sense of the destination proper to each. This *patient* will to hear the other speak did not go, of course, without some impatience on the part of Leibniz, who occasionally speaks of Descartes in terms that many French people still find unjust. To be irritated by this is not to want to understand that the other name of Δίκη is Ἔρις and that periods where the present is without tempest are, as Hegel says, mere *leere Blätter,* blank pages. But Leibniz himself was able better than anyone, thus elevating himself above vulgarity, to characterize properly his own debate with Descartes, whose reputation he was accused of "wanting to ruin."[2] He wrote to Philippi in 1680: "When I speak to headstrong people from the School who treat Descartes with disdain, I emphasize the brilliance of his qualities, but when I have to deal with an overzealous Cartesian, I find myself obliged to change my tone."[3] For imitating, repeating, and 'paraphrasing' a teacher is not "the veritable way of following great men and of sharing in their glory without taking any of it away from them."[4] In this way you comported yourself toward your teacher Husserl, to whom *Sein und Zeit,* which was dedicated to him, is a much greater and more durable homage than the texts of so many overzealous 'Husserlians'.

Yet in what way is the thought of Leibniz, if it is in its relation to Descartes's "langer Wille zum Hören," also "verhaltener Mut zur eigenen Bestimmung"? You do not say it explicitly, since you are content to recall that Leibniz was as German as Descartes was French. Nietzsche will speak well here of the *geschmeidige Stärke,* the supple strength that will permit Leibniz to live "between two contrasts." But speaking in this way still leaves something to be desired. Where is the 'proper destination' of Leibniz as a German? Is it, as you say in your *Nietzsche,* a *Fragezeichen,* a question mark (*N* I 124)? Hölderlin said it in other words that you have taught us to understand:

Aber der Schatz, das Deutsche, der unter des heiligen Friedens Bogen lieget, er ist Jungen und Alten gespart.

But the treasure, the German, lying beneath the arch of sacred peace, has been saved for the young and old.[5]

Concerning the enigma that you evoke, however, you add on the same page of your *Nietzsche:* "One thing is sure: history will ask us to account for ourselves if we do not understand." Allow me to say also of the French what you say of the Germans. Their proper destination is no less perilously enigmatic. But—as you also say—"to no people in history has its truth fallen from the sky" (*N* I 37).

It often seems that it is from listening to another person that one learns most about oneself. Not only because it is here that we experience a strange impossibility, namely that of completely identifying oneself with the other, but also because the way another sees me often enlightens me about myself, since what for me has become habitual can appear strange to another person. It is from a note to the *Observations* or *Beobachtungen* of 1764 that I learnt from Kant what could be peculiar in eighteenth-century French society: "According to French taste, one never says: Is Monsieur at home? but: Is Madame at home? Madame is getting dressed. Madame is suffering from hot flushes. In short, it is exclusively with Madame that all the conversations are occupied and it is Madame who is at the center of all the entertainments."[6] What Madame de Stäel (another Madame) wrote *On Germany* was no less able to strike German readers. And when you came to France for the first time in 1955, a few words of yours helped to reveal Paris to me, as a few of my surprised remarks in Freiburg, Messkirk, or Todtnauberg were perhaps able to help you to see something of your own country. But taking one's leave from the habitual or *Gewöhnliches* does not yet illuminate *Wohnen* or inhabiting itself, although the latter is the secret of the former.[7]

What was from time to time more essential in the course of our meetings—which made apparent to me, in philosophy as in poetry, the very being of the German language, its *Wert und Ehre,* worth and honor, as Hofmannsthal said—was your discovery of a certain felicity of denomination in French, at which you came to marvel. I recall that in 1947 at Todtnauberg, when I said to you that the French *concerné* (*concerned*) could perhaps respond to the German *ereignet* in the sense that you employ it, you said to me: "Ein schönes Wort, denn es sagt zugleich: getroffen, aufgerührt, umschlossen," a beautiful word, for it says at once: to be taken, roused, embraced. And, eight years later, during the ten-day conference at Cerisy, you exhorted your French listeners to hear their own language in underlining that the French *représentation* is as rich in sense as the German *Vorstellung,* although its richness is of another order insofar as it resonates with the secret parenthood of being and time. I also remember that one day you asked what I thought about a German translation of Baudelaire that you presented to me, and I answered: "Doubtless, it is all very good and exact, but one thing is lacking: a relation to the French language." For we have also learnt from you that language is not a system of signs but a relationship with the world; not by the interposition of a world of language between things and ourselves, as Humboldt held, but by the opening of the world itself, in such a way that in turn it opens each individual thing, as Baudelaire said, "to the radiant truth of its native harmony."[8] It is thus that the same world and the same things appear natively at once the same and different within the call of one language or another; and this relation of the same and the other excludes as much any reduction to the identical as it does any nomenclature of differences, in favor of a higher secret of the worldhood of the world and of the thingliness of the thing. Perhaps Aristotle had some inkling of this if his most essential words are τὸ ὂν λέγεται πολλαχῶς, "being is said in many ways."

Your text of 1937, however, is less concerned with the particularities of the two 'neighboring peoples'—so close, as Tacitus said echoing Caesar, that they are separated only *Rheno flumine*, by the River Rhine—than it is with the common origin that is harbored in their vicinity. This is not Europe, as one says today. It is rather what remains hidden in Europe, the enigma that Europe is to itself, or the "unknown mystery of civilization" toward which it is leading, as Balzac said in a relatively obscure text that was discovered by E. R. Curtius, who informed Merleau-Ponty about it, to whom, in turn, I owe the possibility of being able to communicate it to you. The wonder of neighborliness!

It fell to you to speak of the enigma of Europe, the bearer of so many wars, in a way that sought not to explain it, leaving that for the historians and sociologists, but to *think* it right up to the question mark that it is for itself—a question mark that you occasionally name the *griechischer Ansatz*, the Greek beginnings. This was an occasion for one of the most enduring misunderstandings of the sense of your thinking. Heidegger, as everyone almost everywhere says, is the man of the Greeks. He aims to reanimate philosophy in renewing antiquity. In the eyes of certain French readers, this supposed phil-hellenism would only be the alibi of a non-avowed 'Germanism', which would betray itself by a no less supposed hostility to Latin, which of course is as essential as Greek to the 'European balance', whose marvel would consist in the capacity to harmonize everything—Greek,

Latin, and the rest—in a cosmopolitanism without frontiers. People remind you, thus, of what Leibniz wrote to Billettes: "Provided that something important happens, I am indifferent whether it happens in Germany or in France, for I hope for the good of the human race; I am neither αιλέλλην nor αιλορωματος but αιλάνθρωπος."[9]

Leibniz's 'philanthropy', such as it is today to be found in a combative guise within the metaphysical framework of the quarrel "God or Man, Which of the Two Prevails over the Other?" certainly does not constitute the nub of the question for you. From 1947 the *Letter on Humanism* showed in its own way that the supposed *alternative* was only in reality a *dilemma*, and that the task of thought was radical in another way:

> For without being, where it is deployed in an utterance,
> You will never find it.[10]

Hence, in the end, it is necessary to come back to the question of being, the opening up of which was the exclusive contribution of the Greeks. It is in this way, following the trace of Hölderlin, that you wonder more meditatively in what way the Greeks and their enigma are 'indispensable' for us, and whether the stakes concern not only the battle of 'humanisms' but also the "freier Gebrauch des Eigenen,"[11] the free use of what is integral to us.

The Greeks to us are not, as even the greatest thinkers have appeared to believe—such as Racine, perhaps, and Goethe occasionally—'classics' whose 'naturalness' we would have to attempt to equal in measuring ourselves against them. Still less are they 'primitives', whose fire could perhaps once again inflame us in the way that Darius Milhaud believed that he had to produce a 'cannibal' aspect within Aeschylus's *Choephoroe* in setting Paul Claudel's translation to music. To the extent that being opened itself to them as a clearing in beings, the Greeks are much rather *initiators,* but of such a sort that the Greek initiative is in itself only the first epoch of a withdrawal that becomes the fundamental trait of a whole history: our own. A withdrawal of being? This certainly sounds bizarre. Yet does not the masterword of Greek thought, the word ἀλήθεια, point in this direction? In *Sein und Zeit* it was still understood as a *privativer Ausdruck* (*SZ* 222), a privative expression. But in 1942 a few pages of yours on Plato already exhorted us to situate properly what is "positive" in the "privative" essence of ἀλήθεια (*PL* 51). For it is only, as you said in 1943, in the evening of the Greek world and from the perspective of the grammarians that the first letter adopts its privative sense. The 'word' ἀλήθεια does not therefore say simply the triumph of the day, in the sense that the poet writes:

Day comes out of night like a victory.[12]

It speaks rather of a conflict (*Streit*) more essential than any combat (*Kampf*). The conflict that is ἀλήθεια still resonates at the heart of the transcendental dialectic in the *Widerstreit* proper to Reason. The sense of the word here is quite different from that of its merely polemical usage—the one which makes Kant say of two people contradicting each other, with his extremely just sense of language: "Sie haben gut kämpfen," they have fought well (*Critique of Pure Reason*, A 756, B 784). Such a confrontation never leads to any triumph. We are today men of 'combat', the 'champions' of the just cause, in other words men of resentment. We have lost the Greek sense of conflict, which, as you say, liberates both of those that it opposes "in die Selbstbehauptung ihres Wesens" (*HZW* 38), in the self-affirmation of their essence. It was to such a conflict that you exhorted the Germans and the French in 1937. They were thrown into the atrocity of a combat without conflict. Perhaps they are only preserved from it today by what you call "eine vermutlich lange dauernde Ordnung der Erde" (*VA* 83), an ordering of the earth that will probably be long-lasting. This ordering, of which Nietzsche had a presentiment,[13] and which metaphysics at its end diffuses everywhere in reducing man to the figure of the 'beast of work', is not the peace of what is essential, but the equivocation of extreme decline.[14]

It is from you that we know this: the vindictive era of planetary combats in which men clash in view of the domination of the earth— pacifistically or otherwise, and regardless of whether it is a question of national wars or *Klassenkampf*, in relation to which a recent faith expects a "society without classes" as an "absolute form for the development of productive forces"[15]—still leaves us at the surface of a secret history of which the visible history is only the foreground. That of which man is 'the There' reserves for him, perhaps, a quite different destiny than that for which he today busies himself blindly. Beneath what Montaigne named "the din of so many philosophical brains," perhaps this other destiny is what a thinking other than philosophy, such as it impudently delivers itself today to the carelessness of the scientific enterprise if it refuses to furnish for itself the derisory refuge of a religiosity without faith, still preserves for man. This other thinking is poetic language, about which you say, in relation to Trakl, that it is "older because more thoughtful, more thoughtful because more peaceful, more peaceful because more calming" (*US* 55). Such a destiny will not be the end of conflict, which Hölderlin names in *Empedocles* "the conflict of lovers," but the end, perhaps, of conflict as combat.

In the second volume of your *Nietzsche,* whose French translation is still to appear,[16] you evoke enigmatically by the name of *Grundstellung* the possibility, for Occidental man, of another site than that which his metaphysical situation has defined for him. Allow me to repeat without commentary your own words: "The fundamental situation in which the era of metaphysics reaches its end enters in turn into a conflict of a wholly different kind. Such a conflict is no longer a combat for the domination of beings . . . It is the confrontation between the power of beings and the truth of being. To prepare this confrontation is the furthest goal of the meditation attempted here" (*N* II 262).

How, then, could one not think of the 'provisional aim' that the interpretation of being from the horizon of time was for *Sein und Zeit*? How could one not have a presentiment that the provisional aim that you defined on the basis of a meditation on the work of Aristotle already announces the furthest aim, if the very sense of *Sein und Zeit* is to say the *There* of which each one of us is the man, before being the man of a party, a church, a nation, or a profession? Man is the guardian of a more original proximity than that which results from the technological reduction of all distances, and it is toward this original proximity that, without changing place in any way, you have wandered for more than forty years, not, as you say, "with the pretension of a prophetic spirit" but in the light, perhaps, "of a still hesitant dawn" (*SG* 171). To such a proximity belong not only the two 'neighboring peoples' that *Wege zur Aussprache* names, those that emerge from the Greek language, but also, beyond the Greek language, even the most distant peoples, whom we are destined to have to meet one day in their distance. For as you once said to the Hölderlin Gesellschaft that had gathered in Munich, it is no longer possible today for the *There* to remain "in its occidental isolation." But how can a dialogue be opened from "house to house" (*US* 90) with those who inhabit a totally different house from our own? How can we disorientate ourselves in meeting them if we have not already become capable of orientating ourselves to the provenance that we essentially are? If you aspire to hear the other, you should know first how to become what you are. Γένοι οἷος ἐσσὶ μαθών.[17] Such is the secret that carries Leibniz's dialogue with Descartes. Such was the path of Hölderlin and that of Cézanne. Such has been, from the beginning, your own.

To come back to the two 'neighboring peoples', allow me to note one secret of their proximity. You spoke in 1937 of Descartes and

Leibniz, showing how the whole of Leibniz's thought is at bottom a debate with Descartes. It is only through this debate that Leibniz became himself. Perhaps it is necessary here to reverse the relation and to ask oneself if and how Descartes could have become what he is without the resolutely critical meditation of Leibniz. Before Leibniz, and independently of Pascal's reversal, who like any *anti* essentially adheres to what he contradicts, Malebranche and Spinoza are bound to Descartes. Neither the one nor the other is fully in agreement with him, but it is in Descartes that they find, under the title of *Method,* the "spiritual lineage" (Nietzsche) of their philosophies. They differ from Descartes, as Maurice Blondel—whose memory you saluted during your first stay in Aix—said in 1915, only by an *intuition* (the word was fashionable then) or rather, as he said more prudently, by an *intention.* The intention of Malebranche, a 'Christian philosopher', is quite Augustinian. That of Spinoza concerns a theology of a different nature. But beneath the difference of the theological intentions the ontology remains at bottom, and essentially, Cartesian. With Leibniz, on the contrary, there is a breakthrough to an original experience of being itself. It is only from this point that, beginning in philosophy, he finishes as a theologian. Henceforth an essential *conflict* flares up, whereas Malebranche and Spinoza limited themselves to *combating* Descartes on certain points. And it is on the basis of such a conflict that Descartes is transmitted to Kant and then to Hegel, the latter finally telling the entire world that Descartes is a 'hero'. The French have thus, for better or for worse, received from Germany an unknown measure of Descartes to which they have had to resign themselves. It is no less from Germany that the 'View of Descartes' that Valéry proposed to the congress at which you were absent in 1937 is reflected. He receives it, not from Hegel, but from Nietzsche. Not from what Nietzsche had said about Descartes, which is very little. But from the presentiment that it is in the light of Nietzsche that Descartes appears as who he is. Without mentioning the fact that I grew familiar with Cézanne in Berlin, perhaps it would not be excessive to say that at least certain French people have only become themselves on the basis of a stay in the German domain.

It seemed that the idea that the relation of your own thinking with France and the French was something essential, that it was perhaps more essential than your engagement with other countries of Europe and of the world, came to light slowly within you. The marvel here was that a few members of an apparently frivolous people set themselves to work in order to understand better a thinking that initially appeared quite strange to them. Certain people, whom you would not count as friends, are still surprised by it. What a small number brought in their attempt to listen was not, however, a need for exoticism but simply "the singularity of being French," as one of my oldest and dearest friends said one day—a friend who has never, for all that, quite been able to understand why or how *Sein und Zeit* became my book of books. The most pressed for time found 'philosophical novelties' in your work. Others had already gone much further than curiosity. You were not for them a philosopher, still less a Professor, but perhaps a simple schoolmaster who, in the book of Philosophy, would have taught them for the first time to gather letters together, to form syllables, and finally to spell words. They then entered into the long years of an apprenticeship. In this way, none of them resemble in any way Leibniz as a reader of Descartes. No conflict has begun to emerge at the level of what is essential. It is much rather you who said to us concerning Hegel at the Thor Seminar on the 5th September, that every authentic thinking carries an essential limitation. It is only, as you added, when one sees the limits that one sees the greatness of a thinker. And, turning to us, you said: "When you are able to see my limits, you will have understood me. I cannot see them."

Perhaps, as we thought, it is a sign of the times that an avant-garde thinking, invisible to most, has still been able to gain so much of an advance in saying, in letting it be said, not like Hegel before the 'bad infinite', but before the μετά of metaphysics itself, that the task of thought still remains unknown to it: "indem über dies Hinausgehen nicht selbst hinausgegangen wird," insofar as this transcendence is not itself transcended.[18] The more temerarious have thought it possible to impute to you an enterprise of 'overcoming metaphysics', even if you immediately specify that you employ such a locution only in an auxiliary manner (*VA* 71). From the very beginning, in fact, it is not toward such an 'overcoming' that you point but rather, in the opposite direction, toward the "Schritt zurück aus der Metaphysik," the step backwards from metaphysics in disengaging thought from it. Such a retreat is only possible in focusing our attention on what Hölderlin names *das Geringe*—we could say: the almost-nothing. But attention to the μικρόν is here the very opposite to what Plato repelled under the title of *micrology*. In the 'almost-nothing', that with which we are concerned (*ereignet*) is not the diminution of the *Kleines*, the small, but the sparkling of the *Kleinod*, of the jewel, of the κόσμος, of which the prowess of the world of modern technology is certainly the withdrawal, but not the abolition.

That being is of the essence of the jewel [*joyau*]—in which one at once hears the Latin *jocari* and, perhaps, *gaudium*, the game, and even the joy of being, of being able to become the 'least of things' that hides itself away in the invisibility of the insignificant—this is the affair of being and not ours. *Nothing is more proper to coming to presence than hiddenness.* But perhaps the unapparent jewel that the task of thought is to save is for us above all the language that each one of us speaks without reflecting on it. It is up to us, then, to attempt to learn our own language, to hear what it says to us, to speak it as it speaks. If destiny has it that your own path passed through France, this is what a few French people have learnt from Heidegger.

This is why, at the end of my response to your letter of 1937, the one in which you named Leibniz in his relation to Descartes as "one of the most German thinkers of Germany," I would like to allow perhaps the most French of French poets to speak, a poet whose greatness remains unapparent in the eyes of the French themselves, perhaps because his work harbors the jewel of French poetry. His name is Jean de la Fontaine. In the fifth book of the *Fables,* there is one, the sixteenth, which has for a title "The Serpent and the File." One could give it the subtitle "Heidegger and His Critics." Here it is without any commentary:

> A serpent, neighbor to a smith,
> (A neighbor bad to meddle with,)
> Went through his shop, in search of food,
> But nothing found, it's understood,
> To eat, except a file of steel,
> Of which he tried to make a meal.
> The file, without a spark of passion,
> Addressed him in the following fashion:
> "Poor simpleton! you surely bite
> With less of sense than appetite;
> For before from me you gain
> One quarter of a grain,
> You'll break your teeth from ear to ear.
> Time's are the only teeth I fear."
>
> This tale concerns those men of letters,
> Who, good for nothing, bite their betters.
> Their biting so is quite unwise.
> Think you, you literary sharks,
> Your teeth will leave their marks
> On the deathless works you criticize?
> Fie! fie! fie! men!
> To you they're brass—they're steel—they're diamond![19]

DIALOGUE WITH HEIDEGGER

1

The Birth of Philosophy

The title thus proposed harbors a question. We are asking about the possible birth of philosophy. But immediately another question arises: Is our first question not a pseudo-question, like those concerning the origin of language or of inequality between men? Does philosophy really have a birth? Or, like language and perhaps like inequality, is it not always and already there, as far as one goes back, and to some degree everywhere? In other words, are not some things without origin? And would not philosophy be one of them?

So self-evidently is philosophy called the art of developing on any subject ideas that are more or less general and generally contradictory between themselves, as in the French proverbs that teach at the same time that a habit does not make a monk and that feathers make a bird, it is to be presumed that philosophy is as old as the world and that it is from time immemorial that men, since they began to think and speak, must have begun to philosophize. But if philosophy is not simply the exercise of thought, if it is, as Hegel said, a very particular manner of thinking, then things could be quite different. It could be that men have thought, even profoundly and at length, without, for all that, having been philosophers.

This second possibility is what comes to the fore as soon as we are attentive to the word *philosophy*. It is, in our language, a direct and literal transposition of a Greek word. This, in the first instance, is nothing original. Most French words derive from Greek and Latin, or from Greek through Latin, since the latter borrowed much from Greek. But what is interesting here is that it is not only in our language, but in all languages, that philosophy is called *philosophy*. Not only in English or in German, in Italian or in Spanish, but also in Russian, Arabic, and, doubtless, Chinese. Besides, even in Greek the word φιλοσοφία did not always exist. Preceded by the adjective φιλόσοφος that one finds in Heraclitus at the beginning of the fifth century, and by the verb φιλοσοφεῖν that is to be found in Herodotus and thus in the other half of the same century, it makes its entry into language only with Plato in the fourth century. At this time the *Iliad* and the *Odyssey* are already five centuries old. The Greeks indeed thought and spoke in the interval without, however, philosophizing. Plato presents philosophy, which he baptizes as such, as something new and original. This happens at the end of the *Phaedrus*, where, without aspiring to σοφία, which would be the property of the Gods rather than men, the latter seem nevertheless capable of philosophizing—capable, if not of possessing what the word σοφία says, then at least of attempting to acquire something of it, if the gods permit it and without becoming their equal.

But what does the word σοφία say? It is ordinarily translated by *wisdom*, and this enables the translation of φιλοσοφία as the love of *wisdom*. In this way we make quite an advance; we have, in fact, advanced from Greece to Rome. It is the Romans, not the Greeks, who opposed *wisdom* and *science*, and the unity of both terms is to be found in the verb *savoir*, to 'know', which although of the same family as *sagesse* or 'wisdom' signifies also the possession of science. When today, for example, we say *un savant*, it is about a man of science that we are thinking and not about a *sage*. In reality the distinction between *wisdom* and *science* is foreign to the Greeks, a distinction that a peculiarly modern mania sometimes poses as an opposition of *theory* to *practice*. Nothing is more anti-Greek than this opposition. Theory, in the Greek sense, is in no way opposed to practice or, as one says in taking from Marx's German a word that is only a transliteration of Greek, to *praxis*. In other words, the Greeks were in no way men of theory against praxis, but much rather those for whom theory was the highest praxis—theory not signifying for them that they were confined within 'purely theoretical' occupations, but that they had what was properly in question in view as a *task*. In their language Θεωρεῖν was the highest manner of being informed, of having their eyes fixed on what is essential. It was in no way to hide themselves in the world of speculations—a Latin and not a Greek word—in order to escape the harsh necessities of praxis. Otherwise we would be unable to understand why, for Plato, the free man did not have *one*, but *two*, essential occupations; philosophy *and* politics, such as it will be, for Marx, the summit of praxis; and why the same Plato had been able to give to his longest and most elaborate philosophical dialogue the title *Politics*, which was Latinized with the name *Republic*.

But then would for Plato the philosopher essentially be a politician? Of course; and what a politician: a true communist! Doubtless, it is not yet a question, as it will be for Marx, of the socialization of the instruments of production, but rather of the relegation of production to the bottom of the scale, where it still functions socially due to the pressure exerted by the superior on the inferior, that is, of the political on the economic. The result of this is that if the earth is not cultivated in common, then it is nevertheless in thought that the lot attributed to each individual is common to him with the State as a whole, which supposes that the producers are protected from an excess of riches as much as from an excess of poverty. But above this level everything becomes deliberately communal, even women. This applies to the same degree to the guardians of the state as it does to, higher again, those men and women (for Plato also has his moments of feminism) selected from all the classes in view of knowledge, that is, in view of philosophy, who will dedicate their efforts to political affairs, taking the helm successively with solely the public good in sight — not as one receives an honor, but as one fulfils a task, with one of the central aspects of this task being, for the governors, the choice and the formation of their successors. Such was the famous state of Plato, whose uncommon structure will make Aristotle say of his master that it makes him think of someone who always confuses "symphony and unison, rhythm and regularity." At any rate, for Plato, as Léon Robin said when I was a student, "to be a philosopher and to be a statesman are one and the same."

It is clear, thus, that for the Greeks no barrier comes to separate theory from practice. If the privilege of the gods is to be exempt from the second, with men the current does not cease to pass from one to the other, and this at all levels. But what is proper to human practice is that it is established at a *theoretical* level, from which animal nature is quite happily preserved. This is why, as Sophocles said:

> So multiple is everywhere the uncanny
> Yet nothing uncannier than man bestirs itself.

Is this breakthrough of man into the world, however, something specifically Greek? Has man achieved this breakthrough everywhere, before Greece and outside of it? Or is it necessary to say that he had *differently* and perhaps *better* broken though in Greece than anywhere else? This was Hegel's thought in the contrast that he established in the course of his lectures on *Aesthetics* between Greece and Egypt, where the breakthrough of man had only yet made space for the apparition of an enigma, symbolized by the Sphinx. In Greek myth, on the contrary, and as he adds, the Sphinx is itself interpreted as the monster posing enigmas:

> The Sphinx propounded the well-known conundrum: What is it that in the morning goes on four legs, at mid-day on two, and in the evening on three? Oedipus found the simple answer: a man, and he tumbled the Sphinx from the rock.[1]

The *know thyself* that Socrates read much later and meditatively on the inscription at Delphi echoes Oedipus's response. This was not a piece of advice, but a salutation, ἀντὶ τοῦ χαῖρε, "instead of the simple hello." Instead of "take care" the god says from on high: "learn to know thyself" and thus "become who you are," namely a man. But what is it to be a human being? How it is possible to become one? In the eyes of Plato, Pericles was a man, for his speech knew so well how "to be lofty" in its "free flight" without, for all that, losing itself in the clouds. This was true no less, in opposition to Lysias, of Isocrates. But why? As Socrates explains to Pheadrus in the dialogue which carries his name, because "there is, by nature, a sort of philosophy in the thought of such a man." If man is man, therefore, it is by means of this enigmatic 'philosophy'. The question *What is the human being?* hence sends us back to the question *What is philosophy?* Man only truly *breaks through* as man by the *breakthrough* in him of philosophy.

What, then, is philosophy as that which constitutes the very humanity of man in the eyes of a Greek of the fourth century? Do we have a definition of philosophical language—for it is indeed a question of a language—as that which knows so well, as we have seen, how to elevate itself above the matter-of-fact and to take to the heights without losing itself in the clouds? Do we have a properly Greek definition? Yes. But we adopt this definition less from Plato than from his disciple Aristotle. There is, he says, a certain knowledge, we might say a certain perspective, which, *as a whole, brings beings into view insofar as they are.* To be capable of such a perspective is to be a philosopher. But how are we to understand this quite sober definition of philosophy: "as a whole, to bring beings into view insofar as they are"? 'As a whole'—the Greek καθόλου, from which derives our word *catholic*. *L'étant:* this use of the present participle is as unusual in French as it is frequent in German—*das Seiende*—or in English: *a being*. A being is whatever is—a mountain or an animal, my watch, each one of us, a river or a stone, the obelisk at the Place de Concorde, etc. But it is a question of bringing it into view insofar as it is. Here we remain in suspense. How could we bring it into view in any other way? What else can a being do than be? To bring into view a being, is this not necessarily to bring it into view insofar as it is? In truth, the problem is not so simple. One can, in fact, face up to a being or grapple with it without necessarily bringing it into view insofar as it is. One can eat or drink a being, sit on it, dress oneself with it, live in it, describe it or tell a story concerning it, and even expect from it, if it is taken at a sufficient level, the eternal salvation of one's spirit. But is this to bring it into view insofar as it is? In other words, is this to approach it according to the dimension of its *being*? Or, on the contrary, does not such an approach to a being presuppose much more a stepping back from it? Does it not suppose that it is first of all to be left to itself, in such a way that it itself appears, in what it is and as it is, language thus having the task to name, as Aristotle says "what its being already was," before it became the particular, concrete thing before us with such and such a familiar figure: this man, this dog, this book, this house, this tree? In other words, in fifth century Greece a turning occurred.

> Our question is no longer that of a particular being such as a mountain, a house, a tree, in the sense of having to climb a mountain, of living in a house, of busying ourselves with the planting of a tree. On the contrary, it is a question of the mountain, of the house, of the tree as a being, in order to bring into view only what holds itself in reserve in the word being, whether it is a question of the mountain, of the tree, or of the house.

Thus spoke Heidegger some years ago. It is essential here to see clearly that *being* is no longer a quality that one can encompass in the definition of a house, as when one says of a house, for example, that it is a construction that can be inhabited in a bourgeois fashion, or that a tree is a plant with roots, a trunk, and branches. Without doubt, not every construction is a house, not every plant is a tree; construction and plant are something more general than tree or house. But being is still beyond that which is only general. Where, then, does being reside? Not in the foreground of what is, as when I say: this tree is in blossom, nor in the background of what is, as when I say: it is an apple tree. But rather in the much more peculiar proximity in which the tree appears in front of me in order simply to let itself be seen as that which it is. In other words, the question cannot be posed in the terms of a foreground, nor of a background, but in terms of the *ground* itself that carries both, as much the one as the other without being identified with either of the two, and which hence remains hidden in both.

One might say that here there are too many subtleties. Yet it is precisely these subtleties that the Greeks took up as a fundamental question, and it is the elaboration of this question that they named philosophy. They let themselves be provoked by questions only under the pressure and the urgency of a unique question, namely the question of being. Well before Plato and Aristotle, it is what already burst open in the speech of those which modern erudition has named, not without a certain disdain, pre-Socratics, in the sense that one says pre-Columbians, pre-Raphaelites, and pre-hominids. It is the same thing to say, of course, that Ronsard is a pre-Malherbian and Victor Hugo a pre-Mallarméen. Who is not, relatively to some other, in the situation that is said in the prefix *pre-*? The whole question is obviously one of knowing if this *pre-* is only a *not yet*, if it is the *pre-* of a still unrefined primitivism, or on the contrary, if it is that of a precursor, in other words, that of an initiator who opens the way with both a suddenness and a casualness that will never be surpassed, although it is provisionally misunderstood by those who immediately follow him. Aristotle himself was not far from treating his predecessors as *pre-Socratics,* when he presented them as having only, as he says, "spoken falteringly." But, in the end, Aristotle himself is not clear sighted on this point. All this does not mean that what comes before is a priori more perfect than what comes after, the latter being merely the decline of the former, as it is sometimes fashionable to say, but only that in the use that one makes of the antagonistic notions of *progress* and *decadence,* perhaps it is necessary to introduce a little more consideration than one ordinarily does.

To come back to the *pre-Socratics,* who are in no way primitives in the domain of thinking, I propose to you that we read together fragment 18 of Heraclitus. It can be translated as follows:

If one does not expect the unexpected one will not find it: it is unavailable and difficult to compass.

Only the qualities that a being presents, either in the foreground or in the background, are accessible and available. The ground that carries the one as much as the other is, on the contrary, unavailable. It is necessary that our hope and expectancy carry themselves beyond what we can expect, however circumspect we may be, so that the unexpected can happen, namely the *is* itself which secretly reigns in any presence of beings. But how can we name that by which we are more profoundly affected than by the fact that a being presents itself as such and such a being, like this door, for example, that is open or closed, or a man before us who is either welcome or troublesome? Heraclitus names this unexpected, in fact, in several ways, one of which is the Greek word κόσμος. He says, for example:

> This cosmos, which is the same for all, no one of gods or men has made, but it was ever and is now, and will always be an ever living fire, kindling in measures and dying down in measures. (fragment 30)

In speaking this way, what exactly does Heraclitus say? Nothing distances us farther from his words than the common translation of κόσμος by 'world'. Heraclitus would thus say to us that the Great Whole of the earth is anterior to the gods and to men, who would themselves be only details in the Great Whole. But the translation of κόσμος by 'world', or by 'universe', carries us to the antipodes of Heraclitus's words. Κόσμος, rather, evokes an arrangement, a disposition of the things of which we speak. But not just any disposition. It is a question of a disposition thanks to which things appear at the height of their brilliance. This is why, in Homer, the word signifies a *jewel*, the property of a *jewel* being not only to shine by itself, but above all to valorize the one who wears it. The jewel shines less for itself than for something else.

> My dearest darling was bare, and knowing my heart,
> She had only kept her jingling jewels
> Whose rich allure gave her the vanquishing ways
> That Moorish slaves have in their happier days.[2]

Here we have, with the poetry of Baudelaire, the κόσμος in its pure state, which is evidently not the one of cosmonauts, but one which is as close as can be to the κόσμος of Heraclitus. Yet far from adding itself from the outside to what it allows to appear in the height of its brilliance, the κόσμος of Heraclitus is essential to the latter, to the point that nothing would appear without it. But what is this primordial jewel that sparkles in everything and from out of which everything sparkles? It is the secret identity of what the weak in spirit attempt to separate and to oppose as incompatible: "Day-night, winter-summer, war-peace, abundance-penury" (fragment 67). The jewel, the trinket, the κόσμος is the antagonistic ordering of all things, thanks to which they secretly resemble a bow, which only *propels* the arrow by the *withdrawal* of the string, or the lyre which resonates only in vibrating. Even the gods have their divinity in this:

> For if it were not to Dionysus that they make a procession and sing the phallic hymn, they would carry out something most shameful; yet they

are the Same, Hades and Dionysus, in whose honor they go mad and rave. (fragment 15)

They are the Same, Hades and Dionysus—Hades, the master of those from below, as Homer says in the *Iliad,* who, the day of the fateful division of the whole, "received the foggy shadow for his lot" (XV, 187 ff.); and Dionysus, not well known from Homer, but whose followers call for his manifestation as the god who gives *la joie de vivre* such as it is celebrated in the last chorus of *Antigone.* The identity of contrasts culminates in a summit that the fragment that we just read does not mention, seen as it proclaims identity only for *day-night, winter-summer, war-peace, abundance-penury.* This summit is the identity of life and death. Hence fragment 88:

> And it is the same in us that is quick and dead, awake and asleep, young and old; everywhere the former are shifted and become the latter, and the latter in turn are shifted and become the former.

Such is the fundamental *ground,* beyond anything that could be apprehended concretely as a being, which makes *all* beings appear and carries them *all* with their *foregrounds* and their *backgrounds.* The κόσμος of Heraclitus is nothing that can be *isolated* in beings. It is the secret adjoining of what differs only in unison, the madness of men consisting, on the contrary, of separating both sides of the One in attaching themselves to one of the two, only to be immediately dislodged from it by the other.

> Thus they go, here and there,
> Deaf as they are and no less blind, astonished, indecisive races,
> Whose lot is to say as much "it is" as "it is not,"
> As much "it is the same" as "it is not at all the same,"
> All of them, for as long as they are, only ever advance in retracing their
> steps.

These are no longer the words of Heraclitus but rather those of Parmenides, which for more than two millennia the tradition has opposed to the thought of Heraclitus, but who, at about the same time, although at the other end of the Greek world, responds to the latter unknowingly, saying in another guise the unity of the same and the other, whose reign is that of the κόσμος.

The κόσμος of both Heraclitus and Parmenides, as we said, is not the 'Great Whole', but rather the omnipresent sparkling of the marvel of being or, if you will, of the diadem of being. This omnipresent brilliance that, as Aristotle will say, is present even in the smallest of things, is echoed in the poetry of Baudelaire when he writes:

> But the lost jewels of ancient Palmyra
> The unknown metals, pearls from the ocean,
> Mounted by your hand would not suffice
> For this beautiful diadem, dazzling and clear.[3]

In the heart of the landscape of what we have called *beings*, in secret another landscape is open to us, namely that of *being*, solely from which beings take shape. The landscape of being, in its invisibility, is the κόσμος, the *diadem* that always transpires everywhere, as soon as something manifests itself before us. The whole of the thinking of both Heraclitus and Parmenides is a thinking of this double landscape, in which what is more secret carries what is more manifest in deploying itself in the latter, but according to the discretion that befits the secret of the unapparent. Heidegger said one day:

> When, in the early days of the year, the prairies cover the countryside with their verdancy, in the appearance of the green prairies it is being itself that unfolds itself, it is its reign that radiates. But we only ever wander through the verdant prairies, without nature ever presenting itself to us as being nature. And even when we have a feeling of this being of nature, even when we begin to represent to ourselves what we feel, even if we conceptualize it, the being of nature maintains itself in the secret that is proper to it.

Heidegger wrote these lines in echoing a distich of Angelius Silesius, which Leibniz and Hegel had celebrated before him:

> The rose is without why; it blooms because it blooms,
> It pays no attention to itself, asks not whether it can be seen.[4]

The blooming of the rose is none of the roses in flower, but that from which each one becomes what it is, and which consequently gives them all to us without identifying itself with any one of them. It is that to which, at the dawn of our world, an earlier thinking than ours, that of the earliest Greek thinkers, knew how to respond. Perhaps it is permitted to wonder if their thinking did not, from the depths of the forgetting which has become its resting place, say what there was to say more extensively and more profoundly than the exactitude of the modern sciences ever could, including the species of the latter that is botany.

It is necessary to underscore the extraordinary difference that separates the new language of Heraclitus and Parmenides from the ancient language of the poets, from Homer above all, who was the initiator of the poetic word. One can say that the new language expressly attempts to speak of what the poets never managed to name, although it was from its interior that they saw what they named. Homer sees well *in* the κόσμος, but he does not see it *as* κόσμος, for seeing it as κόσμος begins only with Heraclitus or Parmenides, thanks to, as we said, a pivoting such that our regard no longer looks straight — καταντικρύ, as Plato will say — at what appears, but rather at the mode of appearing of what appears. The whole of philosophy emerges from this. It is born from a regard that is fixed on the mode of appearing of what appears, which it determines, first of all, according to the determination that befits such a mode of appearing or, in the Greek sense, such a mode of being. This determination is the marvelous weightlessness of the *verb*, and not the more massive determination that is appropriate for the fixation of what appears, namely the *noun*. Hence the singular taste of the Greek thinkers for what the grammarians will name much later the *participial* mode. The participle — being, singing, living, walking — is, in fact, at once a *noun* and a *verb*. But it names what it names only thanks to the verb. Here we have to do with a denomination that is predominantly verbal. In this sense, a being, τὸ ὄν in Greek, is less the *singular* of the plural 'beings' (τὰ ὄντα) than it is a word that says, from one end to the other of beings, the singularity of being in what is unique to it. This double participation in the nominal and the verbal, but with the predominance of the verbal over the nominal, of whatever is to be thought, and which takes flight from this verb of verbs that is the verb *being*, was perhaps the most lofty of the thoughts that the Greeks formed. It consequently determines a scission in thought that is perhaps unique to the world. Prior to this, thinking could be more or less superficial or profound, melodic or narrative, approximate or exact, expert or unskilled, as it has remained everywhere where humanity has remained sheltered from the Greek inception. Humanity had not yet attained the surpassing that it attains only when the Greeks became those to whom language was freed for a quite different way of thinking and speaking than that of their poets.

In order to clarify this we could do worse than selecting an example. We are, in fact, going to bring together two ways of speaking, which were heard almost at the same time. The first is that of Tchouang-tse, who was one of the continuators of Lao-tse in ancient China, and who lived roughly at the time that Plato lived in Greece. The following is a text of Tchouang-tse, such as I was able to translate something of it, not, of course, directly from the Chinese, but on the basis of a German and a French translation. We can call it:

The Useless Tree

Addressing Tchouang-tse, Hui-tse says to him: "I have on my estate a large tree. Its trunk is so full of knots that it cannot be cut correctly. Its branches are so crooked and twisted that they cannot be worked with a compass and set square. It is on the edge of the path, but no carpenter looks at it. Such are your words, O master, grand and unusable, and everybody unanimously turns away from you."

Tchouang-tse says in turn: "Have you ever seen a marten which, lying flat, is on the lookout and waiting for something to happen? It leaps from place to place and is not frightened to leap too high to the point where it falls into a trap or gets caught in a snare. But there is also the yak. It is as big as a storm cloud. It stands tall, large. Only, it is not even capable of catching mice. You have, as you say, a large tree and deplore the fact that it is good for nothing. Why do you not plant it in a deserted land or in the middle of an empty territory? Then you could wander idly around it or, having nothing to do, sleep under its branches. No saw or axe would be there to threaten it with a premature end, and nobody would be able to damage it. Why should one bother oneself with the fact that something is good for nothing?"

This is a passage that definitely makes us think, and doubtless this is why it has been transmitted to us. But is it a page of philosophy? Or, on the contrary, having issued from this other world that China is to us, does it invite reflection without inviting us in any way to philosophize? We are, at any rate, very far from the enterprise of Plato, who was the contemporary of Tchouang-tse. In the *Sophist*—this is the title of the dialogue—Plato attaches to *being*, understood as "what most accompanies everything," four determinations which all accompany it, but as opposed to each other in pairs: Station and Movement, the Same and the Other. Subsequently, Plato seeks to discern what associations or combinations are possible among these five figures. Henceforth a whole play of passages and impasses unfolds panoramically, one of the fundamental passages being that *being* itself can be understood with the *other* to the point of presenting itself as other than it is, so much so that attaching oneself to being is to be ceaselessly exposed to the risk of error. Error is possible only in the land of being, given that it is also the land of the other, whether this be the fragile which appears solid when a fine layer of ice covers the surface of water, or the path that appears as viable when it is obstructed farther ahead by a heap of rocks that is out of sight. Nothing is more Greek than this interpretation of error. It is easy to say with Descartes that all is our fault and that it is we who become confused. But it is more Greek to say that it occasionally happens to us to be mistaken by an ambiguity that is part of the presence of things. Diderot asks himself: Is it good? Is it bad? to the point of making it the title of a play. How could we know without taking our leave from the relative in-distinction that arises from the Platonic affinity of Being and the Other? All around us abound professionals of infallibility. The Greeks, at the birth of their thinking, were less arrogant. This is why, after catastrophes and even after crimes, they were more inclined to pity the victims than to distribute guilt retrospectively, but this did not, for all that, render them more indulgent. Yet nothing was more foreign to them than what Nietzsche will name much later the "spirit of resentment."

This is, of course, only a parenthesis. But it is essential to see that with Plato we are in a different world than the one from which the words of Tchouang-tse reach us. Hence before speaking of 'Chinese philosophy', as one commonly does, it would be necessary to ask: what is philosophy exactly? It could even be that the thoughts of Mao Tse-tung are today much less philosophical than the thinking of Marx, such as it is borne by the Hegelian, that is, the dialectical, interpretation of being. They are not, for all that, devoid of sense, nor even of depth. They simply derive from a world to which philosophy, far from having been born there, was exported *very late in the day,* in the guise of one of its *late* forms, namely *dialectical materialism.* Besides, it is not only Marxism that has been exported to China. It has no less received by importation the extraordinary conjunction of *knowing* and *power,* such as, three centuries ago, it was formulated in Latin by Bacon and in French by Descartes. To become by means of science "masters and possessors of nature" was a program quite foreign to Greek philosophy, although it is perhaps only on the basis of the Greek turning of thought into philosophy that such a program was able to be formulated later, and its realization to unleash itself throughout the world—an unleashing of which we are experiencing only the very beginning. For what the Greeks set on its way already more than two millennia ago is perhaps the radical origin of what universally seizes us, namely the increasing transformation of our world into a technical world. The advent of technology in the modern sense is by no means something self-evident. To make of it only a "biological event on a grand scale," as does one of the greatest scientists of our time, the physicist Werner Heisenberg, who has shaken to its roots the world of physics with his 'relations of uncertainty', is perhaps to satisfy oneself cheaply. Doubtless, this event would be analogous to what was, toward the beginning of historical time, the enigmatic "migration of the herrings in the seas of the south" with which history began—at least according to the chronology that I was given one day, when as a candidate for the Ecole Normale I was asked to write a dissertation in six hours on the question of the Orient. Six hours is long, particularly given that the chronology stopped about 1870. It is from this that I know the first date of history.

In any event, here we find ourselves, as much in one sense as in the other—in the sense of the migration of herrings or in that of modern technology—quite far from philosophy at its birth. Let us come back to it once more, but this time in order to attempt to illuminate the transformation that Plato and Aristotle effect on the earlier thinking of Heraclitus and Parmenides, which, if you will, is not yet philosophy insofar as *philosophy* is the name by which Plato and Aristotle designate their own enterprise, which their own predecessors had only sketched in a still faltering manner.

Philosophy, as Aristotle says, is the study of beings insofar as they are beings and, in other words, of beings in their being. Such was, as we have seen, the enterprise of the first Greek thinkers, in which their speech became separated from that of the poets. They attempted to unearth the perspective from which the poets themselves saw what they said, but without seeing it or saying it as such. Hence it was essentially a question of saying what one can see thanks to the placing of the conjunction *insofar as* before the word *being*. Hence: taking into view, as a whole, beings insofar as they are beings. It is in this sense that Plato was able to say that, long before him, "something akin to a battle among giants raged concerning being."[5] In this way it appeared to Heraclitus as κόσμος, which is prior to the gods themselves, since it is to the κόσμος that Dionysus himself owes his divinity, and this constitutes his secret identity with Hades. Without the κόσμος, without the *jewel* of such an identity, Dionysus himself would only be a figurehead for the most immodest orgy. It is by the κόσμος in him that he is god, at once life and death and hence immortal. Heraclitus says of the κόσμος, as we have seen, that it is the same for everyone and everything. He also speaks of it as common—ξυνός—to everything. *Common* does not say here something common, that is, something banal, but what gathers the whole and adjoins it as one. When one speaks today of the *common* good, or when one names a *Commune* the smallest territorial organization, or when the Church proclaims itself as the *Community* of the faithful, the word stills guards something of its native vigor. The *common* is thus what is most rare and truly the jewel by which everything sparkles, including the god himself at the height of his divinity. But the word also says its own opposite. It says what equally belongs to several. In this sense the species from which several individuals derive is common, as is the genus from which several species derive. All squares have it in common to be rectangles of which two consecutive sides are equal. The more one goes back, the more the common is impoverished. It was first a horse, then it is only an animal, and then the animal, in turn, is reduced to a simple living being. But what can there be that is more common to everything than being? It is with this superlative that Aristotle, in the end, defines being. It is, at the very limit, a sort of nothing or an almost nothing, which nevertheless remains at the base of everything without yet pointing to anything: "taken in its nudity, being or not is not the sign of anything that we can deal with; by itself it is nothing."[6] Of course, this nothing is not nothing at all. It harbors in itself a secret richness, but one cannot make anything else come out of it other than what one can say of anything.

This is why, as Aristotle seems to say to himself, we would not advance too far in the country of being if we had only a thinking of being as common to everything, if we did not have a quite different thinking, namely a thinking of being as being also the *divine*. Thus God enters into philosophy as equal with being, for which it has become the other name. All this, as it seems, is quite peculiar. How can being let itself be determined at once as what is most common to everything and as what is most *separated* from the rest? To open oneself, on the one hand, to a still more vast community than that of the genus, and, on the other hand, to be a genus upstream from all other genera which are arrayed in tiers beneath it? The collection of texts that has for its ground this strange intertwining will be named by its publishers, three centuries after the death of Aristotle, the *Metaphysics*. To say, as one does today, that metaphysics is as *ontological* as it is *theological* is only to baptize the difficulty: it is not to elucidate the enigma that it harbors. In reality, the word *metaphysics* only serves to designate the situation within which philosophy finds itself grappling with something inextricable. The apparition of the "metaphysical bird," that Valéry sees "chased from post to post, harassed on the tower, fleeing nature, worried in its resting place, spied upon in language, going to nest in death, in tables, in music," can be historically situated. It appears between Heraclitus and Aristotle. But whence does it arise? It does not arrive from the outside, but much rather through the transformation of a thinking that is earlier than it and of which it is the completion or, as it were, the evening. But from Heraclitus to Aristotle would there be, then, no progress in philosophy?

Perhaps not—but perhaps no decadence either. Let us not be too hasty to give names to the secret movement that history harbors. We can dare, however, to wonder whether it would not be slightly naive to imagine that metaphysics is the *nec plus ultra* of thought, even if was reserved to Heidegger alone to pose the question: What is Metaphysics? Twenty years later he will say that metaphysics as a supposed 'doctrine of being' was perhaps only, at bottom, a "phase of the history of being"—the only one, as he added, that exists for us to bring into view, and of which the unfolding of the sciences is, in turn, only a terminal episode. This in no way means, as Valéry thinks, that science would be on the way to unseating metaphysics, our epoch being one of the 'overcoming of metaphysics'. Speaking in this way could well be speaking idly without knowing too much about that of which one speaks. This is, as is known, the most favorable condition for the overabundance of discourse.

To return to Aristotle: we have already met in the words of Heraclitus, according to which even the god was carried to its divinity by the κόσμος, the *divine* that becomes in Aristotle one of two names for being, of which the other name expresses its trans-generic, or, as one will say in the Middle Ages, its transcendental community. But never, for Heraclitus, will κόσμος be able to be identified with the divinity of God. It carries at once the divine and the human, being neither the one nor the other, but their center or their common foyer. Their *fire*, as he said in his brief words. That also of the oven at which he warmed himself in his house, when one day, as Aristotle tells us, he invited some visitors who had stopped at his doorway to come in, in saying to them: "even here the gods are present."[7] But with Aristotle a thinking of the original co-belonging of the divine and the human to the 'invisible harmony'—ἁρμονίη ἀφανής—that only separates them in unifying them effaces itself before that of a causal dependence of both the natural and the human with regard to the divine. Placed above everything as the supreme genus of being where it is separated from the rest, it coexists with a structure of being that remains common to everything, but that is now only a framework that is applicable to anything. Here a question arises: Why does this transformation happen from which it results that, if it is indeed only and always from being that we can know something of the divine, it is in a completely different way than that expressed by the words of Heraclitus? The *why* here is quite ambitious. Let us say only that one possibility wins out over another, the marvel being that the earlier thinking, that of Heraclitus, has, as if in advance, mentioned this possibility. This is what we learn from fragment 32 of Heraclitus, which can be read as follows: "The One, the

Wise, him alone, does not lend itself and lends itself to be said by the name of Zeus."

Does not lend itself and lends itself. In the second case, the study of the One becomes essentially that of the *first* of the gods, of Zeus, but as isolated and cast out from what maintains him at the level of his divinity in the more secret movedness of a unique and *pan-ic* destiny, from which the gods as well as men derive. Henceforth the most proper name of the study of being, having become the bringing into view of the first of the gods, could well be: Theology. What is striking in the words of Heraclitus, however, which speak of a double possibility in the form of a *yes* and a *no,* is that the *no* precedes the *yes. Does not lend itself* has the first rank, and it thus seems to have the upper hand over what only follows it, namely *lends itself*—although there is here no mere impasse, a pure and simple absurdity, but rather a possibility, one that could be developed and even prevail. But, for Heraclitus, it is quite clear that this possibility is not the right one. The One of which he speaks would not be the unhoped-for or the Unexpected that fragment 18 enigmatically names, but something more expected or, as it were, something more accessible, namely the first of the gods. With Aristotle, on the contrary, everything is overturned, and the most proper name of first philosophy becomes, as he says, *theological knowledge.* Not, of course, *Theology*—Aristotle uses the word Theology only to refer back to the poets, to Homer and Hesiod—but much rather *Theological.* The *Theological* is to *Theology* what modern *Logistics* is, for example, to simple *Logic,* or *statistics* to the simple recording of a state of affairs, namely the transformation into a rigorous discipline of a spontaneous but still approximate practice. At any rate, with Aristotle theological research seems to become the very heart of the inquiry into beings as beings, and hence the most proper task of philosophy.

Evidently, with this theological transformation or mutation of an earlier thinking the possibility of a properly religious exploitation of Greek philosophy is opened—open as soon as a religion will decide to preoccupy itself with it. Such was par excellence the destiny of the Christian religion upon the decline of the antique world. But it is only in the thirteenth century that the philosophico-religious syncretism that ends up in naming itself 'Christian philosophy' will adopt the imposing proportions of a *Summa,* which is the *Summa* of Saint Thomas. The heart of the matter here is no longer, according to the formula of a quite remarkable historian of scholasticism, Etienne Gilson, the definition of being in the last analysis by the divine, as it was for Aristotle, but the veritable "identification of *God* and *being.*" This means: the identification of God, who according to the *Letter to the Hebrews,* after having formerly spoken to our fathers by the Prophets, has just spoken to us by his Son, and of *Being,* such as it was the proper enterprise of Greek philosophy. Such a convergence would be truly the eighth wonder of the world if it did not rest, as I fear, on a fundamental misunderstanding. It is necessary to make this point clear. It is made apparently possible by the theological mutation of the meditation on being, as it was accomplished from Heraclitus to Aristotle. But the *Theological* in Aristotle's sense and the Theology of Saint Thomas are different to such an extent that it seems difficult for the second to graft itself onto the first, which was, however, its deliberate project. Doubtless, there is as much of the Most High in Aristotle's *Metaphysics* as there is in the *Summa* of Saint Thomas. But the Most High, as Aristotle understands it with a Greek ear, is an essentially verbal definition of a mode of being. It is on no account the *nomination* of a being. The beings of this mode of being, as Aristotle says not without humor, "I leave to those wiser than I am the care to count if they are 47 or 55." He does not speak in this way because he is Greek, and thus as one says rather too liberally, polytheistic, but because the *unicity* of the divine as a mode of being has strictly nothing to do, in his eyes, with the reduction to a *numerical unity* of a possible plurality of individuals. In other words, Aristotle could have quite easily professed *even* monotheism, as he almost does in the last book of his *Physics,* without ceasing in any way to be a philosopher. Making Monotheism the truth of truths, on the contrary, is to cease to be a philosopher in Aristotle's sense. It is a question here only of a nuance, certainly, but it is on nuances of this sort that depends the discernment of what is a path and of what is an impasse in philosophy.

Consequently, between what comes to us from the Greeks, namely philosophy, and what does not, namely revelation, there is not and there cannot be the slightest shadow of contradiction—and no more the slightest shadow of non-contradiction. In other words, to the question Where do the worlds of philosophy and faith meet? the most radical response is perhaps: *nowhere*! The collisions are feigned. Philosophy and religion are neither contradictory nor non-contradictory. For two propositions to be able to be contradictory or not, it is necessary, as Leibniz said, that they have something in common on the basis of which they can contradict or not contradict each other. In what he named the *disparate,* however, contradiction is not even possible. Between Pythagoras's theorem and "The café has closed its shutters," there is neither contradiction nor non-contradiction. We are within the disparate. There is nothing to be found in seeking to determine whether Carnot's principle is or is not contradictory with the *Marseillaise*. So would philosophy and revelation, then, be disparate in Leibniz's sense? Perhaps. What is revealed to us in faith remains, at any rate, entirely at the level of beings and derives in no way from the question of being, which is the sole basis on which philosophy can receive information about the divine. The God of revelation announces himself, on the contrary, directly. "I am who I am," as he says to Moses. This in no way means, as Saint Thomas thought: I am what the Greeks sought with the name being. Nietzsche could have the last word here when he says in an aphorism of *Beyond Good and Evil:* "It is truly from refinement that God learnt Greek, having resolved to become a writer — and that he did not learn it better."[8]

The moment has come to conclude. To conclude means to come back once again to the subject. The subject was: the birth of philosophy. Perhaps it has become clearer that philosophy is not an eternal necessity that would have always accompanied the march of man on the earth, but that it has a birth, a country of birth, a cradle. It was on the shores of Ionia and also of Italy that one day it was born, Mediterranean, before coming, toward the evening of the Greek world, to inhabit Attica. It was not too well received here, if we are to judge by the banishment of Anaxagoras, who was the first arrival from Ionia to Athens, but who had to leave despite the friendship of Pericles, and by the death of Socrates slightly later, which was an even more radical form of exile for him. Evidently the Athenians did not take too kindly to philosophy. They had, as is said, an 'old soldier mentality' from the Medean and other wars. This is indeed why Socrates was accused of corrupting youth, that is, the old soldiers of the future. Besides, the Athenians hardly had any time to accustom themselves to philosophy, for in Greece, as Schelling said, "everything happens at an incredible speed." If everything, for our concerns, begins in the fifth century with the point-blank thinking of Heraclitus, it finishes with Aristotle, slightly more than a century afterward, but, as we have seen, after such a decisive transformation from the initial starting point that one cannot fail to wonder at it.

> Greek philosophy finishes with Aristotle, who was followed by mere men of discourse or simple commentators, not to mention the numerous jugglers who emanated from the diverse sects that emerged from the primitive ground without adding anything to it.

Thus spoke, in the last century, August Comte, who notwithstanding an extravagant life occasionally had good ideas.

One happily speaks today of an *acceleration of history*. This is to satisfy oneself cheaply. I fear that in this formula, introduced by Daniel

Halévy, history is confused with means of communication and transport. Perhaps, on the contrary, we are relatively *stagnant* with regard to the forerunners who preceded us so far in the distance, whose short race was the setting off of our own history.

For this scission of language and in language that was, at its birth, philosophy, such as the Greeks instituted it, brought us into the world in endowing us with an instinct that is contrary to all others. Valéry marveled at it in naming it: *l'instinct de l'écart sans retour*—the instinct of an unbridgeable gap.

It is perhaps no longer only Greek philosophy but philosophy itself that lies behind us today, leaving its place to the sciences that escaped from it. The force that they exert in the world is on the way to leading us somewhere, but nobody knows where. Yet if we are thus transported without being able to do anything about it, perhaps it is from this forgotten and distant birth that was the birth of philosophy. This is why it is perhaps unwise to expect from philosophy and what arises from it a warding off of the perils that its destiny was precisely to incite. But perhaps it is no wiser to believe that it is possible to dispel them by means of external assistance, which only ever is, as Nietzsche said, an escape route. Are we, then, in an impasse? Do we only know ourselves there? Or do we not have a lot to learn on this point? If we begin, however slowly or slightly, to confront such questions so that they become more and more thoughtful, then it is not in vain that we will have paused to meditate upon the enigma that the birth of philosophy is for us.

2

Heraclitus and Parmenides

To René Char

If the world that is said to be pre-Socratic is rich in original historical figures, Heraclitus and Parmenides are the most radiantly central figures of this world. With Heraclitus and Parmenides the very foundation of occidental thought is accomplished. It is to them that what is still alive and vivacious at the bottom of our thinking goes back, as if to the secret of its source. It can be said that it is through them that we think, even if we do not think of them, for they are the light in which the depth of our world is originally revealed—a depth which we always and already *are* and which remains all the more enigmatic for us, and thus all the more concealed, in that we belong to it in the heart of the history that has come to us and that is still to come.

From Heraclitus of Ephesus, named Heraclitus the Obscure, we have a collection of sentences that are called fragments, around a hundred of which can be held to be authentic. These fragments are perhaps so many citations of a once extant work. They are nonetheless fragments, drawn haphazardly from a block of which we know only the splinters. The fragments of Heraclitus are such splinters or, if you will, so many lightning flashes that reach us from the origin of the ages, like the fulguration of a storm that would have mysteriously withdrawn. If Heraclitus was named from antiquity the Obscure, then this is certainly because of his style, which is already fragmentary and aphoristic in the full sense of the word—the aphorism literally being this circumscribed meditation that both separates and draws out what is essential in a phrase that concerns our destiny.

From Parmenides of Elea, who would seem to have been slightly younger than Heraclitus, what we have is quite different. Parmenides is the author of a Poem that once existed in its entirety, although there remain only fragments of it. Yet the word has here a wholly different sense than when one speaks of the fragments of Heraclitus. If Heraclitus is essentially fragmentary, Parmenides has become fragmentary only over time. This is why the ancients did not count him among the Enigmatics, but rather placed him beside Xenophanes, Plato, and Aristotle, among the masters who did not deign to explain themselves, taking care, as Simplicius will say, of "those who understand superficially." In any event, the fragments of Parmenides that we still have, like the Parthenon among Greek temples, are the most important and the most coherent of the world before Socrates.

It is customary—the custom dates from antiquity, for we find it well established in Plato—to oppose Heraclitus to Parmenides as two gladiators crossing swords at the origin of thought. Is the former not the philosopher of universal movement, the latter proclaiming, on the contrary, the radical immobility of being? An irreconcilable adversity concerning the movement of being would constitute, then, the dawn of philosophy. All things are flux, says Heraclitus, πάντα ῥεῖ; and as Plato, who did not take too kindly to this way of speaking, adds in the form of a caricature: he diagnoses everywhere a universal debacle, as if "someone with a cold pretended that it was not him, but the Whole that has a streaming nose and suffers from catarrh."[1] Being *is*, says Parmenides, on the contrary. What happens is only an illusion, for if we are searching for a path, no path in which we could have confidence can be cleared between the viability of being and the non-viability of non-being. Having thus begun by a simplistic clash of contradictory propositions, it would only remain for us to continue valiantly the polemic from which philosophy was born, perhaps using any means possible, and Cicero would not have been mistaken to write: "it is impossible to invent anything so absurd that it would not have been said by one philosopher arguing against another."[2]

Things, however, are perhaps less simple. It is necessary to recall, only for the record first of all, that the famous πάντα ῥεῖ which is so universally cited, and which Plato seems to take for a sufficient summary of Heraclitus's thinking, is not part of the aphorisms that are the most authentically attributed to the Ephesian. Of course, an image of a river that flows without end is to be found in Heraclitus, but in naming the river the thinker opposes its permanence to the flowing of the water. The sun also is new every day, but it never oversteps its own limits, for the Erynnies, the guardians of justice, are always watching over it.

Similarly, if fire becomes sea and the sea becomes earth, the sea derives from that against which it measured itself before becoming earth. The permanence of measures that ceaselessly reigns over movement is more radical than movement itself. But this thinking of permanence does not intervene in forming an island of calm where we could find refuge. For if such a permanence assigns to movement its limits, it never stops the latter anywhere, a thing being only what it is in being at once the same and other at the heart of a unity wherein difference never ceases to transpire. This is why "the God is day-night, winter-summer, war-peace, abundance-penury, and thus takes various shapes, just as fire, when mingled with different spices, is named according to the savor of each" (fragment 67). God? Who is this Heraclitian God that is always other? His real name is combat. "*Polemos* is the father of everything, king of all: it is he who makes some appear as gods, others men and who reveals some as slaves, others free" (fragment 53). This unusual God-Combat is, thus, the original unity of contrasts that is maintained right up to the most extreme point of their antagonistic tension, yet without either of them being able to prevail over the other. Another name for such a God is Harmony. But here the Greek word ἁρμονίη excludes any reference to the mawkish appeasement that, since Plato, we call harmony. Heraclitian harmony speaks of the pressured junction of opposing forces. It is at work only in the adjoining of adverse tensions, thanks to which alone the bow projects the arrow—the bow whose Greek name evokes at once life, βιός, and the redoubtable weapon of Artemis, βιός, the one from which springs death. Here language philosophizes by itself, and it is a play of words that precedes thought, for it is in this play that the unity of contraries is directly articulated. In this unity it falls to us to be in the world, at once too old and too young to live and to die, but living our death and dying our life according to the law of God, Combat, and Harmony, of which a fourth name is Αἰών, Time. "Time is a child who plays draughts, he plays in moving the pieces of his game: O kingdom whose prince is a child" (fragment 52). Any commentary here could only weaken this original evocation of the innocence at the heart of harmony, of the dissension from which the world is formed as our world, the one whose law it falls to us to defend in fighting for our city walls.

Nothing, therefore, is more foreign to the spirit of Heraclitus than the supposed doctrine of universal mobilism that a lazy tradition transmits to us from him. And if we want to maintain as authentically Heraclitian the words πάντα ῥεῖ, we have to think them through anew in order to discover their true sense. What such words say to us is perhaps less a simple flux than the essential relation of the latter to the counter-current of the reflux. The contrasted movement of flux and reflux is no longer that of being at full steam and being adrift, but it establishes a *level* whose at least relative permanence allows boats to be afloat, and thus to take to the open seas as much as to return to port. The movement of flux and reflux is the very movement of struggle. Far from simplifying everything in a unilateralism, the struggle never ceases to appropriate each side in its opposition to the side that opposes it. It is their clash that the words force us to consider, and it is as a phase of this clash that the λóγος defines what we can hold for constancy only if we still remain capable of conquering it.

Heraclitus enjoins us to recognize in this λóγος, which composes the universal opposition whose well-adjoined collection is the combat of the world, the specific virtue of fire. He thus appears to inaugurate a 'vulcanist' cosmology that would contradict the 'neptunism' of Thales of Milet. To believe the Stoics, he would even have held that fire never stops advancing to the point where everything becomes periodically inflamed in a universal conflagration. In reality, the fire of which Heraclitus speaks is less a basic element that would end up prevailing over others than it is that against which everything else is exchanged "like wares against gold and gold against wares."

If fire is exchanged against everything, a thing only ever being what it is in opposition to itself, then this exchange only has meaning in fire thought as the living center of all opposition. Such is fire, in fact: it is from it that everything takes its measure. It is diversified in a world of contrasts, for it is in itself an original contrast, at once flamboyant light and smoldering ardor. For if φύσις (fragment 123) is the emergence whereby each thing attains clarity, this clarity can be what it is only by the retreat in it of a more secret ardor, the foyer of all clarity and brightness. Consequently, it is in the clear-obscure of the fire whose "expansion is gathered within itself" that the visage of the world is animated. This is a continual emergence and a continual withdrawal, the emergence liking this withdrawal, from which it never ceases to radiate as a challenge to all decline. Those who know how to stoke the fire in the hearth without letting it die know much more about this than the vain *polymathy* of the lettered ever could. Heraclitus was of the former. Aristotle recounts that to some strangers who had come to see him, and who appeared taken aback to find him warming himself by a stove, he said in order to encourage them to approach: "But here also the gods are present."[3] How are we to understand this *here also*? Does it merely concern the simplicity of a humble abode? Should we not rather understand that the humble stove remains, in spite of everything, the place of the fire that is always life, of the fire that is older than gods and men, and whose light is only a reflection of the still un-deciphered enigma that Greek thought presents to us? Yes, at least if the secret of such a thinking is maintained in the strangeness of a noun that we translate as truth only in being inattentive to the more original clearing that is the Greek world itself, which the language of this world had named ἀλήθεια.

Already misunderstood by Plato and increasingly deformed and misrepresented, the thinking of Heraclitus will remain a well-kept secret of history, and we have to wait more than two millennia for something of it to come to light. It was, in fact, barely two centuries ago that three friends were born who shared the same student rooms for five years at Tübingen, namely Hölderlin, Hegel, and Schelling. They chose as an originally common subject of study the *One-All* of Heraclitus, in liberating themselves of any simply *mobilist* interpretation of his thinking. It is, thus, not by chance that in his novel *Hyperion or the Hermit in Greece* Hölderlin evokes Heraclitus, whose "grandiose phrase" he transcribes thus: "the One that is endlessly differentiated in itself." Concerning such a thought, he adds: "only a Greek was able to find it, for in it the very essence of beauty is to be discovered, and before this revelation there was no philosophy."[4] We are so close here to Hegel's declaration that if the Greeks instituted the thinking of being, then it is only for having recognized the truth of being in the splendor of the beautiful! And if Schelling, attentive to so many other oracles, seems only to mention the Oracle of Ephesus in passing, Hegel, on the contrary, will attribute to him a decisive importance in the history of the world: "There is no proposition of Heraclitus that I have not taken up in my Logic."[5] In this Logic, which so little resembles what one ordinarily designates by this title, Hegel interprets philosophy as infinite thought. Finite thought is thought that allows everything to fall back to the inert simplification of unilaterality in seeing only one side of things. Infinite thought, however, is thought that also discovers the other side of things, and that consequently allows opposition to appear as the unique foyer of all life. For the contraries are not qualities that would first be established in themselves and that would have to clash subsequently in order to engender anything, but it is rather at the very heart of what is that they work ceaselessly in opposite directions. Consequently, Hegel's dialectic and its Marxist version both echo Heraclitus's thinking and respond to it through the centuries. And it is, in the end, from the same origin that an other echo resonates in Nietzsche's meditation, when the 'last philosopher' dares to reveal the *eternal return of the same* as the ultimate secret that the determination of being as *will to power* conceals. At this *summit of meditation,* the soul becomes true being, that "in which all things have their currents and counter-currents, their ebb and flow."[6] For the soul thus transfigured the *innocence of becoming* is finally re-established, and time, having become once again a playful child, opens a future forever delivered from the *spirit of resentment,* which the mirage of the past when it is only the past continually nourishes.

Hence modern metaphysics, by all that carries the seal of greatness in it, attains the height of the imposing peaks that appeared at the origin of our world with Heraclitus's thinking. It is at Heraclitus's height that Hegel and Nietzsche meet in following paths whose divergence nevertheless converges. But this grandiose return of modern thought to a long forgotten origin, far from happening as a reception that responds to the origin, is perhaps the most extreme forgetting of it. Such a forgetting that names what effaces itself in it, and that even pretends to recognize and honor it at its own level, is not a simple intermittence of memory, an accidental ignorance to which the progress of knowledge would finally furnish a cure. It is a forgetting of what is essential. It is by forgetting what is essential that even Hegel and Nietzsche claim to draw their inspiration from Heraclitus in celebrating him as the initiator of philosophy. For both have access to the clearing of the Greek world only within the horizon of their own problems: for the first, the modern problem of absolute certainty; for the second, the bringing into question of the latter in the still more modern problematic of value. But the dimension in which the thinking of Heraclitus moves, which is the dimension of ἀλήθεια, derives in no way from the scales of certainty, and it no more allows itself to be measured as value. In a world that has become increasingly delivered over to their measures, certainty and value are much rather the now worrying and pale light of the originally animating fire that was, at its dawn, the λόγος of Heraclitus. Yet if the transmutation into philosophy of an earlier thinking opened the history of a long decline, poetry is a quite different affair. This is why Hölderlin's poetic relation to Heraclitus situates him in the closest proximity to the latter's thinking, from which, on the contrary, the philosophical veneration of Hegel and Nietzsche is removed. When Hölderlin names nature, when above all in his last poems he hesitates to name nature again as the sacred awakening of light that shines only in concealing itself at the heart of its own brilliance—and that saves, thus, those that it illuminates—poetic discourse is once more a discourse of being, being as it gives itself in the enigma of its withdrawal. For it belongs to poets, not to resolve problems that metaphysics refuses according to the measure of its concepts, but rather to be for us the vigils of the enigma. "Heraclitus, Georges de la

Tour." The insolence of this vocative, this throw of the dice by René Char, is at the very heart of the same enigma. It invokes the thinker of the meditating fire, whose clarity veils itself in shadow, and the painter of the lucid flame, which preserves the enclosure of night, into the same presence. But, in the helplessness of proofs, poetry and thought respond to each other. All the signs are concordant. Nothing arbitrary anywhere, but everywhere the same craft: *Mon métier est un métier de pointe* (My craft is an advanced craft)."

If there is a difference between Parmenides and Heraclitus, then it has become difficult for us to reduce this difference to the too universally received opposition of a philosophy of becoming and a philosophy of being. But if Heraclitus is not a thinker of becoming, does not the Poem of Parmenides remain as a meditation on being? How it would be superficial to understand it as the proclamation made in the name of being that becoming is only an illusion, thus remaining faithful to a tradition no less inveterate than that of 'Heraclitian mobilism'! Is not summarily concluding from the language of being that what is not being is non-being tantamount to ignoring the very letter of an instruction that, after having named the truth or the way of being in the face of the non-truth that is the impasse of non-being, immediately evokes a third way from which it is no less important to distance ourselves, but which can be followed as the way along which ordinary mortals are always misled? The nine verses that constitute one of the most celebrated fragments of the Poem attest to fact that the assignation of this third way as the way of deviation is essential to Parmenides' thinking:

> Thus it is necessary, to allow to be said and to guard in thought,
>   Beings-being,
> But without opening is the nothing; this is what I bid thee ponder.
> Above all, hold thee back from this way of inquiry
> And from this other also where mortals knowing naught are lost
> In two minds; for it is a lack of expertise
> Which moves the wandering thought in their breast;
> Deaf as they are and no less blind, astounded, stupefied races,
> For whom both being and non-being, being the same and not
>   the same, are one,
> Wherever they go, they only ever advance in retracing their
>   steps.

Distinct from the *Polyphemic* way of being and from the inaccessibility of non-being, another path is opened before us whose detours reveal a quite particular domain, for no solid habitation can find a site there. In this domain of ambiguity where things can only appear at once as the same and as other, all presence is at once its own absence, abundance is already penury, warmth is coldness, and winter is at the heart of radiant summer. But if there is only presence by the absence in it of what is opposed to it, then this other side of each thing, however absent it may be, is never annulled, and it can suddenly become presence while the first side disappears into absence. Such is the world where the weak intellect of men is both here and elsewhere, endlessly seduced and always rebuffed, floating at the whim of contrary currents. Are we so far from Heraclitus? But does not Parmenides consider such a world of illusion, where what negates a thing always transpires in everything, to be simply an illusory world, thus reducing to nothing the wisdom of Heraclitus? Does he not teach us to stamp it with inanity in opposing to it the eternally immobile sphere of being as a unique plenitude? Such will be, slightly later, the call of Platonic metaphysics: the injunction to flee to the heart of being from a groundless world of appearances where we would only be led astray. But if the sinuous play of presence and absence, the game in which we ourselves are at stake, was only a vain inconsistency for Parmenides, why would the divinely spoken Truth undertake to reveal its meanders for us with so much detail, substituting the *disconcerting texture* of the words that evoke them for the *discourse of faith* that they suddenly suspend? Such words are indeed quite disconcerting, for they never stop turning from one term to its opposite without ever fixing themselves anywhere. And yet it is without ever being at all discredited that they come and go in the second part of the same Poem, which consequently appears to announce the duality, day and night, of the things of this world, just as deliberately as it had exposed the unity of day without night, with which it is now contrasted.

In this way the meditation of Parmenides' Poem leads us to the heart of a difficulty that already seemed inextricable to the ancients. The words that unequivocally revealed to us the truth of being now confront equivocation and seem to revel in it. What are we to understand, then, from this disconcerting to-and-fro of the word of truth? Would it be there only to highlight in the things of this world the radical invalidity of the equivocation where being itself is lost in the disappearance of meaning? If this was the case, there would be hardly any difference between Parmenides' Poem and the much later philosophy of Plato, who never hesitates to conclude that equivocation is illusion, everything that can suffer equivocation thus finding itself radically separated from the *portion of being*. But does the contrasted structure of the Poem, whose unity of tone is nevertheless never anywhere broken, really invite us to such a disjunction? Would not the word of truth, when it undertakes to traverse the contraries from both directions, much rather teach us to take our leave from equivocation without invalidating the world, in denouncing in the equivocation itself, rather than the things of this world, what thinking is enjoined to overcome? The commentators have hardly entertained this second and quite un-Platonic possibility. And yet is it not in this sense that Parmenides' Poem speaks to us in its entirety if we attempt to understand it without any Platonic assumptions? If it puts us on our guard against the ambiguity of the naive knowledge that the Greek tongue names δόξα, it nevertheless does not reduce naive δόξα to a mere source of confusion that we would consequently have to reject—both it and its δοκοῦντα —in the groundless inanity of a pseudo-world. It is not in a vacuum but rather in a plenitude that it is able, with every right, to be a capacity to receive, and if such a reception will always deviate into errancy, then it is nonetheless at bottom a positive encounter and an essential correspondence. Thus δόξα in Parmenides' sense has a completely different character than δόξα according to Plato. It can give way to illusion only at the heart of a clearing which itself is non-illusory, for it is there and only there that the portion of adversity that takes hold of us, and that we have to learn to confront, is revealed to us as a universal splendor.

But if δόξα is not purely and simply illusion, if it is *on good grounds* (δοκίμως) that it brings us into the world, it nevertheless remains destined to wander ceaselessly on the path of errancy where any step only ever progresses in being thrown back in the opposite direction, and thus forever to float along this path without ever ending up at anything. Such is the destiny of the artless regard that it can radiate at the heart of the clearing only in being surprised by an abundance that everywhere overwhelms its reception. If the first regard thrown on this adverse splendor already corresponds to what positively concerns us, then it is not yet open to the fully deployed depth of its own horizon. It belongs to the nature of δόξα, thus, to remain the prisoner of a perspective in which it naively perceives only the foreground of things. Short-sightedly opposing presence and absence, it is fascinated by all that appears in presence only subsequently to disappear. It attempts to grasp a presence that escapes it and that gives itself over to a no less precarious absence, and it is in this way that mortals experience to their cost the correlation of the contraries; they say *this* but it is *that*, they bet on one or the other only to be disappointed each time. Thus we ceaselessly err, *bicephalized* as we are by the universal ambiguity that is, on the way of deviation, the double game of presence and absence. If, however, the horizon came to reveal itself to the point of enabling us to see that presence and absence, far from being opposed to each other as two separate figures, can deploy their contrast only in the initially unapparent unity of a reciprocal belonging, then errancy would be surmounted, the contradiction resolved, equivocation finally undone, but in this world, which consequently would be fully coherent and a domain of being. Yet is this not what an isolated group of four verses, a fragment in which the secret unity of the whole of the Poem is articulated, precisely enjoins us to meditate? At this summit of his meditation, Parmenides' thinking gathers itself into a supreme conclusion:

> See them as the same, what is absent and what is present, see
> them, in the thinking regard, in the full vigor of being
> For such a regard will not cut off what is from its holding fast to
> being
> No more when what is is dispersed wholly and completely in
> absence, as befits the adjoining of being,
> Than when it is gathered in a presence.

What these four verses that radiate from the very center of the Poem say to us is in no way the in-distinction of presence and absence in a pure and simple confusion of both. They much rather say to us that disappearing in the night of absence is on no account a dispersion of being, for it is only in it that absence can take place. Not that being would first have to stand in itself, elevated as a superior genus above presence and absence: on the contrary, it is according to a more essential relationship of the one to the other that its plenitude unfolds. The opposition of presence and absence, far from constituting a decisive break that would separate them without recourse to each other, *is* itself this *unitive* correlation where we are in the presence of presence-absence. If, therefore, absence appears apart from presence, then this is only when our vision remains restricted, as in the completely naive *reception* that is δόξα. But it is not at all the same for whoever has good eyesight, and that is to say, in the more sagacious *collection* by which thought responds fully to being. In this way the understanding of being has already surmounted the disjunction of presence and absence that the horizonless separatism of δόξα imposes on the two-headed races of stupefied mortals. Being draws back to itself, in the unity of the Same, the alternating that plays with us in these scintillating things that are the δοκοῦντα. We can learn to see such scintillation in its unique and fixed light, if we know, through a veritable knowing, the things present and absent from the perspective of the singularity of being, whose divine words alone are able to speak of its splendor. For if presence and absence are qualities that never stop alternating in beings, this can occur only within the immutable horizon of being. Being itself is never a being, but the measure according to which all beings can just as much enter into presence as they can withdraw themselves from the latter, thus disappearing. More original than the presence-absence of beings is the universality of being that, unscathed from its sharing in such a vicissitude, contains the latter without dissolving itself in it, and consequently concerns us in a more insistent manner. But if this is the case, the words that have a *disconcerting texture,* the words that, from the end of the eighth fragment, twirl around in apparently breaking the unity of the Poem still fall under the discourse of being—it is the thinking of being that animates them and prolongs itself in them. Such words can be said to twirl around insofar as they ceaselessly come and go from one or other of the two sides of things that are presence and absence. But these twirls that shake the presence-absence of the δοκοῦντα from so near, far from losing themselves and us in the endless meanders of their labyrinth, are much rather the grace that liberates us from the latter, in leading us to recognize the unique radiation of being in presence as much as absence.

Parmenides' meditation is thus a *pan-ic* of being that no presence will ever exhaust, whose plenitude is not lacking in any absence. How distant it remains from the procedure of Plato, which will bring non-being into presence itself as a result of its finding itself exposed to absence, however slight this may be, and which will define being by the permanence of beings! But if the time is short from Parmenides to Plato, a world already marks the transition. The absence that for Plato is the empire of non-being belongs, on the contrary, entirely to the problematic of being in Parmenides' Poem, where non-being itself is not at all absence. Even absence is eliminated from non-being. For the word that names the latter is there only to brand the very opening of being as forbidden to it, in leading presence and absence to a duel in which both clash only in the name of being and in its light. Hence it is as the unity of presence and absence that being is opposed to non-being, which itself holds both in check. A bottomless abyss without depth, non-being is not even an abyss, and no language will ever say anything of it.

If Parmenides is the thinker of being, we can understand now that this thinking of being overshadows change no more than a thinking of change, such as Heraclitus conceives it, destabilizes a fundamental permanence. Movement appears to Heraclitus only upon a back-

ground of permanence, and when Parmenides thinks the permanence of being against non-being, it is as an unmovable horizon of
presence-absence that is the essence of all change. Far from rising
from the dawn against each other like the champions of an inaugural
polemic, Heraclitus and Parmenides are perhaps both, despite the difference of their words, listening to the same λόγος, to which they both
lend the same ear at the origin of occidental thought. At bottom, there
is perhaps no more immobilism in Parmenides' Poem than there is
mobilism in the fragments of Heraclitus, or rather permanence and
change are to be found to the same degree in both. In this way the two
languages diverge without, however, contradicting each other. Both
expose the Greek knowledge of being, a *knowing of being* that unfolds
in the element of presence without forcing or tormenting anything,
without shying away or becoming strained, without compromise or
excess.

It remains the case, however, that if a long-secret truth of Heraclitus is finally beginning to break though the veil that hid it, it is not so
with Parmenides. Nietzsche himself continues to take him for the
adversary of change, the one who held appearances in contempt, the
fanatic of another world from which an illusory world separates us,
and which would be the forever frozen world of the eternally identical. Similarly, in an illustrious strophe of the "Cemetery by the Sea,"
it is as a dreamer of eternity that Valéry evokes Parmenides through
his disciple Zeno, who was Parmenides' favorite according to Plato.[7]
And in an epigraph that is no less illustrious, but that Valéry wrongly
considers as contrastive, the poet appeals to the sobriety of Pindaric
wisdom against the metaphysical madness into which the Eleat
would have let himself be dragged. A poet can thus fail to understand another poet, and philosophers are not the only ones to err. Is
this not the highest sign that Parmenides' spirit, yet more than that
of Heraclitus, continues to hide itself in the defensive position of a
thinking that is still without access among us?

Near and yet far from us, the two figures of the origin that are Heraclitus and Parmenides have not ceased to wait, to surprise, and to provoke questions—whether the questioner is a painter: Braque, a poet:
Char, a philosopher: Heidegger. And perhaps this is, in the end, the
strange marvel: that poetry and thought can occasionally end up finding and joining each other, meeting and understanding each other in
this first dawn where words are still signposts. "The lord, whose oracle
is at Delphi, neither reveals nor conceals: but shows with signs" (fragment 93).

3

Reading Parmenides

Parmenides' Poem, whose fragments were gathered together by Theophrastus in the time of Aristotle and by the neo-Platonist Simplicius in the time of Justinian, would seem to date from the beginning of the fifth century. No one in France studies it in depth, but this does not prevent the 'experts' from knowing exactly what it says, thanks to the constancy of a tradition that, from Plato to modern philology, gives a virtually uniform interpretation of it. According to this classical interpretation, Parmenides would have taught at one extremity of the Greek world the opposite to what, in the same epoch, Heraclitus said at the eastern extremity of the same world. Heraclitus, as Plato declares, held that everything flows like the water of a river, and that stability is only ever a mere appearance. Parmenides would have adopted the opposite position. According to him, becoming would be the mere appearance against which one has to maintain the immobile unity of being as the unique truth. From the beginning of his poem does he not hold the 'opinions of mortals', in whose eyes nothing is real that is not multiple and changing, to be inadmissible?

Opinions are unanimous on this point. Differences intervene only with the question of the precise nature of the developments in the poem concerning the world of illusion and error. On this point, since the end of the nineteenth century, and during the first fifteen years of our century, three interpretations arose consecutively:

1. Primarily the interpretation of Diels, Professor in Berlin, who undertook the first critical edition of Parmenides' Poem in 1897.[1] The

error that Parmenides denounces as barring access to the truth of beings has, according to Diels, two levels. First, the confusion of what is with what is not in the multitude's devotion to mere appearances. This is the common fate of man. Yet on another level it is a question of the more erudite opinions of those who teach falsely with Heraclitus that the essence of being is change. It is, therefore, not only the naive error of everyman, but the philosophical error of Heraclitus against which Parmenides vituperates, and his tone would pass from pitiful indulgence to implacable severity according to whether it is a question of the one or the other. In the eyes of John Burnet, however, who studies the same question at the same time but in England and from a slightly different perspective, Parmenides speaks less against Heraclitus than against the Pythagorians, who apparently "were far more serious opponents at that date in Italy."[2]

2. Diels's interpretation, from which that of Burnet is virtually indistinguishable, is contested two years later by Wilamowitz,[3] who is or who will become the colleague of the former at the University of Berlin. In truth, as Wilamowitz writes, Parmenides does not speak against anyone in particular. For the opinions that he holds to be inadmissible are maintained, at bottom, as a sort of inferior truth, a hypothetical or relative truth for the use of those incapable of attaining the true heart of the matter. Such will also be the interpretation of Theodore Gomperz. But in opposing Diels, Wilamowitz and Gomperz only return to the oldest interpretation of the poem, one that had already been formulated by Theophrastus, Aristotle's contemporary and the first editor of the work of Parmenides. For Theophrastus, it is "according to the opinion of the greatest number" that Parmenides posed "two principles in order to account for the genesis of phenomena."[4]

3. But in 1916 Karl Reinhardt, who taught at Frankfurt and whom I once had the chance to meet on the shores of Lake Maggiore just after the Second World War, dismisses the interpretations of both Diels and Wilamowitz. This is neither a polemical refutation nor a concessive hypothesis; what Parmenides explains, after having opposed truth to error, is quite simply how it would be impossible for error not to seize the minds of men from the very beginning. The power of error over men responds, as Reinhardt says, "to a sort of original sin" of pre-history.[5] The site of this error, that is, opinion or δόξα, ceases to be, therefore, a mere adventitious juxtaposition to true knowledge, ἀλήθεια, in the Poem; it becomes an integral part of a whole to whose unity it belongs as that to which true knowledge is contrasted. In France, Diès is, as it would seem, repulsed by Reinhardt's interpretation, which he summarily qualifies in 1923 as "very

adventurous" in a note within his edition of Plato's *Parmenides*.[6] After this no one will say one word more about it. The reason for this national protectionism is perhaps that Reinhardt is not very easy to read, and is thus destined at the very most to augment those infamous bibliographies that occasionally dazzle naive students, subjugated as they are by what they take to be the omniscience of their teachers.

Reinhardt's interpretation remains today that of Hermann Fränkel, who has taught for some years at Stanford. It is also that of Johannes Lohmann, who teaches comparative grammar at Freiburg, according to what he wrote to me some years ago in a letter which took up and prolonged a conversation that had begun at Freiburg station at the beginning of October 1959. The originality of this interpretation is that, according to it, the words of the Goddess that we are going to hear in a moment do not express, as Diels and Wilamowitz both thought even if they did not agree on the details, a simple bipartition: on the one side truth, on the other side the error of the opinions professed by mortals, the question being whether the latter is to be completely refuted or partially tolerated. The words of the Goddess rather express a tripartition: truth, error, and the truth *of* error, which is to say, a study of the ground of error itself.

The argument that there is a tripartition where a bimillenary tradition has only been able to see a bipartition, is, I believe, the veritable acquisition of Reinhardt's study. Yet whether this tripartition is exactly as Reinhardt determines it remains as questionable.

It falls to Heidegger to have raised such a question eleven years after the publication of Reinhardt's book, on page 223 of *Sein und Zeit* (1927), that is, four pages before the incomplete French translation published in 1964 by Gallimard as a supposed first volume of the text mysteriously comes to a halt. Heidegger says in a note: "Karl Reinhardt was the first to conceptualize and solve the hackneyed problem of how the two parts of Parmenides' poem are connected, though he did not explicitly point out the ontological foundation for the connection between ἀλήθεια and δόξα, or of the necessity of this connection."

I attempted to elucidate this point within a brief study in 1955 in homage to my pupil and friend Jean-Jacques Ranieri, to whom a few years before I had recommended the study of the philosophers that one calls pre-Socratic. I mention this only for the sake of memory, having been informed by the learned *Revue de métaphysique et de morale* that I was fantasizing, since I was not in agreement with any of the specialists who constituted the authority until then; and by the no less learned *Revue philosophique* that the interpretation I proposed, in a style that was, to tell the truth, otiose and precious—you know, one writes as one is able to write—was "perfectly arbitrary" given that it contained an evidently provocative reference to Heidegger. It is a fact that the intrusion of a philosopher in the private hunting ground of philology that the pre-Socratic world had become was a scandal from which the example could only come from Heidegger. Doubtless, at this rate the interpretation of the *Critique of Pure Reason* will soon come to be purely the business of Germanists.

To return to Parmenides, the exact nature of the tripartition with which the two learned journals that I have just evoked were by no means concerned is what seems, elsewhere if not in France, to constitute the point that requires elucidation. Is it a question, as Reinhardt thought, of the tripartition: truth, error, and truth of error as original sin? Is it a question of something other? But of what exactly? Can we draw it out from a simple translation? Yes, but on condition that this translation is not simply a movement of the text to us, but rather a movement on our part to Parmenides' words. Not, of course, in order to burden them with presuppositions that have come from elsewhere, but to attempt to hear in them the simplicity of what they say. And here philology, as erudite as it may be, remains insufficient. For it is above all philology that is far from being exempt from philosophical presuppositions. When Fränkel says, for example, in echoing the public rumors concerning the ideas of the learned, that Parmenides "refutes the sensible world in denouncing it as an illusion,"[7] perhaps he expresses less the result of a critical reading than the condition that renders his reading fatal from the very beginning. The reading that I have had occasion to propose is not a *lectio difficilior* in the sense of philology, but in the sense of philosophy. It is not a question of substituting a supposed spirit for the letter, but of preparing one's spirit for the reading of the letter, which itself is something altogether different than a message that remains to be decoded. It is, therefore, a voyage to Elea that I propose to you and not the opening of a dig that, according to the latest information, has now begun.

I visited Elea before or almost before the opening of the dig. Slightly to the south of Paestum, and almost opposite Cape Palinurus, Elea, from plateau to plateau, steps down toward the coast where once the Acropolis stood on a hilltop before the sea, which is crowned today by a tower bequeathed by the Middle Ages. There remained, however, the charm of the Promenade that looks onto Monte Stella, the whole length of the ramparts that Parmenides had seen, but that have also become fragments, like the Poem whose emergence they protected. The relative contrast between the relative mobility of the sea and the no less relative stability of the promontory and of the mount, in particular, evoke the unique and *pan-ic* permanence where everything is written, even absence, and which cannot be compared to anything. That is Elea. It is here that one day and forever the fabulous carriage departed at a gallop, which today reaches us after its more than bimillenary race, only in order to go, perhaps, farther than where we are.

> The steeds that carry me as far as my heart ever desired were advancing. They had led me on a road rich in lessons of divinity, the road that carries the man who knows through the houses. It is on it that I was borne, on it that the wise steeds coupled to my car led me, while maidens showed the way.
> And the axle, glowing in the socket, gave the strident cry of a flute, urged round by the whirling wheels at both ends, when the daughters of the Sun, hastening to convey me into light, threw back their veils from off their faces once they had left the abode of night.
> There are the gates of the ways of Night and Day, fitted between a lintel above and a threshold of stone below. They themselves stand luminously in the air with the fullness of their vast doors, and powerfully rigorous Dike keeps the keys that fit them. In entreating her with gentle words, the Daughters of the Sun found the art of persuading her. For them she unfastened the bolted bars without demur. Then the doors flew back, leaving the space of the doors gaping. One after the other, in their housing, the brazen posts fitted with rivets and nails swung back. And it is here, passing through the doors, straight on the broad way, that the young girls guided the horses and car.
> And the Goddess welcomed me also, favorably. She took in her hand my right hand, and here is what she said in singing it for me:
> "Welcome, O youth, that is escorted by immortal charioteers, that by the gallop of horses reaches our abode! It is no ill chance that led you to take this road, far as it lies from men and their path, but Themis, but Dike. And now you must undertake to learn all things. As much the Open-without-hiddenness, a well-rounded sphere with an unshaken heart, as the opinions of mortals, where nothing stands in the Open-without-hiddenness. Yet you shall learn this also: how it is the destiny of what diversely is to be seen to show itself on a good ground, which, traversing everything, transpires everywhere."

We have understood: it is indeed a question of a tripartition: *this and then this but no less that* and not of a simple bipartition: *first of all this and then that.* How were Diels and Wilamowitz not able to see it? It is because they wanted to learn from the Poem only the dichotomy of the Open-without-hiddenness, ἀλήθεια and the βροτῶν δόξαι, the opinions of mortals who are subjugated by appearances where nothing has any foundation in the Open-without-hiddenness. Such an opposition evidently leaves no room for any other possibility. This is why Diels and Wilamowitz interpret the last two verses, those that seem to open a third task for thought, as a simple paraphrase that comments on what precedes them. Diels arrives at his ends thanks to a heroic amelioration of the text, a veritable philological putsch, which allows him to read it as follows: "Having learnt the truth as well as the error of mortals, learn also how this error must be rectified." Wilamowitz draws back from the violence of the modifications that Diels makes the text endure and reads: "Having learnt the truth as well as the error of mortals, understand also that this error is not pure nonsense, that it is not inadmissible as would be saying that non-A equals A." Since the world of appearance is not contradictory, it is possible to give a consistent representation of it that will take the place of truth for those unable to attain the heart of truth itself. For example: if Copernicus and Galileo attain the very heart of truth, our representation of the sun as turning around the earth is indeed an illusion. But such an illusion is not an absurdity. One can even expose in all coherence a system of the world in starting from the idea, though it is false, that the sun turns around the earth. Ptolemy's system, even if it is not the equal of that of Copernicus, is not without merit, and can quite easily suffice for non-specialists.

But here the interpretation of Wilamowitz, safe-keeper of the text, perilously weakens the opposition of ἀλήθεια to the βροτῶν δόξαι. Nothing, in fact, is less concessive in Greek thought than truth. This is why Diels does not hesitate to modify the text with the aim of saving its meaning. In relation to Wilamowitz, who loses the meaning in order to save the text, and to Diels, who alters the text in order to save its meaning, the originality of Reinhardt is that he asks philology for the means to save both the text and the meaning. Philology offers, as he says, a *third* possibility. It consists in reading: "Having learnt to know the truth as well as error, you will learn also how fatal it was that error seized from the beginning the knowledge of mortals." Such a reading is quite possible. It amounts to saying: "Having learnt the system of Copernicus as well as the illusion that it denounces, you will learn also how it was fatal that men had to remain under an illusion until Copernicus." But does there not still remain a *fourth* possibility, distinct from the one that Reinhardt discovers, and to which philology, still a good girl, is not opposed any more than it is to the preceding ones? It would consist in reading what we have read thus: "Having penetrated to the heart of truth and well understood the errors to which men are subject, learn also how things, such as they show themselves, carry themselves quite well in their own way." With Parmenides, let us call things in the way that they show or manifest themselves τὰ δοκοῦντα. Reinhardt continues to interpret the δοκοῦντα pejoratively. They are the illusion that, following God knows what 'original sin of pre-history', will fatally subjugate each one of us as soon as he opens his eyes. Such is Plato's interpretation. Is it, for all that, that of Parmenides? Does he not say quite simply that mortals, before being enlightened by the word of ἀλήθεια, see badly what is there before their eyes? So would Parmenides' thinking cast no aspersions on what Plato disdainfully calls the sensible world? Would it not commit us to sacrifice the δοκοῦντα to the *über-schmale Wahrheit*,[8] as Reinhardt says, to the 'more than meager' truth of being? Not at all. The life of the δοκοῦντα is without original sin. The world of illusion is not an illusion of world. "Good health to the δοκοῦντα!" says Parmenides, in the sense that Char will say "Good health to the Snake!" The δοκοῦντα are this serpent itself. But it is necessary to learn to see it *snake*, which is difficult. It is much easier to be taken in by one's own game. But we are getting ahead of ourselves, and we should progress in measured steps. Let us listen to the Goddess:

> Come now and I will tell you, and you shall be the guardian
>   of the words spoken.
> What paths of inquiry are to be thought.
> The first of the paths shows that it is without it being possible
>   for it not to be.
> Have confidence in this path, faithful as it is to the Open-
>   without-hiddenness.
> As for the other, namely that it is not and that it must not be
> On this track, I warn you, no step will be assured
> For you cannot know non-being, which leads to nothing, or
>   utter it.
>
> The same, in truth, is at once thinking and being.

We have just heard two fragments, which, perhaps, are only one, for if the fragment that says the *Sameness* of Thought and Being is joined to the two final words of the preceding fragment, it forms with them a complete hexameter.

In the first of these two fragments, the previously announced tripartition seems to be reduced to a simple bipartition: being, non-being. But this, as we will see, is only an appearance. In reality, the bipartition appears here only in the service of the tripartition already announced by the Goddess. Here we are at the point where two paths go their separate ways, only one of them 'following ἀλήθεια'. Would the second, then, deviate in leading us into error? Not at all. Error is met no more on the one than on the other path, even though only one of the two is the true path. Is there, then, something more radically contrary to truth than error? Absolutely. Such a contrary is already said in the Greek word ἀλήθεια. In ἀ-λήθεια there is to be heard: λήθη. This is generally translated as *forgetting*. This translation is very exact, except that it evokes nothing of the loquacious relation of the one to the other. At bottom, ἀλήθεια is truth no more than λήθη is *forgetting*, except in the dictionary. This is why we have translated ἀλήθεια by *Open-without-hiddenness*.[9] The word λήθη speaks on the contrary of the withdrawal that is sheltered and reserved in what comes out of its retreat in appearing, without the non-retreat of appearance ever being able to relinquish the omnipresent possibility of its own withdrawal. To emerge in maintaining in itself the power not to emerge, and even the secret of a refusal to emerge in the sense that the desert refuses to flourish, such is the marvel of being and of its relation to non-being, which as a desert of being, a desert that points to nothing, is its most imminent danger and is already there as soon as being is open to us. If, therefore, being is the path of ἀλήθεια and if non-being is a path, then the latter is the path of λήθη, a path that does not open onto anything, a path without issue, a path that is a non-path.

The nomination of nothingness as an echo of being is not, for Parmenides, a mere stylistic exercise, a simple rhetorical to and fro that would send us gently to sleep, but an experience, whose depth and amplitude, once deployed by him, will persist from one end to the other of the philosophy that it founds, which will be the history of philosophy.

Bergson writes in *Creative Evolution*: "The philosophers have hardly occupied themselves with the idea of nothingness."[10] Perhaps it is much rather the philosophy of Bergson that never properly occupied itself with the thinking of philosophers. Heidegger will say a quarter of a century later: "The question about what is not and about Nothing has gone side by side with the question of what is since its inception. But it does not do so superficially, as an accompanying phenomenon; instead, the question about Nothing takes shape in accordance with the breadth, depth, and originality with which the question about beings is asked on each occasion, and conversely. The manner of asking about Nothing can serve as a gauge and a criterion for the manner of asking about beings" (*EM* 18).

It is here that we arrive at the following fragment, which itself is only one fragment of verse, but which we ought to name, with Valéry, "the pearl of the sphere."[11] Let us listen to it one more time:

The same, in truth, is at once thinking and being.

We find ourselves, then, with a second bipartition. Not one that is *separative* as is that of the preceding fragment, the one that opposed being and non-being, but *unitive*. From the perspective of being, standing before non-being in its contrast with it:

The same, in truth, is at once thinking and being.

Parmenides does not say here that thinking and being amount to the same in the sense that 7 + 5 amounts to the same as 10 + 2, but rather that if the two can be distinguished from each other, then this is only ever at the heart of a belonging together that is defined as Identity. Far from it being the case, therefore, that Identity belongs originally to being, in the sense that Aristotle will articulate the principle of identity as a fundamental trait of being, it is rather being itself that belongs to Identity, which is higher than it, and which is its identity with thought. How are we to understand such an Identity, at once unique and dual, wherein both thinking and being are each for the other, without either of them being able to prevail over the other in dissociating itself from the other in order to impose itself on it? Parmenides leaves us here before the enigma. Philosophy will find it difficult to maintain itself on this inaugural peak, even though, in all the forms that will be given to it to adopt, thought will never stop calling out to being, which itself ceaselessly responds to the call of thought throughout a history that is rich in metamorphoses, whose episodes will only ever be, however, but the periphrases of a more original evocation of Identity, such as it is signaled to us in Parmenides' Poem.

It is possible to recognize in the Identity that Parmenides names the most constant theme of occidental thought. The two contrasted positions of realism and idealism between which philosophy has floated for centuries only disable this more secret Identity. "Man thinks, therefore I am, says the universe." It is enough to invert this phrase of Valéry, an idealistic phrase, for it to produce: "I am, therefore man thinks, says the universe." In this game of inversions it is clear that idealism is at bottom only a closet realism, the realism of thought,[12] and that realism, in turn, remains in the grasp of idealism, its highest achievement being, as if by chance, the explanation of ideologies and of the action they exert on that from which they are supposed to derive. But Parmenides' phrase is beneath both. It is deployed at a level where the one as much as the other fall away. Doubtless, this is why it is reserved for the most audacious thinking, when it frees itself from a quite secular bewitchment, to find itself at Parmenides' level. This memorable repetition, the word repetition not signifying a simple reiteration, but an *asking-again,* a *reprise* and return to the source, was, almost two centuries ago, the *Critique of Pure Reason.* Kant writes: "The conditions of the possibility of experience in general are, at the same time, conditions of possibility for the objects of experience."[13] How can we not recognize that this enigmatic formula and, particularly, the *at the same time* insist upon the echo of Identity, of the Sameness at the heart of which being and thinking began by responding to each other before becoming separated in such a way as to continue to point to each other from both sides of their scission?

With Kant, however, we are no longer in Elea. The big difference between Parmenides' aphorism and the aphorism of Kant is that the latter bears on thinking more than on being. It teaches us that it is thinking that procures for being, which has become objectivity from the fact of the reduction of beings in their being to the state of a 'correlate' of scientific judgment, the possibility of manifesting itself as an object of thought in the unity of experience.[14] Parmenides' aphorism bears, on the contrary, not on thinking, but on being. It does not say that thinking dictates to being its conditions, but that it is only where there is being that thinking no less originally emerges. In other words, it says that being is the country of thinking, or, if you will, its most proper landscape by the grace of which alone thinking opens itself to being in welcoming it and letting it be before it. "I'm his," thinking says of being, without in any way saying to it: "You're mine." It is in this way that it responds, as Heidegger says, to the 'call of being'. Is being, then, a person? In actual fact, being is neither a person nor even a thing. "It is, in truth, being." But language is the 'house of being'. To be concerned by being is, thus, an affair of language and what it says. But we only *say* in *letting ourselves say,* in the sense that Cézanne knew how to let himself say, to let Mont Sainte-Victoire be said to him. The Same, in truth, is painting and being. Painting is not an after-the-fact and more or less adequate expression of being. It belongs to it at the heart of a more secret Identity than any adequation, in which it is being, however, and not painting that has the last word. Cézanne's painting would thus be still closer to the word of Parmenides' than Kant's philosophy, even though it responds to it from nearby only in the sense that poetry and thinking respond to each other, and that is to say, across the greatest distances. Braque, one day and from afar, says to Heidegger: "Echoes respond to echoes and everything reverberates."[15] But where? In the Identity that alone carries the distance and to which Parmenides' words respond from the origin of the ages:

The same, in truth, is at once thinking and being.

But let us continue our reading. In a fragment that has been placed here for no particularly apparent reason—it would be desirable for more hypotheses to be advanced concerning its situation—the two contrasted figures of presence and absence suddenly appear in their relation to being. Even absence is not the abolition of being, for it belongs to its harmony, since it is also a mode of presence. It can even be said that nothing is more present to the meditation of being than what, in absence, distances itself. No ab-sence is ever ab-solute.

> See them, even being far from here, as solidly present for thought. For it will not cut off what is from its holding fast to being, no less in the total dispersion of absence—it belongs to the harmony of being—than in the gathering of presence.

In the text that we have just heard, absence, presence, and being are named. Being, in other words, is named three times, first of all in its relation to two prefixes, then absolutely. The two prefixes are παρά and ἀπό. παρά speaks of an immediate vicinity in the sense that a parasite is a person's companion at the dinner table. Ἀπό, on the contrary, speaks of distance in the sense that a planet's apogee is its greatest distance from the earth, and that with an apology we can often deflect, and thus distance, an accusation from ourselves. Yet nothing is more intimate to the being of beings, at least insofar as Greek experience responds to it, than the contrast that is said by these two prefixes παρά and ἀπό—a contrast that is so intimate that without it the word being, understood in isolation, loses the essence of its meaning. Heidegger recalls: "In the Greek εἶναι there is always to be thought conjointly what is often said thus: παρεῖαι and ἀπεῖναι" (WD 143). Instead, therefore, of beginning with being, which would supposedly be known in itself, in order to annex presence and absence to it secondarily, it is necessary to begin with the play of presence and absence in being to understand the latter properly, for the prefixes that accompany it are not *adventitious* but rather *essential*. Otherwise expressed, being is, at the very heart of beings, the play of which these prefixes speak, the incessant play of presence and absence, which play brings beings closer to us than presence itself, whose opposition to absence is only an opposition in the foreground. This is why, says Parmenides, even what is absent is present in a certain sense. Doubtless, not in the sense of what immediately and for the moment occupies the foreground, but in that of a more secret presence, but which is no less solid, as in the adverb βεβαίως, which specifies that absence is not a groundless abyss, but a ground on which it is possible to gain one's footing in such a way that walking on it remains possible. It may even be that, from the bottom of absence, a still closer presence than immediate presence occasionally reaches us. It was, in fact, not in Brittany, but in the confines of Beauce and Perche that what Chateaubriand named *Apparition de Combourg* took place for him, when hitherto the chateau of his childhood had only been a chronological reference for him.

Thinking at the level of νοῦς is thus to pull oneself back from the short-sighted opposition between presence and absence that the myopia of mortals makes absolute at its own level, in order to open oneself to a dimension where even absence becomes a mode of presence. Such is the dimension of being that deploys itself in everything as an original dimension of absence as much as of presence, whose relative opposition is, for beings, κόσμος, or, better, κατὰ κόσμον, in conformity with the harmony of beings. Consequently, in the country of being, nothing appears whose presence is not secretly permeated by absence, and which does not shine, at the heart of absence, with a secret presence, for being is in the closest proximity to what is. Hence being is that *from which* beings are as present, without being this forever, as they are distanced in absence, without, for all that, being abolished. It is forever the *collection* of presence and absence, their λόγος, in opposition to non-being, which on the contrary is forever the radical abolition of both. But then being is not at all a being, for no being is forever present, if its relation to being consists as much of absence as presence. It is not, therefore, somewhere in beings, but rather transitively to them that we can meet it and say *It is,* in its contrast with nothingness, which, on the contrary, cuts short our speech. Here we see the extent to which Parmenides' meditation is still far from metaphysics, for which being will be, such as Plato and Aristotle will determine it at the level of beings, the culmination of a presence sheltered from any absence by the fixity of the divine that is higher than the sky. Here the divine is not yet the last word of being. For even the divine has his own time. And also his withdrawal, but without being able to desert being, which remains all the more as the place of his absence when, in the night of the world, the certitude of his presence is more vigorously trumpeted by some and that of his absence by others. Nothing, therefore, is more foreign to Parmenides' thinking than the 'identification of being and the divine', such as it will announce itself in Aristotle to triumph subsequently with scholasticism. Being, then, is not the divine but the dimension where the divine itself is as much absent as present and, in the most intimate heart of absence, solidly present, as befits the harmony of being. Such a thinking of being is not, therefore, 'theological'. Should we name it 'ontological'? No more than 'theological'. For being cannot, if it is not the divine, be understood—as in Aristotle's ontology, if it is reduced to its narrowest confines—as the most common of all predicates, the one which would float above all others without properly determining anything. It much rather names the unique singularity of the gathering from which, transitively to beings, arises the measure that maintains everything, even the divine, in its limits. As neither ontology nor theology, but beneath both of these, perhaps Parmenides' thinking is all the more thoughtful, and not all the more rustic, in opposition to what is supposed by those for whom metaphysics is the salt of the earth just as much as by those whose appetite for primitivism seeks to satisfy itself with the 'pre-Socratics', as one says, with something prehistoric or pre-hominid, or at least with something slightly cannibalistic.

But let us listen to what Parmenides says in the three following fragments, of which we will comment on the second and third.

> Already gathering everything, such is that from which I begin, for I will return here once again.

> > Thus it is necessary
> > To allow to be said and to guard in thought
> > Beings-being.

> There is in truth being; nothing on the contrary is not; it is this that I exhort you to meditate. From this path, my words hold you back.

> But from this other also, along which mortals knowing naught wander two-headed. For it is helplessness that moves the wandering thoughts in their breasts. They are borne here and there, deaf as they are and no less blind, astounded, undiscerning races whose lot is to say as much: "it is" as "it is not," "it is the same," and "it is not at all the same." All of them for as long as they are advance only in retracing their steps.

> By no inquiry will you ever equate being with non-beings. Restrain your thought from this path of inquiry and let not rich habitual experience constrain you to send one eye there so as not to see, an ear full of noise, a tongue, but, letting what is be, think for yourself the difference, the one that is brought into question by the test involving great struggle, of which my words speak to you.

The two latter fragments, which Diels deliberately separated in his first edition of the Poem, making fragment VII the finale of fragment I, visibly go together. It is even possible to wonder whether they do not form a single whole. In both cases, a path is in question that is not, like that of non-being, a non-path, since it is the path that mortals follow, but it is nevertheless not the path of being. It is, says Parmenides, the path of the Shocked, the Dazzled, or the Astounded.

But whence does such astonishment arise? Hardly have they said "it is thus" when it is already no longer thus. Consequently, they no longer comprehend anything about what happens in their little heads. For as soon as they have leapt from *it is* to *it is not but it is,* it has once again become other or is once again like before. It is at once here and elsewhere. This is why the mortals who cannot see anything are described as *double-headed.* To learn to see is, on the contrary, to learn in what dimension being thus and being otherwise both belong to the nature of what changes and which consequently is not. Whoever limits himself to saying "It is day" understands nothing of the nature of the day which, according to a phrase of Blanchot's who 'Parmenidizes' unwittingly, "is only day by the night implied in it." But is it all so simple? No, it is not as simple as all that to understand what "is the same, in the living and the dead, the awake and the asleep, the young and the old, the one everywhere the inversion of the other which, once there, returns to the former." But, as one will say, it is not Parmenides that speaks here but Heraclitus (fragment 88). Of course. But where and from whom have we learnt, astounded as we are in Parmenides' sense, that Parmenides and Heraclitus do not say the Same, if it is not from the lack of discernment that makes us distribute the *it is* and the *it is not,* the *it is the same* and *it is not at all the same* according to our first impressions, in being *double-headed* toward and against everything. As Wahl wrote around ten years ago, among the myths that Heidegger seeks to propagate—and God knows there are a few of them—it is necessary to put at the head of the list that of "a fictive author, Parmenides-Heraclitus, invented by Heidegger." Everybody knows perfectly well, for having learnt it on school benches, that Parmenides and Heraclitus are irreducibly opposed to each other. Both are there from the origin only in order to say the opposite of what the other says. Otherwise what would become of philosophy and what purpose would there be in philosophizing? If, on the other hand, it is taken as given that in philosophy everything begins by a good old contradiction, then at least we have some bread on the table. Fortified by this origin, let us shamelessly deliver ourselves over to the pleasure of contradicting, in the way Hegel's striplings "give themselves, the one saying A when the other says B in order to say B when the adversary says A, the pleasure of contradicting each other by the contradiction of each with himself." The relation of thought and contradiction, contradiction understood at its lowest level, is for Hegel "the same conjunction of the sublime and the inferior that nature expresses in all its naiveté in the living organism, by the conjunction in the same organ of the highest function, that of engendering, with another, *nämlich des Pissens,"* as he says resolutely (it is a Swabian speaking).[16]

We should also note that the antagonism, so dear to many, is today losing its currency. On the 450th page of a thesis on Aristotle defended in 1962, in fact, we find the following remark: "Heraclitus and Parmenides say much more fundamentally the same thing than Aristotle pretends to think."[17] In truth, Aristotle does not pretend at all. He understands the words of Parmenides and those of Heraclitus as Saint Thomas will understand the words of Aristotle long after him, without being able to understand them in a different way. Yet what is remarkable here is that this quite audacious remark is presented without any reference, as if it was due to the author himself. In truth, it takes up for the author's own account only what thirty years earlier Heidegger, against the elements, was the first to discover. As he said in 1955: "Heraclitus, that one opposes brutally to Parmenides in attributing to him the doctrine of becoming, says in truth the same as the latter."[18] Let this be said in passing in order to signal how a literature of borrowed plumes occasionally finds what it is looking for even in the work of a thinker whom one will not forego mistreating from time to time. Braque said to himself one day: "The artist is not misunderstood, he is unknown. He is exploited without anyone knowing who he is."[19] Is exploitation always as artless? We should come back to Parmenides.

No less than fragment VI, fragment VII has the value of a warning against the path that is followed by mortals, for whom it is "helplessness that moves the wandering thoughts in their breast." Fragment VII begins with a verse that we have read thus:

By no inquiry will you ever equate being with non-beings.

Plato twice cites this verse and the one that follows it in the *Sophist,* but he lends absolutely no attention to the plural with which the first ends. What we have translated by 'non-beings' is: μὴ ἐόντα and not: μὴ ἐόν. Reading μὴ ἐόντα as if it was μὴ ἐόν, Plato makes of the verse that he cites only a tautological repetition of fragment II, in which Parmenides had said of being that it is impossible or rather forbidden for it not to be: οὐκ ἔστι μὴ εἶναι. It can be deduced quite logically from this that it is forbidden for non-being to be. This is what Plato does. In reality, the plural ἐόντα does have a meaning. It is not the reiteration of the μὴ ἐόν of fragment II, which is a singular, but that of another plural. This other plural is to be found in fragment I, in a guise that is not negative but positive: τὰ δοκοῦντα. The μὴ ἐόντα of fragment VII are well and truly the δοκοῦντα of fragment I, not the μὴ ἐόν of fragment II. But we had learnt in fragment I that the δοκοῦντα, what appears in all its diversity, were held to show themselves as they must. Why, then, do they become negatively: μὴ ἐόντα? I think that here it is necessary to be aware of the nature of the negation, which is μὴ and not οὐ. The δοκοῦντα are μὴ ἐόντα not because they are nothing at all, but to the extent that they cannot identity themselves, even in the case of a god, with what the verb *being* says, given that if they are, they are at once this and something else. This is precisely why, without being the μὴ ἐόν in any way, they are μὴ ἐόντα, that is, what on no account should be confused with the unicity of being. If they should not be confused with being, they have to be differentiated from it. But this differentiation is itself completely different from that of being and non-being to which Plato, whom many scholars have followed on this point, assimilates it. In this latter case, it is a question of the distinction of two singularities, whereas in the other it is a question of the distinction between a singular and a plural.

Does the discernment, the 'crisis' that is in question in the penultimate verse of fragment VII, conceal in itself a double difference? Of course. "Turn away from this way of inquiry *and* from this other also where stupefied mortals are lost." The difference now emphasized is essentially one that stupefied mortals do not make. Not only the difference between being and non-being, but that which no less ceaselessly reigns between the singularity of being and the diversity of 'non-beings'. Mortals go everywhere searching for a being that could constitute unreservedly the subject of the verb being, for a being that *would be* without reserve: *ostendens,* as Saint Thomas will say, *suum proprium nomen esse: Qui est*—"showing that his own proper name is: The One who is."[20] Long after Parmenides they will find it in the Scriptures, whose God—who seems to be being—makes of non-being what is not himself. Nothing is more foreign to Parmenides. Even god is only god from being, which itself is not a being, for if being was god it would not be being. The identification of god and being, such as it constitutes according to Gilson the basis of what he names Christian philosophy, jauntily repudiates the difference of being and beings that Parmenides, on the contrary, unfolds and decisively puts to the test, a test in which ἀλήθεια and not πίστις, belief, convokes the one to whom she speaks.

We have rendered the Greek ἔλεγχος by 'test'. It is not impossible, as the philologists say, that this ancient word still vibrates in the Latin *levis,* and it contains the idea of lightening, and thus of discrediting someone in making him lose his *gravitas.* This was the case with the arguments of Zeno of Elea, who 'lightened' his adversary in showing that the logical development of his thesis was much more ridiculous that that of the thesis that he derides. Ἔλεγχος is spoken of here as πόλυδηρις. A 'test involving great struggle', as we translated, in insisting more on the difficulty of the unique combat that it presupposes than on the variety of the multiple combats that it would have enabled. It is ἀλήθεια itself that convokes us to such a test. In an epoch which is almost that of Parmenides, the poet Bachylides said: "It is pancratic ἀλήθεια who puts the valor of the virile to the test": ἀνδρῶν ἀρετὰν παγκρατὴς ἐλέγχει ἀλήθεια—the ἀλήθεια that, as Plato will say, οὐδέποτε ἐλέγχεται,[21] can never lose face. Ἀλήθεια challenges, therefore, the one to whom she speaks to reduce the singularity of being and the diversity of non-beings to each other. Doubtless, not in order to reduce non-beings to nothingness, but so that what they are is on no account confused with that from which they maintain their health, namely the forever unscathed singularity of being. The test to be undergone, then, is to think in the word ἐόν the unitive difference of ἐόν and the ἐόντα, that is, of the μὴ ἐόντα, for which ἐόν is not only one singular among others, but above all the *singularity* of being, with which beings, ἐόντα, however vigorously they may appear, are not to be confused. They are thus: μὴ ἐόντα.

Heidegger will characterize this difference much later in naming it occasionally, after *Sein und Zeit, ontological difference,* or simply *Difference.* He will later say that such a diptych Beings-Being is the most proper concern of metaphysics. This is, as Wahl says, a myth, since Parmenides never "concerned himself" with such a difference, given that he could not have done so, not having read Heidegger. Indeed. But it is, in fact, exactly the opposite that is true. It is Heidegger who reads and who has read Parmenides, and not the inverse, as does occasionally happen. Perhaps even his most proper originality consists in *reading,* whereas others have only "[sent] one eye there so as not to see, an ear full of noise, a tongue" that happily cackles. In their adventures they have simply forgotten the λόγος. Of course, they have done this with the best of all intentions, namely for the advancement of science, but for a science of which the least that can be said is that Parmenides comes back to us as more and more pre-Socratic, that is, as more rustic than ever, developing truisms with the same serenity as Joseph Prudhomme or Polonius in *Hamlet.*

If, however, Parmenides does not at all resemble this supposedly scientific caricature, and if his Poem constitutes a dawn of thought, we should not be surprised that immediately after the evocation of the 'test involving great struggle' in fragment VII, the long fragment VIII that follows the presentation of the Difference is the presentation of being itself in its difference from beings, that is, from what appears only in disappearing. If we are attentive to this fragment with "an eye to Difference," as Heidegger will say in 1957, we no longer risk taking being in the way that for Parmenides it ceaselessly 'points' to us, for an anachronistic, though still pale, prefiguration of the eternal Father. Diels wrote in 1897:

> With Xenophanes, who is rightly taken to be the precursor of Parmenides as a poet and thinker, divinity and world are one and the same, and it is the theological element that always predominates in his somewhat meager pantheism. In Parmenides, on the contrary, along with the terrestrial world whose reality he denies, the transcendent counterpart of this world, namely divinity, falls also. It is, however, in a visibly intentional way that in his doctrine of the One-All, such as he presents it in his peculiarly difficult manner, he avoids the name God. He was wary of compromising the august majesty of his eternal Ἐόν in mixing it with the concept of God, inaccessible to men in his purity. The phantom-like aspect of his divine figures, something unimaginable for a Greek, have their origin in this. He could be said to be a Nordic reasoner who delivers himself over to speculation, while all around him shines the splendor of green prairies.[22]

All this shows clearly, as Diels concludes emphatically, that Parmenides was not a poet.

Here the eminent philologist surpasses himself. Reading fragment VIII of Parmenides' Poem as a piece of abstract supertheology blended with Nordic ratiocination is the height of confusion. We are in Elea, not in Copenhagen. But let us listen to the strange discourse of the Poetess in its Eleatic sobriety, such as it announces, in and through every being and whether or not it is present, the singularity of being.

> Henceforth a single path remains open to language, the one that it names: it is. On this abound many tokens that being is uncreated and indestructible; complete, immovable, and without end.
>
> Nor was it ever, nor will it be, since now it is, all at once a continuous whole, unique. What kind of origin could you find for it? In what way and from what source could it have grown? From non-being? This is what I let you neither say nor think; for it can neither be thought nor uttered that it is not, nor how. And if it came from nothing, what need could have made it arise later rather than sooner? It must therefore be either completely or not at all.
>
> Nor will the force of any assurance concede that something other than it arise besides itself; this is why Dike does not loosen her binds and gives no license to anything to come into being or pass away, but holds it fast. The question thereon depends on this: it is or it is not. Having thus decided, you must at all cost set aside one path as unthinkable and

nameless, for it diverges from the Open-without-hiddenness. The other, on the contrary, is open and is the real path. How, then, can what is be going to be in the future? How could it come into being? For, if it has become it is not; nor is it if it must one day come into being? Thus is becoming extinguished and passing away beyond inquiry.

Nor is it divisible, since it is everywhere alike, and nothing more can happen to it to hinder it from holding together, and nothing less; but it is a whole, full of being. Wherefore everything is held in it, for being is in contact with being.

Moreover, it is immovable in the limits of powerful binds, it is such, without beginning and without end, since birth and destruction have been driven afar, and it is assurance, open to the Open, that has cast them away. Remaining the same in the same state, it rests in itself and remains in the self-same place; for Necessity, in its vigor, maintains it in the binds of a limit that everywhere encloses it, without allowing it to be in-finite: it is, in fact, in need of nothing; not being such it would stand it need of everything.

Thinking and that by the grace of which a thought emerges is the same. For without being, where it has deployed itself in an utterance, you will not find it; nothing was, nothing is, nor will anything be other than being and beside it. Since its destiny maintains it in binds as a plenitude at rest, it is thus that it will name all that mortals have been able to fix for their own usage, assured that nothing more remains in hiddenness: as much being born as perishing, being there as not being there, changing one place for another and appearing with a continually different color.

But if it has a furthest limit, it is complete on every side, like the mass of a rounded sphere, identically radiating from the center in every direction; for it cannot be greater or smaller in one place than in another; for there is no nothing that could keep it from reaching out equally, and nor can anything that is have more being here and less elsewhere, since it is, as a whole, inviolable. Equal to itself from every point, it resides equally in its limits.

The commentary required by this fragment would necessitate a paper of its own, if not several. This is why we limit ourselves here to two remarks.

The first remark is that the presentation of being consists in linking to it a whole range of either negative or positive epithets. In these epithets, Parmenides opposes the κόσμος, the *jewel* of the 'signs of being', such as it appears 'on the path of ἀλήθεια', to the turning back on itself inherent to the path of the δοκοῦντα, on which "nothing is grounded in the Open-without-hiddenness."

The legendary interpretation of Parmenides, the one that has been current since Plato, sees here only the opposition of the world here-below with its, as Nietzsche says, "multi-colored, blossoming, decep-tive, charming and vivacious forms" to the "sphere" of another world that would mark the first with inanity. On this point, Nietzsche goes as far as to feign a prayer of Parmenides that would summarize the es-sence of his poem: "Allow me one certitude, O gods, even if it is only a mere plank on the sea of incertitude, just large enough to stretch myself out on it! Keep for yourself all that is becoming, the multi-col-ored, blossoming, deceptive, charming, and alive forms and give me one single thing, mere poor and completely empty certitude."[23]

In truth Parmenides says nothing of the sort. The 'sphere' of which he speaks is not beyond this world, it is everywhere where the things of this world are themselves in view, the task of thought being to see them "deploy themselves as they must," and not as they seem to be," and that is to say, according to the myopia of mortals.

The second remark bears on the evocation of what we have trans-lated by Destiny and by Necessity. If the word of Parmenides is that of ἀλήθεια, the ground of ἀλήθεια itself, or its other name, is μοῖρα. As μοῖρα, ἀλήθεια holds being in the binds of a necessity that it never anywhere releases. The essential thing here is to hear with a Greek ear what the Greeks named μοῖρα. It is not a question of a *fatum* that would float over us and to which we could only submit ourselves, but rather of the *lot* with which we are originally invested. *Fatum* is indeed the Latin translation of μοῖρα. It is also the most complete forgetting of what the Greeks understood with this name.

It is *by* μοῖρα, which even holds being itself in its binds, that, as Par-menides says, what men call unilaterally, in other words *oppositively,* "being and non-being, being born and perishing, leaving its place for another or appearing with a changing color" will be named. Will be named? Not *flatus vocis,* a simple sound proffered by the mouth with-out anything being there to correspond to it, as when, as Aristotle will explain much later, I say *tragelaphos,* I say with a word "what does not even exist." Parmenides' μὴ ἐόντα are in no way 'things that do not exist', that is, pure illusions having no other support than one that is merely verbal, but rather things that do not exist *separately,* their truth demanding that the *being otherwise* that their *being thus* presupposes be itself taken into view, which mere δόξα is not able to do. Δόξα is con-sequently not pure deception but is rather well and truly grounded. It is necessary to understand the verb ὀνομάζειν here in the sense that we say 'to label', as when Valéry tells us concerning the *isms* that we are today so fond of: "One neither gets drunk nor quenches a thirst by the label on the bottle."[24]

Parmenides' phrase, then, is to be understood thus: "It is from the fact of μοῖρα that all that mortals have been able in manifold ways to label for their own usage, in being assured that nothing remains hidden, always comes up short." The 'nominalism' of Parmenides, to take up one of the *isms* of which Valéry speaks, is therefore not a nominalism in the usual sense of the word, the one according to which thinking would only be, as the tradition that is still alive and well today has it, a set of 'simple names'.

It is because μοῖρα withholds being in its binds that δόξα is limited to simple denominative representations, but these representations are such only from the fact that, without any access to the ἐόν, it is reduced to receiving only what it encounters and no more; the 'no more' being what is higher and more ample, as when before a house that he does not recognize as a house someone distinguishes and names full and empty spaces, walls and openings, a framework and compartments, thus considering himself to be in the truth, whereas all this has meaning only by the still unapparent house. Hence: "It is thus that all that mortals have been able to label for themselves, assured that nothing else remains hidden, will be but an 'it is only'" and, in other words, that they are the inhabitants of what Nietzsche will name the 'house of being'.

To be only an 'it is only' is not to be a *flatus vocis,* but to be only an isolated part of a whole, solely in relation to which the part has a sense. The ὀνόματα are not, therefore, pure φωνήματα, but they remain δηλώματα in which the δήλωσις stops short.

Insofar as they are not οὐκ ἐόντα, the μὴ ἐόντα fall under the problematic of being, but for the one who does not have being in view they appear onomastically as so many *it is only's,* whereas in the regard of being and of its μοῖρα, there is nothing that would only be a *nothing other than.* Whoever limits himself to saying "it is day," as when the sun is at its zenith, is limited to living from day to day without knowing anything of the being of the day. The marvel here is that it is from the first path, that of being, that everything is determined, although this path is never isolated, but is rather always in connection with the two others. This is why Heidegger writes in *Introduction to Metaphysics:*

> So the man who truly knows is not the one who blindly runs after a truth but only the one who constantly knows all three ways, that of Being, that of non-Being, and that of seeming. Superior knowing—and knowing is superiority—is granted only to the one who has experienced the sweeping storm on the way of Being, to whom the terror of the second way to the abyss of Nothing has not remained foreign, and who has still taken over the third way, the way of seeming, as a constant urgency. (*EM* 86)

What storm does Heidegger here speak of in relation to Parmenides' first path? He will evoke it again, some twenty years later, in naming it, this time in relation to Heraclitus, the 'storm of being'. Is he not misled here by what some hold to be his romanticism?[25] In truth, the storm in question is much rather what Plato named, at the end of the *Republic,* βροντή τε καὶ σεισμός, "thunder and trembling,"[26] which, in the middle of the night, suddenly throws those who have drunk the water of the river of forgetting outside of the country of λήθη and into the world of birth, ἄττοντας ὥσπερ ἀστέρας, like shooting stars.

We stopped our reading before the end of fragment VIII, for the words are suddenly going to change their tone. After having made the 'signs' of being appear, such as they point to the name of *Dike* from the bottom of absence as much as in the presence of beings, the Goddess comes to the second of three tasks that she had proposed to her listener in fragment I: to learn what the opinions of mortals, captivated by appearances, consist in, only to pass immediately to the third task: to understand "how, in its diversity, the Appearing was destined to present itself on a good ground, which, traversing everything, emerges everywhere." It is essential here to understand well the repetition of the tripartition announced in fragment I:

> Here shall I bring to an end for you my trustworthy speech and the knowing that delimits the Open-without-hiddenness. Henceforth learn the beliefs of mortals, lending an ear to the disconcerting order of my words.
>
> Mortals have established two figures to name what they have in sight, one of which they should not name, and this is where they go astray. They have opposed their frameworks in dissociating them and have assigned to them marks that they placed apart from one another: here the ethereal fire of the flame, the favor giving fire, very light, everywhere identical to itself, without anything in common with the other, and there, opposed to it, this other that they have also reduced to itself: the night without light, compact in its body and no less oppressive.
>
> Their adjoining in a world, such as it everywhere unfolds as it must, this is what it falls to me to tell you, so that no opinion of any mortal will ever outstrip you.

What, therefore, is the origin of the fact that the supposed knowledge of mortals is in reality only deviation? Exclusively this: that mortals, too docile to appearances, separate both sides of what appears to them, without being able to catch sight of the adjoining of what they separate. These two sides had been defined in fragment VI as presence and absence. They are now the flaming of the fire and the obscurity of the night. In the fragment that follows fragment VIII, Parmenides will say more briefly: 'light and night'.

> But everything having been named light and night, everything that, according to its respective powers, has its place here as much as elsewhere, everything is full of light and of night without light, each equal to the other, for there is nothing which does not share in one of them.

Light and night. Nothing is more Greek than to name in this way the double aspect, presence and absence, of all beings. Everywhere, says Oreste in the *Choephores* (verse 319), σκότῳ φάος ἀντίμοιρον, "to the night, light is a counter-destiny." But it is enough for one of the two aspects to occupy no longer the foreground for it to appear to desert the other. This is what is desired by the separatism of names, whose short-sighted opposition denatures what is to be thought in making it appear only as a 'this and not that'. Nothing is further from the language of being—where solely νοεῖν, the understanding, is πεφατισμένον, having found there and there only the plenitude of its saying—than onomastic sectioning in the way that it points toward this as much as toward its contrary, according to whether the former or the latter comes into the foreground. The gathering of the λόγος thus disintegrates into partial denominations, of which each is always refuted by an other which hastily comes to substitute itself for the former, but only to become, in turn, untenable. It is thus, as Kant will say in the second Preface of the first *Critique*, that as long as metaphysics has not found the "sure path of a science," whoever lends his efforts to it "must forever retrace his steps, for the road that he has just followed does not take him to where he wants to go."[27] Kant's phrase is the distant echo of the words of Parmenides'. Fifteen years earlier, Kant had already evoked the *Umkippungen*, the games of inversion, that remain its lot, as long as it remained incapable, in running blindly after names, of formulating synthetically the relation of what still only appeared to it within the disjuncture of the choice for or against. For it was not χωρὶς ἀπ' ἀλλήλων, apart from one another, that the antithetical aspects of what had already been thought had to be thought, but rather according to a more essential unity that, as Hegel will say, saves each from the other in a sublimation whose benefit consists in relieving the field of thought from their contradiction, and that is to say, to have become capable of excluding the summary *duel* of the antagonists, which has become merely apparent, to the profit of their *dia*-lectical unity.

Not that Parmenides is a dialectical thinker in Hegel's sense and, more than two millennia before him, his disciple. It is much rather

Hegel who unwittingly echoes the thought of Parmenides and responds to him in his own way. But it has only become easier to stress that the summary dualism, the δύο of the figures isolated from each other, which characterizes the errancy of mortals at the *caesura* of verse 53, is surmounted in verse 60 by the thought of the διά of a διάκοσμος, which the Goddess commits herself to reveal as a whole, so that, as she says, "the sense of mortals never outstrips you."

In my opinion, it is here that it is necessary to separate ourselves resolutely from all previous interpretations. Parmenides describes the διάκοσμος in the understanding that surmounts the duality which leads mortals into illusion as ἐοικώς. This participle means that that of which it speaks is in order, as is fitting. But what? The διάκοσμος and that is to say, the world such as it is seen to *de*ploy (διά) itself by mortals, whose opinions are without truth. Fränkel will translate, therefore, with Diels and Reinhardt: "Of this world of error, I will give you an exact account." Philologically all this is quite possible. But why would the διάκοσμος in question be a 'world of error'? Why, if it is not because this must be the case for the no longer philological but philosophical reason that Parmenides is supposed, according to Fränkel, "to refute the sensible world in denouncing it as an illusion"? But what if Parmenides did not 'refute' anything at all here? What if he spoke of things in the site of their appearing, not, of course, as mortals hold them to be, separating the two figures that they present, but such as one who 'can see' lets them be said to him (fragment I), going back from the duality that is everywhere apparent to the unity that it everywhere conceals, a unity from which every duality is born and of which it is only the bifurcation?

But what unity? Is there any other unity in Parmenides' Poem than the constancy of being such as it is established in fragment VIII? But how could unitary and immobile being, without birth or decline, centered on itself like a sphere, constitute the bind of what never stops twisting and turning in the last fragments of the Poem? Of course, if being was only a being, frozen in itself like a world beyond the world, this would be quite impossible. But far from being that of a being, is not the fixity of being rather that of the *Di*-mension, of the διά, which differs from beings only in such a way that every being belongs to it in the most intimate heart of the duel that is always at work in it, the duel of their appearing and disappearing? Being would henceforth be the joint, invariably unique, of the one and the other, and thus the unity of both such as it escapes the myopia of mortals, but that thought catches sight of when the duality which first of all besieges it becomes once again the bifurcated simplicity that it has never stopped being.

Would this, then, be the sense of Parmenides' Poem? It is possible to think so. But then in spite of all that we have learnt about it from ancient times to Nietzsche and beyond, the Poem would cast no aspersions on the sensible world to the profit of a world of being, at the cost of which the first would be only an illusion. Parmenides' Poem is well and truly the apology of this world. It speaks entirely "to the good health of the δοκοῦντα," as we said at the beginning. We find Parmenides' δοκοῦντα, the Appearing, once again in Plato. But here they do not at all have the same sense. To appear is now to seem, and Plato's δοκοῦντα are only in fact mere 'semblances'. But semblances of what? Semblances of what they are not. The beauties of this world, for example, a beautiful girl, a beautiful horse, seem to be the Beautiful itself, but they are not it, for the beautiful in itself resides in a supercelestial world, forever inaccessible to the double insult of birth and decline, while the beauties, let us not speak of them! Parmenides' δοκοῦντα are also, in one sense, mere 'semblances'. But, at the very most, they seem only to be the latter in excluding the former, without it yet being known that in the truth of being they are as much the one as the other. Far from Platonically opposing the sky to the earth, then, Parmenides' Poem says the sky on the earth as the unity of *Differents*, a unity whose secret is open only to the one who knows how to open himself in thought to the difference of being and beings. This difference, such as the dawn of Greek thinking discovers it, is the one that Parmenides as much as Heraclitus names κόσμος. This is not a question, of course, of the great Whole, but of the secret adjoining that carries every visible adjoining, and in other words, of the jewel that the visible conceals in its heart, by virtue of which everything sparkles. In Homer κόσμος means 'jewel', and a jewel shines not only by and for itself, but also valorizes or illuminates the one who wears it. This is why the κόσμος is διάκοσμος. Without letting itself be isolated to the profit of a particular being, it dispenses and diffuses itself, radiantly unique, throughout beings. This is what the Goddess says of the adjoining of Day-Night, not *in order to* show, but *after* having shown in what, in its separatism, the errancy of the errant consists.

Presence and absence, day and night:

> Their adjoining in a world, such as it everywhere deploys itself as it must, is what it falls to me to indicate to you, so that the opinion of no mortal will ever outstrip you.

The fragments that follow, numbered from X to XIX, quite probably relate to the exposition of the διάκοσμος. Not of a *world of error,* but of the *truth of the world* such as it is resplendent for those who know how to think it, without this truth falling under any other, without the world ever being the reflection of another world or of a world behind the scenes.

The principal difficulty of this second part of the Poem, as it is commonly described, is that its fragments become more and more lacunary. Yet it remains the case that they allow us to apprehend that true knowing must think an identity instead of the mere disjunction that mortals find. According to Diogenes Laertius, Parmenides is even supposed to have been the first to discover the identity of the Morning Star and the Evening Star. Where we see and say *two*, it is therefore *one* that it is necessary "to allow to be said and to maintain in thought." Unfortunately, the text is lacking, and this is, according to Diogenes Laertius himself, only a rumor. But, in the end, the two stars amount only to one, like Night and Day, like everything that mortals name separately. Diels goes as far as to say here that Parmenides lets himself go to the point of "Heraclitizing despite himself"; *Parmenides heraklitisirt wider Willen.*[28] In Diels's eyes, it is quite evident that it is against Heraclitus, whom he would—why not?—have heard something about, that Parmenides stands and speaks.[29] In opposing the harmonic identity that all separation presupposes to the separating power of names, it is thus to Heraclitus that, despite himself, he returns—the Heraclitus who said: "God? Day-Night, Winter-Summer, War-Peace, Abundance-Penury: it becomes always different, just as fire, when mingled with spices, is named according to the savor of each" (fragment 67). In reality, everything rests here on the presupposition that Parmenides refutes Heraclitus, the harmony of the Heraclitian κόσμος becoming for him the κόσμος of the 'signs of being', such that it would oppose itself pre-Platonically to the διάκοσμος that is only an illusion of mortals. As we have seen, it is much rather the κόσμος of the signs of being that is the διά, the very dimension of the διάκοσμος. Parmenides does not refute Heraclitus any more than he is influenced by him. The one and the other, although in different words, say the Same and respond to each other with an ear to the One that the duality everywhere apparent conceals in its heart, and that the knowing of mortals can only allow to lapse into a nomenclature, "thus sure to have entered into the Open-without-hiddenness." This 'allowing to lapse' which can be understood in the Greek κατατίθεσθαι, and which returns three times in Parmenides' Poem, each time in liaison with the verb ὀνομάξειν, to 'name', speaks of a 'fall' that is much more original than any original sin. It is to the κατά of this fall, after more than two thousand years, that the *Verfallen* of *Sein und Zeit* responds in interpreting it. "Without any negative connotations," it speaks of the fall of human speech, to a much lower point than the possible plenitude of its saying, in the daily comfort of conversation where we are limited to exchanging propositions. Xenophanes, who in the course of his travels perhaps passed through Elea, where it would not have been impossible for him to have met the young Parmenides, already knew something about this. And it is no longer Parmenides who speaks here but Xenophanes:

> By the fireside in the winter-time, this is what you should say,
> As we lie on soft couches with a full stomach,
> Drinking sweet wine and crunching chick peas:
> "Of what country are you? Of your years, good sir, give us an account,
> And how old were you when the Mede appeared?"

There is nothing low here, nothing guilty or reprehensible. Chatter and curiosity are simply accounted for: we can inquire about something, we converse, we can even endlessly discuss something in "calling something A when a neighbor says B, B when he says A," without ever taking our leave from the inconsequentiality of propositions or ever risking being disturbed by encountering a thought. Such is the happy state of fallenness from which Parmenides aims, on the contrary, to take his leave in going back from *words* to the *word* that disorientates us, in leading us away from rumor as much as from any concern for what people will say, solely in order to say what is.

Let us listen then to the song of the διάκοσμος, not as a song of error, but in the way that it offers a toast to 'the health of the δοκοῦντα':

> But you will know the luminous unfolding of the ether, all that, in the ether, points, the consuming work of the brilliant sun, pure torch, and whence they derive; you will learn also the effects and the circulation of the moon with the round eye and how it was formed. You will know also the sky that withholds everything in surrounding it, from where it emerges, and how the necessity that directs it fixed limits on the course of the stars.
>
> How the earth and the sun and the universal ether of the sky and the celestial Milky Way and the most remote Olympus and the burning force of the star were thrown into birth.
>
> The narrowest rings are full of fire without admixture; those that come after are full of night, but between them both a portion of flame penetrates. In the center is the divinity that governs everything, for it is everywhere the origin of the giving birth of Styx and of coupling, sending the female to be unified to the male and the male to the female.

> First of all the gods, Eros, it is he who was contrived.
> Clear in the night with borrowed light, around the errant earth.
> Always carrying its worried regards toward the rays of the sun.

Responding each time to the mêlée of his members everywhere stirring, it is thus that sense appears in man. In the same way, what it is concerned with responds to it as a physical emergence, for everyone and in everything; a plenitude, in truth, is thought.

This last fragment for a long time has been one of the most studied and one of the most controversial. Aristotle cites it in book III of the *Metaphysics*. He comments on it as follows: to change one's way of being is to change one's thinking. Fränkel is quite right to underline that here Parmenides announces something new. The Poets had said that the thoughts of men varied according to the manner in which Zeus presented things to them. Parmenides says rather that everything varies according to the constitution of every person, whatever it is that he encounters. Reinhardt will write: "One grain more or one grain less in the blend of contraries is what the thought of men depends on." And he adds, developing an indication of Theophrastus:

> Consequently, knowing is in no way a characteristic which man and animals would have the privilege of possessing in distinction from the rest of beings; wherever two blends of the same type are in contact in the world, there is also knowledge. We say that the cadaver is dead, and we refuse to attribute sensation to it, and yet it does not see any worse than us; the unique difference is that its mixture is contrary to ours; it thus sees what we do not, namely obscurity; and what is true of the cadaver is no less true of all that is reputed to be dead in this world.

But how can we reconcile the relativism that seems to emerge from this fragment with the immutable constancy of the day *without shadow* that fragment VIII had made appear as the fixed dimension of the play of the διάκοσμος? There is no contradiction here. The nature of the bodily emerging in each and every being contributes to making men more or less aware of one or more of the constraints of beings, and it is in this way that "flair or sense appears in men." But νόος, the sense named here, is only an advance indication of the "letting be said and guarding in thought" of fragment VI, which in attending to beings-being appears, as fragment I said, only to the one "who walks at a distance from men and their path." In the first case, it would be only a question of what could be anachronistically named Parmenides' anthropology, his 'psychology' as Reinhardt says—and even of an anthropology or psychology in which the ἄνθρωπος is not structurally different from the animal, or from what is simply vegetal, or even from what is mineral, which never lacks its own 'flair'. In the other case, it is still a question of what appears to man, but when under the guidance of *Dike* and *Themis* he has opened himself to the word of ἀλήθεια. Such a man remains no less, however, φύσις μελέων, and that is to say, a physical emergence. It is only when the physical emergence is at its height that thought occurs. Parmenides does not say anything else to us about this *height,* except that such a height is perhaps an advantage because of the ambiguity of the word πλέον. But what he says here shows us all the more acutely that nothing is more foreign to him than the distinction, so "easy" to Descartes, "of the things that belong to intellectual nature and of those that belong to the body" (Synopsis of the *Meditations*).

Mind and body are not for the Greeks two 'substances' that could be determined apart from each other. Even in its most profound recesses thinking remains, relatively to what it thinks, a 'physical emergence', and on the other hand there is no 'physical emergence' that does not open itself in some way to whatever con-cerns it. Aristotle will situate the most rudimentary form of sensibility in 'tact'. But the most accomplished thought still has the nature of tact, tact in its highest form: θιγεῖν καὶ φάναι (*Metaphysics,* Θ, 10, 1051 b 24). Such is the fundamental trait of what he studies under the title of Ψυχή, the latter being the *appearing of a physical body* (εἶδος σώματος φυσικοῦ, *De Anima,* I, 412a 20). For us such propositions seem to be the height of peculiarity. This is because, according to Cournot's phrase, we have had "other preceptors than the Greeks." Perhaps it will be reserved to phenomenology to rediscover, without any hint of 'materialism', something of a knowing that today has been forgotten, the one in which the Greeks had their most proper residence. Without thinking of Aristotle, Merleau-Ponty says to us: "It is by his body that the mind of the other is a mind in my eyes."[30] And Heidegger, for whom *Leiblichkeit* is essential to *Dasein* (*SZ* 108): "we do not *have* a body, but we *are* corporeal" (*N* I 118). However, before the phenomenologists, it was the poets who were the guardians of the enigma. It is Goethe here who echoes Parmenides, in coming back to him through Plato:

> If the eye was not sunny,
> How would we see the light?
> If the vigor of the god was not living in us,
> How could the divine call enrapture us?[31]

We are almost at the end of our reading. The two following fragments, of which one consists of only a few words, while the other is known only from a Latin translation that it is possible to consider as either admissible or inadmissible, both go back from man to the gestation of man. They speak of the genesis of the child whose sex depends on the direction of the spermatic jet and the accidents that it implies. But this snippet of genetics that completes the anthropology of fragment XVI precedes a final fragment, about which it is not forbidden to think that it may well constitute, in summarizing everything, the very end of the Poem, whose last three fragments we are going to hear. The end of the Poem? Reinhardt is inclined to think so, for to him it appears separated from the rest like the total on a bill is visibly separated from the amounts added by a horizontal line.

> On the right boys; on the left girls.
> When a man and woman blend at the same time the seeds of love, the force in the veins that is constituted from the different bloods, if it maintains a correct temperament, forms sturdy bodies. But if, born from blended seeds, the forces are hostile and refuse to be united in the body issuing from the blend, they will irritate the sex of the infant from their double origin.
> It is thus, in the course of their appearing, that things here come into being, the ones that now are, and in time they will develop and pass away. But to each of these things men have assigned a fixed name that designates them separately.

What characterizes this 'conclusion' is that in its first verse the word δόξα appears in the singular for the first time in the locution: κατὰ δόξαν. Before this point we have only ever encountered it in the plural (βροτῶν δόξαι, for example). Everywhere it is said that Parmenides' Poem treats the relation of ἀλήθεια and δόξα, in other words, that of *truth* and *opinion*. Everybody from Theophrastus to Fränkel, including even Nietzsche, thus interprets the κατὰ δόξαν of fragment XIX as saying: according to opinion.

> It is thus, according to opinion, that the things here are born . . .

It can all the more easily be deduced from this that everything that has come before, from the end of fragment VII, was only an exact account of the opinion that misleads mortals, which one must either refute (Diels), partially rehabilitate (Wilamowitz), or fully elucidate (Reinhardt). But if this interpretation is, as we have tried to show, unacceptable, then the κατὰ δόξαν of fragment XIX is questionable. We translated it by "in the course of the appearing of things," giving to the word δόξαν an *objective* sense and not the *subjective* sense of opinion, against which, I think, philology can really have nothing to say. Δόξα θεοῦ is still in the first *Letter to the Corinthians gloria Dei*. It is in this objective sense of the word that man, as Saint Paul says, is the glory of God, while woman is only δόξα ἀνδρός, *gloria viri*, the glory of man. She shines only in the light of man, which is to her, like that of the moon in fragment XIV, a 'light from elsewhere'. Concerning things, therefore, κατὰ δόξαν can easily be understood as: in the light of their appearing.

But it can also be understood in a still simpler manner, but without in any way resolving to lend to the word δόξα the meaning of opinion. In Homer δόξα quite often means, here from the perspective of man and not of things, waiting, namely waiting for something to manifest itself. What is παρὰ δόξαν is distanced from waiting. One can therefore read κατὰ δόξαν as saying the opposite of παρὰ δόξαν, or of ἀπὸ δόξας: "It is in this way that without any paradox . . ." It would therefore no longer be a question of opinion, except for those who begin from the *a priori* idea that Parmenides, from the end of fragment VIII, gives a detailed exposition of the *trügerischer Bau*, the 'deceptive structure', as even Reinhardt still said, of the διάκοσμος. But what if the διάκοσμος that Parmenides brings to light is not a deceptive structure, what if it is, on the contrary, truth itself and the well-being of everything that is fittingly deployed in it in traversing everything and transpiring everywhere? What if it is only 'deceptive' by the founding of a bimillenary error on an ancient misinterpretation? In this case it would be necessary to read κατὰ δόξαν not as 'according to the mistaken opinion of mortals', but either as we did before in saying: in the course of the appearing of things, formed at once by presence and absence, absence belonging no less than presence to the harmony of being; or as we are going to do now in opposing κατὰ δόξαν to ἀπὸ δόξας or παρὰ δόξαν, and that is to say, in understanding it as the disposition of men who, enlightened by ἀλήθεια, have learnt to expect that things are what they are.

We now find ourselves at the terminus of our journey in the country of being, or, better, of beings-being, and that is to say, in the country where beings, although they are not being, fittingly emerge from being, at least for those who, attentive to the marvel of the κόσμος, have learnt the διά of the δύο, or, as Heraclitus said, the σύν of the διά, in letting themselves say and guarding in thought that which is, with the unique concern not to miss the secret adjoining of all manifest presence. More arduous than corresponding *separatively* either to the night or to the day is the art of knowing how to respond *unitively* to the rhythm of Day-Night, which is the being of the day as much as it is of the night.

This properly Greek sense of rhythm is precisely what Aristotle reproached Plato for having deserted, in becoming, as he says of his master, "similar to someone who reduces symphony to unison, rhythm to the regular step."[32] Would Aristotle have rediscovered rhythm? Does he not also, the Platonist that he remains, lead us to desert it, losing from his sight what, well before philosophy, the language of the poets of the Greek world, to whom Parmenides is so close in his own way, had celebrated in evoking it enigmatically with the name of καιρός?

This enigmatic name, if it is not to be found in Homer, appears in the poetry of Hesiod and Pindar to mean 'the best in everything', καιρός ἐπὶ πᾶσιν ἄριστος. One can happily make of it the 'opportune moment', if opportunity is to arrive at the port without missing the passage.

Such is, at least at its dawn, the Greek knowledge of being, the knowing of being that is unfolded in the element of presence, without tormenting or forcing anything, without hiding away from or grasping at anything, without compromise or measurelessness. A unique marvel with two distinct aspects, it is henceforth the grace that man breathes from being and the casualness that becomes his own in his fascination with beings. We occasionally gain a glimpse of such a marvel in a smiling face, in the simplicity of a landscape, in the imposing lines of a column, or before the Apollo of Olympia, but also, perhaps, in learning to read Parmenides' poem. While the sun sets over Elea, let us once again lend an ear to the Greek word, the one that Parmenides heard in listening to ἀλήθεια, the day of the birth of a world.

> This is what she says in singing it for me:
> The Same, in truth, is at once thinking and being
> For without being, deployed in a saying, you will not be able to
>   find it.
> See them, even being far from here, solidly present for thought
> For being is to what is in the closest proximity.
> Presenting the shape of a perfect sphere, from the center, in all
>   directions, identically radiating.
> It is the same, thinking, and that by the grace of which a
>   thought emerges.
> The Same, in truth, is at once thinking and being.

4

Zeno

What is moved moves neither
where it is nor where it is not.

With Zeno thought falls well below the summit at the height of which
it had established itself with Heraclitus and Parmenides. Zeno, as Aristotle would have said, is 'the inventor of dialectics'. Such a remark is
not complimentary in the slightest, since dialectics, like sophistry,
only has the appearance of philosophy for Aristotle. The theme is no
longer that of beings insofar as they are and in their direct and primi-
tive truth, but merely what follows, as a consequence, the presuppositions which are supposed to determine it. The true philosopher
looks and makes us see. Zeno cares not a whit for looking and makes
nothing visible. He is attentive only to what happens if. This is why he
never ceases advancing along the path of his proofs, while we find
ourselves caught in a trap without ever having been enlightened. Inventor of dialectics, Zeno is the first of the rationalizers. Their proofs,
says Braque, 'tire' a truth that has previously been brought to light.
They advance with their eyes closed to the world, a world brought to
light by someone else before them, refuting each other in a polemical
blindness. "Fight as they may," as Kant writes, "the shadows which
they cleave asunder grow together again forthwith, like the heroes in
Valhalla, to disport themselves anew in the bloodless contests."[1] It is
the same with all contesting, which in order to make the adversary fall
from his own error into that of the other contestant, excels in substituting the forced march of constraining argumentation for the pensive repose of originative wonder.

In Plato's *Parmenides* the young Socrates reproaches Zeno for being

64

but the epigone of Parmenides: "It is clear to me, Parmenides, that Zeno's intention is to associate himself not only to your friendship but also to your work. In a way, his book states the same position as your own, but in varying the form he tries to delude us into thinking that his thesis is different." In the face of an attack of such candor, Zeno seeks to excuse himself in passing off his book as a youthful aberration: "This is where you are mistaken, Socrates, for you imagine it was inspired, not by a youthful eagerness, but by the ambition of the older man" (128a–128e).

Whether or not what Zeno says is true, it is essential to understand how he is bound to Parmenides—his elder, his friend, his teacher—and how he nevertheless remains original. Many are those who have attempted to hold Parmenides' thesis up to ridicule in showing that if there is one, then the consequences and contradictions that such a thesis will have to bear will be grotesque. Zeno's text is, therefore, a retort that returns the ridicule with interest in aiming to make it appear evident that if there are several, then the consequences will be still more grotesque for those concerned to develop them. Taking as given the thesis of his adversary in this way, Zeno's dialectic consists in showing that if this thesis seems, in the first instance, less paradoxical than one that is apparently inadmissible, then its logical development will lead us no less to the height of extravagance.

What could be more natural than opposing plurality and movement to the Parmenidian unity and immobility of being? We shall nevertheless do this in order to see what happens. In both cases we will be constrained to affirm something and its absolute opposite. Our statements are thus going to become similar to those of the ventriloquist Eurycles mentioned in Plato's *Sophist,* whose stomach has already said the opposite when his mouth utters a word. Is not making such a ventriloquial effect appear in the development of an opposing thesis the best means of reducing it to naught with the invincible weapon of ridicule? Zeno goes about things in this way, inaugurating a tradition that Kant will allow to flourish once again in the *Critique of Pure Reason.* Kant shows that whoever considers himself, in all the naiveté of seriousness, to be able to speak rationally of the world as a supposedly complete totality or in its supposed exhaustive division speaks of it at once as finite and infinite. This ventriloquism of reason that Kant denounces under the name of antinomy brings us back to Zeno. Hence the respect with which the critical philosopher evokes "the subtle dialectician, reprimanded erroneously as a mischievous sophist by Plato, who thinks that it is only in order to demonstrate his skill that he proves one thesis by specious arguments in order to immediately overturn it with other arguments equally strong."[2]

We shall try, against Parmenides' thesis, to compose being out of elementary units. Consequently, it becomes several. But the constitutive unity, in order truly to merit its name, must be indivisible, and thus without extension; and yet it must have extension for otherwise the repetition of this extension will not allow us to escape from the non-being of non-extension. Consequently, let us listen to Zeno: according to the hypothesis of several,

> It is necessary that everything, if it is, has extension and thickness and that one of its sides is at a distance from the other. And the same remark applies to what, in a thing, is at the forefront; this also will have extension and something in it, in turn, will be at the forefront; it is evidently the same thing to say that it is a unity and that it is without end; nothing of this kind taken from the thing will be ultimate, nor any side without relation to an other. If therefore there are several, things will be necessarily at once small and indeterminately large.[3]

Zeno seems to say that there is no element of extension, taken as thickness, which has not in turn, however small it may be, a front and back side, and that is to say, no element that could exist without there being extension in it—and, therefore, that it is impossible to arrive from the whole at elements that would not already have the extended nature of a thing, and that would not, therefore, be divisible. Only that which has no thickness would be properly indivisible, a component in the last instance; but this would be nothing, which, composed with itself, would not allow us to get to something. The conclusion is that in the hypothesis of divisibility and plurality, everything is at once small and large. It is small to the point of having no thickness; large with an indeterminable extension, that is, without us being able to know either to what extent or from what it is so. It is in developing the thesis of plurality in this way that Zeno turns the laughter back against the pluralists and ensures the triumph of Parmenides.

The Palamedes of Elea—as Plato still calls him—passes for having composed four arguments of the same sort, "speaking each time with an art that is capable of making it appear to his listeners that the same things are similar and dissimilar, one and many, or even as much immobile as in movement."[4] These words of Plato's evoke Zeno's four most famous arguments, those that Aristotle relates to us. Enumerating in his Poem the signs that define the lot of being, Parmenides characterized it not only as one, but also as immobile:

But immobile in the limits of powerful binds
It is without beginning and without end, since birth and
   destruction
Have been chased away into the distance where assurance,
   open to the Open, has repelled them.

Let us follow, then, the hypothesis of movement and see what happens. The development of the paradoxical consequences of this apparently plausible hypothesis takes place through four figures that a
poet's memory carries to us in a faultless strophe of "Cemetery by the
Sea."[5] Not only will the light-footed Achilles never catch the tortoise,
but never has anybody even begun his first step. For how can we
traverse a distance without having first of all traversed the half of it,
and previously the half of this half, etc., in such a way that the shortest
distance is at the same time an infinite distance? Such are the first two
arguments. The following two, in maintaining the indivisibility of the
instant, constrain us to say that the arrow in its flight is frozen at each
instant, and that it is impossible for those who race in opposite directions in the stadium ever to meet each other. The first two arguments
appeal to the infinite divisibility of all space. The latter two appeal to
the decomposition of time into indivisible instants within which
nothing can happen. For if, in the instant, a distance could be traversed at a high speed, a higher speed would traverse the same distance in less than the instant, which would cease in this way to be the
indivisible instant. Consequently, the arrow can only be in flight as in-
stantaneously immobile. Immobile and not at rest like it is in the
quiver of the archer. Rest is completely other to this suspense in
which the mobile suddenly freezes, which itself is as foreign to rest as
it is to movement, like sound, says Aristotle, is foreign to visibility. De-
mobilized rather than immobilized by the spell of the instant, such is
Zeno's arrow. The same applies, in the wind of the race, to the teams
racing at the same speed in opposite directions. Try as they might,
they will meet only if the half of the time is equal to the whole of
which it is the half.[6] From Zeno's perspective, then, things are deserted by what Aristotle will name the 'life' of movement, of which
rest is a moment but without it attaining the divine sphere of the First
Immobile. It is therefore necessary at all costs, says the Stagirite, to
break the spell—otherwise physics is done for.

   It falls to Hegel to honor Zeno's subtlety at its proper level and in its
relation, against the 'pitiful' critique of Bayle, to the no less misunderstood acuity of the Aristotelian critique. It is on the occasion of an examination of the Kantian Antinomy of Division that Hegel evokes

Zeno's arguments in his *Logic*.[7] He declares them to be "infinitely more rich in sense and more profound" than Kant's argumentation, which remains, as he says, "confused and embarrassed." Zeno goes much more directly to what is essential, which is the discovery of the two intrinsically antagonistic moments that any extension contains: continuity and discretion. It is the still unreflected dissociation of these two moments that makes possible the double offensive of dialectical argumentation, of which the whole art will consist in opposing to movement the insurmountable obstacle of either a distance that never ceases to surge back toward its own origin or of an atomized instant within which all movement remains held. But such a dissociation is precisely what the speculative power and amplitude of Aristotle's thought overcomes in establishing the unity of the concept of extension in the very duality of its moments—the highlighting of the one supposing the ever present immanence of the other. Discretion, in fact, only ever appears upon the background of continuity, and there is no continuity that does not preserve, in its own heart, the permanent possibility and imminence of a break. For extension is precisely a flux whereby it never ceases to go out of itself, yet without ever ending up as something qualitatively different, "as when one says, for example, that in the place of this stone a tree could be found." Henceforth, the infinitely divisible continuity of distance does not prevent the cadence of steps of which each is one, any more than the actually indivisible unity of the instant blocks their passage. Such is the secret that escapes the separatism of the dialectician, but not the gaze of the physician. The arrow, thus, flies in an undivided flight, and Achilles, advancing with undivided steps, overtakes all the tortoises in the world. But he can also, if he chooses to, slow the cadence of his step and allow himself to be left increasingly behind. One measures here, through Hegel, the magisterial superiority of the Aristotelian analysis to Bergson's rhetoric, which opposes to Zeno the indivisibility and not the indivision of Achilles' steps. The Achilles that Bergson aspires to save from Eleatic immobility falls back, in the end, to the caricature of Zeno's Achilles that Giradoux's Cyclops offers us in Elpénor: "believing himself bound to walk with indivisible steps, he threw his foot forward like an ataxic."[8] How could one not prefer to this indomitable walker the infinitely more subtle Achilles of Zeno, who has his feet trapped in his halves of halves until Aristotle gently frees him. But is it not, perhaps, the destiny of an epoch that has once again become barbarous to have no opening onto the increasingly veiled word of the Greeks?

To conclude, we shall pose one more question. So far, we have related Zeno to Parmenides as if he had only ever been the brilliant second of the incommensurable Eleatic. This is Plato's view, and it is undeniable that the texts that have been historically transmitted to us go in this direction. But what is announced by the other titles that the doxographical tradition has conserved for us? At bottom, as Diès remarks following Gomperz, it seems that "the historical Zeno owes his role as a faithful squire uniquely to Plato's dialogue." Yet in Plato's dialogue the reduction of Zeno to this role is not only intentional, but it also fails to eclipse another figure of him. It is, in fact, less in the honor of Parmenides than to hear a reading of Zeno's text that the group comes together. It is less a question, then, of witnessing the final triumph of the thesis of the One than it is of admiring the work of a dialectical virtuoso. How could it not be concluded from this that there is a distance between the Zeno as disciple that Parmenides presents and the Eleatic Palamedes that the *Phaedrus* names? Zeno would thus only have occasionally put his own technique in the service of his master; a technique which could, in the event, equally turn back against the thesis that it was happening to defend. Indeed, does it not unsettle as much as it defends it? What Zeno shows, in effect, is not that Parmenides is right, but much rather that his adversaries are still more ridiculously incapable than he is of accounting for the fact of movement. Henceforth, the λόγος of Parmenides appears at the very most as stronger or, if you will, as less weak than that of his adversaries. The shadow of skepticism floats over the whole enterprise. We feel a world emerge within which the public confrontation of two adverse logics, like in a cockfight, is substituted for the meditation that gathers itself upon the original reciprocity of λόγος and ἀλήθεια. This will be the still little-known world of sophistry.

"The walk to the star," says Braque: "those who go to the front carry a crook, those who walk behind hold a whip, and at the side, the horrible overseers keeping all in line."[9] Heraclitus and Parmenides take the lead and are ahead of everything that follows. Zeno is not one of those who carry a crook, but his whip is still only irony. Perhaps it is reserved for us to live in the time of the horrible overseers keeping all in line.

5

A Note on Plato and Aristotle

Plato's philosophy is the first breakthrough to philosophy itself. To philosophize is, in the Greek sense, to apply oneself thematically to the study of beings *insofar as* they are beings. Philosophy supposes that beings, such are they are individually named and instead of being taken as they come—as the man to whom I address my speech, as the table at which I sit down, as the tree that blossoms before me—are to be understood first of all in their *being*, which is the properly *verbal* modality that is harbored in any *nomination* of beings. It is not by chance that the master-word that says in a single word the very question of philosophy at its birth is ὄν. Grammar, in the language of Platonism, will characterize this much later as μετοχή. The Latins will say *participle*. The participle points both to the nominal and to the verbal aspect. Tὸ ὄν is at once the singular of τὰ ὄντα, beings, and the singularity that is, for all beings, the verb εἶναι. The Greek locution τό ὄν will, thus, be translated as much by *being* as by *a being* or *beings*. Here, however, the Greeks do not think in modeling themselves on grammar, which does not yet exist. On the contrary, it is grammar that much later models itself on Greek philosophy and, particularly, on the Platonic philosophy of participation.

Although Greek philosophy does not model itself on grammar, it does respond to the Greek language. The Greek language is, in fact, the sole language in which what grammar will call the participial mode sets the scene, and this from the perspective of what, in Greek at least, is the verb of verbs, namely the verb *being*. In Latin, *esse* has no

70

participle. The word *ens* is a late invention, clumsily fabricated in order to translate the Greek ὄν. In French, 'being' (*être*) is only ever employed as an auxiliary, and 'beings' (*l'étant*) came into common use only on the occasion of the translations of Heidegger. Before this, one used to say *un être* and not *un étant*. The English 'being' is consonant with the Greek ὄν, but to the profit of beings rather than being. The English are not the Greeks of the modern world. Whether as logisticians or moralists, they are as far as possible from philosophy in the form in which it became the destiny of the Greek world. Only German, when it begins to philosophize, this beginning having from its birth the dimensions of a *Critique of Pure Reason,* clearly distinguishes *das Seiende* (beings) and *das Sein* (being). This is why in the *Critique of Pure Reason* Kant finds himself, perhaps unwittingly, in a dialogue with Plato and Aristotle.[1]

If the philosophy of Plato is the first breakthrough of philosophy itself, to which it even gives its name, it is not, for all that, an absolute beginning. It is on the basis of an earlier discourse than philosophy that it has a ready tongue. This discourse is the thinking of Heraclitus and Parmenides. Neither describes himself as a *philosopher,* although the word is employed once by Heraclitus (fragment 35), but in a sense that is possibly pejorative. The verb *philosophize* appears slightly later with Herodotus. So were Heraclitus and Parmenides not, then, philosophers? Not if one hears in the word the technical signification that Plato gives to it.

It is necessary to be clear on this point. The difference of being and beings, which is the fundamental trait of the philosophies of Plato and Aristotle, already carries the thinking of Heraclitus and Parmenides. Both thought beings in their being instead of merely narrating the vicissitudes of beings. They posed the question of being for the first time. But to believe that Plato and Aristotle took up this question only in order to promote and develop it is not to see in what way the question itself has radically changed from Heraclitus and Parmenides to Plato. Plato and Aristotle are completely unaware of such a change. For them, Heraclitus and Parmenides still 'speak falteringly'. Thus Ronsard, in the eyes of Boileau, will only, in relation to Malherbe, 'speak falteringly'. One might as well say that the Cathedral of Chartres is only the first, still gothic faltering expression of what the Chateau of Versailles will be, and that Giotto is only a still inarticulate Raphaël.

The words of Heraclitus that say for the first time the dual unity of being and beings are: Ἕν πάντα, One—All. The One, in the One-All, is the ξυνόν of the πάντα. Not what they *have* in common, but what they all essentially *are* when we look at them ξὺν νόῳ, with the regard of νοῦς—when, in other words, we follow the track right up to what is the 'unapparent adjoining' of all things. When Heraclitus says: "If all things became smoke, noses would distinguish them" (fragment 7), he only says in other words: ἐν πάντα. To be familiar with this is to know how to correspond (ὁμολογεῖν) to the One-All, in which "the secret adjoining prevails over that which is only apparent." The mode according to which morning, noon, and night compose the unity of the day is apparent, as is the way in which the cycle of the seasons gives rhythm to the year, and also the way that life stretches from youth to old age through maturity. The unity of contrasts, however, such as day-night, winter-summer, war-peace, abundance-penury, Dionysos-Hades is secret, as is, and more so, the withdrawal that the unity of emergence (φύσις) harbors in its own heart. Although emergence can only open out and close itself off in coming out from the retreat of the crypt, nothing is more proper to it than this withdrawal in which it hides itself—not in order to eliminate and abolish the emergence, but rather to preserve it all the more in holding itself back while manifesting itself: φύσις κρύπτεσθαι φιλεῖ. In this way the words of Heraclitus speak of the heart of being as differing from beings, without anything of the order of beings being able to take up on its own account the clearing of being, whether this be the first of all beings and even Zeus himself: "The One, the Wise, it alone, is little pleased although it is pleased to be said by the name of Zeus" (fragment 32). The first place given to the negation does not occur, as Heidegger says, merely by chance. It has its ground in the thing itself as it opens itself to thought. "Zeus is not in himself the One, even if, manipulating the clearing, he accomplishes the dispensations of destiny" (VA 224).

It seems, therefore, that for the first thinkers of Greece, what is given to thought is held to be essential beyond—or rather beneath—a distinction that will become decisive for philosophy, namely the distinction of the divine and the human. The gods as much as men come under another dimension that is for them a sort of common destiny, on whose basis alone they are all what they are, although they are subject to this destiny or lot (μοῖρα) in different ways. Φύσις and λόγος, μοῖρα and ἔρις, ἀλήθεια and ἐν are, first of all, the fundamental words of an earlier thinking of being than philosophy.[2]

The ground of philosophy remains the thinking of being, but thought in a philosophical mode being is immediately determined as a common property of all beings, which themselves become at bottom identical by the presence in them of this common property. This fundamental community or identity has the inaugural import of a leveling. Evidently, such a leveling does not suffice to draw the figure of a world. For there to be a world, it is necessary that a principle of differentiation, one that is at work wherever there is λόγος, completes the principle of leveling. Hence a double necessity appears in being, by which it constitutes as much the universally common base as the singularly unique summit of everything. In this way, in Plato's philosophy the assignation of being as εἶδος and the eidetic leveling that it institutes occur in tandem with a hierarchical subordination of the εἶδος to the ἀγαθόν, although the later remains an ἰδέα. In the dual unity of Being-beings, being undergoes a doubling which makes it appear at once as a common property, in which all beings are leveled, and as a unique summit, from which everything is animated. It is with this doubling of being that philosophy begins as metaphysics. Aristotle, taking no notice of Plato's reserve, will not hesitate to name τὸ θεῖον, the divine, this 'sublime point' of being, in which its basic determination is exalted. For, as he says, if the divine is present somewhere, it can be only at this level. Henceforth, philosophy is at once the study of being at its summit, a study that Aristotle, using a word that was older than him, characterizes as theology, and also the study of being as the most common property of all beings. This second study will remain anonymous until the seventeenth century, for it is only around 1646 that Clauberg, the friend of Burman, who had been to Holland to interview Descartes, will create, symmetrically to theology, the name *ontology*. One can say, however, that long before this creation philosophy is the *onto-theological* interpretation of the being of beings.

To try to understand what happened with Plato and Aristotle, let us compare a phrase of Heraclitus and a phrase of Aristotle. The phrase of Heraclitus, one that perhaps carries all his others, is ῝Εν πάντα, One-All. We also find the ἕν and the πάντα, which are named from the perspective of the ἕν, in book Λ of Aristotle's *Metaphysics*. The philosopher says: πρὸς μὲν γὰρ ἕν ἅπαντα συντέτακται,[3] "it is in view of the one that each thing receives its due place." Here the One of Heraclitus has become the focal point supposed by the alignment of everything. To the Greek τάξις the Latin *ordo* responds as a translation. Therefore, according to Aristotle, it is as centered on the One that all the others are 'ordered'. The image of the strategist 'on whose account' the army is deployed in order is related to this. Aristotle's image will be taken up quite naturally by Plotinus: "If, therefore, there is a great strategist at the helm of everything, what could escape from the alignment?"[4] Plotinus also says: "So multiple are beings, and not the same, there must be a first, a second and so on, each according to its worth."[5] This order of precedence carries us far, very far from the thinking of Heraclitus. For him, the priority of the ἕν in relation to the πάντα has in no way the superlative character of a precedence. This is why the ἕν πάντα is κόσμος, and not, as for Aristotle, τάξις, which is to say, *ordo*. Is the world of Heraclitus, then, in disorder? Not at all. It is no more in disorder than it is in order. It is κόσμος. It is this in the sense that fire, which lives without end, kindles and dies down everywhere without ever losing its reserve.

The idea of alignment and the injunction to align oneself begin to break through only when thinking becomes philosophical, and that is to say, with Plato and Aristotle. Τάξον αὐτὰ ἀνὰ λόγον, "align them analogically," as Plato says at the end of book VI of the *Republic*, in speaking of the segments of a line that he has cut in two, and then each of the segments once again in two. Consequently, we begin to recognize that analogy is itself only a mode of alignment, one that Saint Thomas will privilege after Plotinus, who said: συνέχει τὰ πάντα ἀναλογία, "analogy maintains the whole together."[6] For Saint Thomas also, it is analogy that keeps all things in line, as the following passage from the *Summa*, a veritable feast of order, says: "Nam ex patre familias dependet ordo domus, qui continetur sub ordine civitatis, qui procedit a civitatis rectore: cum et hic contineatur sub ordine Regis, a quo totum regnum ordinatur" — For the order of the household derives from the father of the family, which is held together under the order of the state, which proceeds from the governor of the state; since this too is contained under the order of the King, by whom the whole kingdom is ruled.[7]

We have become accustomed to living in the orthodoxy of the line to such an extent that our Platonic atavism discovers alignment everywhere, even when there is no trace of it to be found. For Heraclitus, however, κόσμος is without τάξις, for the κόσμος as 'syntaxized' ἐν συντάξει μιᾷ, as Plotinus will say,[8] begins only with philosophy. "He confuses symphony with unison and rhythm with the regular step," as Aristotle had said of Plato.[9] But of which philosophy would it be possible not to say this? Although Aristotelian τάξις is no longer the κόσμος of Heraclitus, it is not yet, however, the Latin *ordo*, still less the scholastic *ordo*, whose ground is creation: "omnia creata ordinantur in Deum" — all created things are ordered in God. This representation of order from the perspective of God the creator is as strange to Aristotle's thinking as the monotheistic individuation of the divine that it presupposes, which excellent commentators nevertheless do not refrain from positing as the ground of his theology. Did not Hamelin write: "The object of first philosophy is an Individual"?[10] In reality, Aristotle's θεῖον, like the φύσις that it carries, is essentially γένος. Not a "class of beings," as Gilson will say,[11] but much rather a dimension of being, which is, in truth, its supreme dimension, "whether or not there is one or several there."[12] Having been born and having their roots (γένος) there, it is from this *a priori* determined dimension that, first of all, the Immutables derive and 'emerge', with perhaps one of them being at the very most Homerically primary in relation to the others,[13] in the sense that Zeus is the first of the gods. If, however, Aristotle is too Greek to profess dogmatically the monotheistic reduction of the divine, his own way of being Greek is already quite different from that of Heraclitus. One can say that with Aristotle an inversion occurs in the relation of being to the divine; with him the ἐθέλει gains precedence over the οὐκ ἐθέλει in fragment 32 of Heraclitus, whereas for the latter the opposite was the case. It is with Aristotle that first philosophy adopts the name of *theology* for the first time — this theology rigorously understood being a *theiology* more than a *theology* — which is quite foreign to the earlier thinking of Heraclitus. For Heraclitus, as for Pindar, the distinction of god and man is not yet ultimate, if it is true that for the gods and for us, ἐκ μιᾶς δὲ πνέομεν ματρὸς ἀμφότεροι, "it is thanks to a unique mother that we breath, the ones as much as the others."[14] Sophocles echoes the plural πνέομεν when the god says to Oedipus in *Oedipus at Colon:* "Well, Oedipus, Oedipus, why are we waiting to take our leave?"[15] More essential than the distinction of god and man is the strange *we* which only brings god and man together in maintaining them at a distance, and which is the very site of prayer in the Greek sense. With Aristotle, on the contrary, it is already the self-sufficiency of the divine that carries the human, which already aligns itself on him, although we have not yet reached Leibniz, when he says much later of what he will call *ultima ratio rerum:* "Uno vocabulo solet appellari DEUS" — The ultimate ground of things: in one word, it is wont to be called God.

In this way, the path is long from the earliest thinking of being in its priority to the primacy of the divine in being, and from the Aristotelian primacy of the divine in being to its scholastic reduction to monotheism. In other words, as Heidegger says: *Sein — und Zeit.*

If monotheism, such as Kant celebrates it,[16] has today become what Nietzsche named one of our "highest ranking atavisms,"[17] is this a sufficient reason to deny, in the name of this *atavism,* the more secret ascendance that the monotheistic fixation implies? Do we not rather have to learn how to feel, with Nietzsche, "our feet on a still trembling ground,"[18] or, as Heidegger says, to become once again attentive to the "call that leads us back to ourselves in our long history."[19] Thirty years earlier, Heidegger had said (*KM, in fine*):

Or have we already become so much the fools of the organization, of the universal hustle and bustle, that we are no longer able to befriend the essential, the simple, and the constant? It is in this friendship (φιλία) that the turning to beings as such takes place, from which the question concerning the concept of being (σοφία) — the grounding question of philosophy — arises.

Or do we also first need remembrance for this?
So Aristotle offered the saying:

Certainly and from the beginning, and now and without stopping, what we are looking for and grappling with is: what is being?

Let us return from Aristotle to Plato. If one can speak only rigorously of an onto-theological structure of metaphysics from Aristotle onwards, such a structure, as we have seen, is already announced with Plato in that he uniformly reduces οὐσία to the εἶδος only in order to subordinate this eidetically reduced οὐσία to the ἀγαθόν. The fixation of οὐσία as εἶδος entails, for the εἶδος themselves insofar as they remain τὰ (πολλὰ) εἴδη, the necessity of an over-determination, itself eidetic, but which defines the *One* of this *several* that they still are, in an *Idea of Ideas,* an exclusive prototype of their plurality, without which philosophy would remain with the multiple rather than advancing toward the *One,* or rather toward the identity of the One and the Multiple that is the ground of ἀλήθεια, as we learn in *Philebus.* To find for the πολλὰ εἴδη the ἕν that they demand, such is the task of Platonic philosophy.

We should make this clear. Things, for Plato, are only in the figure or aspect that they offer. The little of being that this table here possesses, for example, consists in being trapezoid. But the εἶδος τῆς τραπέζης? It is, in turn, like all the other Ideas, *agathoid.* But the ἀγαθόν itself? Here the upward movement stops: the ἀγαθόν is in no way *oid,* for as we read in *Philebus:* ἱκανὸν τὸ ἀγαθόν. The ἀγαθόν fully suffices in itself.

All this, then, is quite clear. Only a sole point remains obscure. Why is the εἶδος *agathoid* and not, for example, *ovoid* or even *phalloid*? One ordinarily responds thus: because for Plato, as it will be for Kant much later, the big question is morality. In reality, the philosopher of the ἀγαθόν does not moralize at all. The εἶδος is *agathoid* because it is, in οὐσία, what is "right." But in what sense? "I fear that the head of the pope is not quite right," as Bossuet wrote one day. In no way did he want to say that there was immorality in the head of the pope, but rather that he was a birdbrain, that he had lost his head, and that like Madame Jourdain he was falling apart at the seams. It is in the same sense that Plato was already thinking. Without the εἶδος, everything falls apart in οὐσία. There would no longer be anything βέβαιον or ὑγιές, no longer anything *solid* or *healthy*. On the contrary, πάντα ῥεῖ: "it is not only my nose but everything that is running!" But whence can it come to οὐσία? From what, if not from what by itself, is *healthy*? From "great health"[20] as Nietzsche will say. If "great health" does not reign at the foundation of being, nothing will ever be healthy. Evidently, what Nietzsche understands by "great health" is the Dionysian inversion of Platonism. It nevertheless remains the case that Nietzsche says again what Plato's philosophy already said. If the εἶδος brings forth and maintains οὐσία in health, this is because the ground of being is "great health," the communicative health of the ἀγαθόν, without which becoming would win over being. "To the good health of οὐσία" says the ἀγαθόν, "and shame to Heraclitus and to his world which will never manage to get over the metaphysical catarrh by which it is so unfortunately afflicted!"

It is in this way that the uniformly eidetic determination of οὐσία supposes the culmination of the ἀγαθόν, itself ἰδέα τοῦ ἀγαθοῦ. Henceforth it is the whole of philosophy that without discontinuity will be the correlation of a basic determination, here the εἶδος, and of a determination of the summit, here the ἀγαθόν, in which the basic determination returns to exalt itself. The base is held in place only by the summit, which can define itself only relatively to the base and thanks to it. We have here to do with a circle, of which the circle pejoratively named Cartesian is only a particularly manifest figure. The Cartesian circle is in no way specifically Cartesian. Such a circle never stops being reproduced from one end to the other of philosophy. The philosophy of Hegel is no less circular than that of Descartes, by the correlation in it of the absolute as Spirit and becoming as a dialectical process, each one being supported by the other. The Absolute is nothing without the dialectical process, given that it is only the Absolute as its Result. But the dialectical process only properly begins from the Absolute that results from it. The Nietzschean correlation of the will to power and the eternal return is no less consonant with the Platonic structure of philosophy. The will to power responds so well to the εἶδος that its study will, in fact, be called *Morphology*. On the other hand, the eternal return as the 'summit of meditation' is the ultimate exaltation of the will to power, in the sense that the ἀγαθόν is the supreme exaltation of the εἶδος. The whole of philosophy thus unfolds in the echo of this doubling at the heart of being, its first figure being Platonism. Such a doubling is not a juxtaposition of perspectives, but rather an identity of two extremes which never stop turning, onto-theologically, the one around the other, without philosophy ever being able to think the circle that carries it, for it is precisely by means of such a circle that it is philosophy.

In essence, as we have said, Plato's philosophy is the communal determination of being as εἶδος, as figure or aspect. But this Platonic attention to the visage of beings itself has several aspects:

1. *Primarily*, the intrepid figure of youth. This characterizes Socrates on the day on his death, when more than ever he proclaims that being is *idea*: τῷ καλῷ τὰ καλὰ καλά, he says, "it is by the Beautiful that beautiful things are beautiful." But where does the Beautiful itself reside? *Over-there*, says Plato, and that is to say, elsewhere than the beautiful things here. It resides, therefore, in another world, the one that perhaps Socrates is going to visit after having drunk the hemlock. It is with this strange dislocation that philosophy begins. In what, however, does the relation between the Beautiful there and the beautiful things here consist? Is it a presence (παρουσία) in each one of them of the Beautiful itself? Is it a community (κοινωνία) of another sort? Which exactly? 'For the moment', and that is to say, just before drinking the hemlock, Socrates abstains from clarifying this.

2. *Next*, the more reflective figure of maturity. Socartes, who has just died in front of our eyes, is suddenly rejuvenated, and it is from the distant Elea that the old Parmenides arrives to take charge of the philosophical game. After one brief dialogue, Socrates is convinced that explaining the καλά by means of the καλόν in which they 'participate' is pure verbiage. What, then, is to be done? Gymnastics, as the old man answers, who is once again willing to set the example despite his age. Hence the great exercise that is carried out without any concern for any supposed participation of things in the two Ideas that are the One and Being. In the course of this exercise the result is sought, for the One and for 'the others', of the 'hypotheses' that the One *is* One or that the One *is*, as well as of the negations of these hypotheses. In the *Sophist* this game that originally bears on three figures only, namely the One, being, and what is other than One, becomes a game of five figures. At its head is *Being* as, in the words of Montaigne, the 'band sergeant', and then there are two couples of contraries: *Station* and *Movement, Same* and *Other*. From the possible combinations of these five figures there results a sixth figure that is no less magisterial than the first five: the λόγος itself, which in this way "is born to us."[21] But where are we exactly? In the world of pure Ideas, and that is to say, *over-there*, and Plato seems in no way to be concerned about it.

It is also on this occasion that he resolves, as if in passing, a question from *hither* that had been left in suspense in an earlier dialogue between Socrates and Theaetetus, the one entitled, precisely, *Theae-tetus*. How, as Socrates asked, can this disgrace occur to thought: being false? At the time it was a mere game for him to disconcert Theaetetus in showing him that all his answers were tantamount to saying tautologically: "Error, is to be in error concerning . . ." Now, however, in speaking to the very same Theaetetus, the Eleatic of the *Sophist* reasons thus: without blending in general, there is no λόγος, since it is from the blending of the figures that it is 'born to us'. But without the blending of the λόγος with non-being, there is no possibility for the former to say what is not. Yet how could the λόγος be exempt from sharing in non-being, given that the nature of non-being, in the guise of the Other which is the fifth figure of the game, is to find itself in a 'state of distribution' throughout being and all the other figures. It specifically belongs to the λόγος, then, to be "double, true as well as false."[22]

3. *Finally*, the more serene figure of old age, about which Heidegger says that with those who "know how to grow old" it "frees the young for what is original." This last figure of Platonism seems to correspond to an attempt to re-conquer at least something of what an all too impatient beginning had sacrificed: the things of this world, and that is to say, the 'the path of this world'. It appears first of all in the *Timeaus* through the development of a *myth*. Timaeus, who is a foreigner, having come from Italy, recounts how a certain god produces by his art τὸ πᾶν τόδε, 'this whole here'. But this is only a *myth*. Aristotle will ask: Where has anyone ever seen such a thing? The myth of the *Timaeus* is, thus, not at all 'likely' as it is customary to say in translating the Greek εἰκώς poorly: the demiurge of the narrative of the *Timaeus* is, in Plato's eyes, as *likely* as the Evil Genius will be for Descartes. It is much rather *fitting, expedient, in the right place*. With the *Philebus*, however, we come back from myth to philosophy, and this is also the return of Socrates.

Like the stranger in the *Sophist*, the Socrates of the *Philebus* begins by setting up the figures of a dialectical game that will also be five in number. It has been argued both that they respond to the figures of the *Sophist* and that they differ from them completely.[23] These figures are, first, *Limit* and the *Unlimited*, and then *Blend* of the two and *Cause* of the Blend. Only at the end of the dialogue does the fifth figure enter the game, having a diacritical or 'separatist' function. Plato continues to name these figures *genera* or *ideas*, as in the *Sophist* and *Parmenides*. It could be, however, that a secret change has occurred. The One and Being of the *Parmenides*, as well as the five figures of the *Sophist*, did not expressly force us to emerge from the 'super-celestial' world. This is no longer the case with the *blends* such as they result from the combination of limit with the unlimited under the guidance of the cause (the Good). Doubtless, the blend can be a pure idea. For example, number, which is an idea, results from the insertion of limit in the infinite variation toward the more or less of quantity, which ceases in this way to grow or to endlessly shrink. But the grammatical accord of words, the harmony of sounds, or even the health of the body have no less the nature of the blend. There are, then, blends that are in no way ideas but are among the things of this world that can claim to have a good constitution. Even pleasure, which is so obviously something from *hither,* will no longer be, as in the time of the *Phaedo,* shamefully dismissed, but admitted to its place in the 'share of the Good'. The Socrates of the *Philebus,* therefore, seems to return from the flight and the asceticism to which the Socrates of the *Phaedo* invited us. There is, however, still something concessive about his language. Plato remains so subjugated by his first conquest that it is only at the behest of the young that he finally allows, to the point of determining them as akin to the idea, some of the 'sensibles' that he pardons to pass to the side of the good. The others remain outside of the horizon of philosophy. It is only with Aristotle that a decisive inversion will be accomplished.

What Aristotle never stops staying and repeating is that if the εἶδος belongs essentially to οὐσία, then the εἶδος alone does not suffice to determine it as οὐσία. Certainly, *being* remains a common property, and even the most common of them all, but what is the most common to all beings is that in its being each one of them is, first of all and above all, 'this thing here', τόδε τι. This man or this horse, for example, as he says. But why does Aristotle speak in this way?

Being, for Aristotle, is first of all and above all ὑποκεῖσθαι, to lie at the base as constituting the ground of what is in sight. Being is also, but more weakly, συμβεβηκέναι, to accompany what already lies as the basis, which itself does not accompany anything else. The being sought by philosophy is thus the ὑποκείμενον πρῶτον, the one that is this in 'lying-beneath everything else'. Here Homeric language gives us the best of examples: "There it lies (κεῖται), quite low, the farthest forward in the sea, toward the sunset, leaving the east and the west to the others."[24] But what? Ithaca, the unique center of the whole of the Odyssey. It is the island Ithaca that is, in its κεῖσθαι, the ὑποκείμενον πρῶτον.

But according to Aristotle, who remains the pupil of Plato, the master word of philosophy, οὐσία, names not only what πρῶτως κεῖται, like Ithaca, but also "the aspects (εἴδη) according to which beings in the first sense of the word already reign." For whatever is presence in the first sense of the word is no less immediately εἶδος or aspect. Everything that is 'primarily presence' always and already manifests itself eidetically: Ithaca, for example, *as* 'an island'. This is true to such an extent, as Aristotle notes, that the most immediate manner to be in the presence of something, namely αἴσθησις, is already in itself τοῦ καθόλου. It brings us "into the presence of the universal"; we see the man named Callias advance toward us *as* a man, far from seeing only Callias. Similarly, in the *Odyssey,* Athena appears to Ulysses "in the figure of a large and beautiful woman" or, just before the 'discovery' of Ithaca, "in the guise of a young man, a goatherd, as free as the son of a lord." She is Athena, but also, and at the same time, one of the figures according to which she is already there.

Yet the εἶδος thus determined does not reside, as Platonic separatism supposed, in an intelligible heaven. It is the 'this here' that shows itself immediately as εἶδος: Napoleon, before Goethe, *as* 'a man', Ithaca *as* 'an island'. But *where* can such an extraordinary phenomenon take place? In the primordial space of *language,* which says of Napoleon: 'Now that is a man' or of Ithaca: 'That is an island'. The εἶδος is itself carried only by language, which says it of a 'this here', not as constituting only a part of it, but as co-extensive with its appearance. To speak of a 'this here' as *eidetically* manifest — Athena as a woman — and from there, but only from there, as capable of being accompanied by other characteristics, which, instead of having the constancy of the εἶδος, can vary between contraries — 'a large and beautiful woman' could be small and ugly — is the work of whoever has language, ἔργον τοῦ λέγοντος.[25] As λόγος ἀποφαντικός, this language is what reveals the appearing itself.

If Aristotle does not explicitly treat this marvelous property of the εἶδος to appear not καθ'αὑτό at a super-celestial distance, but co-extensively to that of which it is the aspect, this is because it is always presupposed in everything that he says. He was once led, however, to bring to language this pre-supposition, when he specifies in book II of the *Physics* that the εἶδος of which he speaks is not the εἶδος in Plato's sense, but that one must take it οὐ χωριστὸν ὄν ἀλλ᾽ ἢ κατὰ τὸν λόγον,[26] "not as being separated, but only according to language." Ordinarily, this remark in the *Physics* is translated in saying: "Not as being separated, save conceptually." This is, in my opinion, if not non-sense, then at least a radical misunderstanding of the sense of ἀλλ᾽ ἤ. As Bonitz remarks, if the locution has occasionally a sense close to *save* after a negation, the particle ἤ can equally reinforce without further ado the *but* that precedes it.[27] Aristotle, in truth, opposes to Plato's εἶδος χωριστὸν ὄν the one that he names τὸ κατὰ τὸν λόγον, which is the εἶδος of the apophantic proposition. The very sense of this proposition is to allow the particular thing to appear *as* what a man is, for example, or as what a horse or tree is. It is only with language (λόγος) that the thing appears in what it is and as it is. But language as λόγος is not what the philology of today knows of language, namely a symbolic expression. It belongs and responds to the very emergence of being, of which it is the gathered presence (σύμβολον), for it is being that speaks wherever there is language. Doubtless, being does not tend its voice in the way that the Eternal, from the bottom of a bush, spoke to Moses, but in the sense that it is 'language' (λόγος) that is, from top to bottom, the very appearing of the thing *as* this thing here. It appears *as* a man or as a horse, the one as much as the other manifesting itself, in turn, *as* large or small, *as* young or old, *as* robust or feeble, etc. It is always according to the inaugural import of this *as* that beings allow themselves to be said in their being and thus, having become sayable, to show themselves in the light of a world that only ever opens itself in becoming language. Language is thus what Nietzsche called the *house of being*,[28] through which alone we have movement and rest. "When we go to the fountain or when we walk in the forest, it is through what 'fountain' or 'forest' says to us that our path passes, even if we do not speak aloud and think of nothing that relates to language" (*HZW* 286). Here it is not Aristotle who speaks, but Heidegger. But these words that treat language return to the listening station that is thought in its beginning, where Aristotle, listening for the λόγος, hears in it, in his own way, the *apophantic* language of being.

We are here at the very root of the opposition of Aristotle to Plato. But how is this opposition to be determined? It can be said that Platonism is the eidetic reduction of being, the determination of the latter exclusively by the εἶδος. The rest is only ever secondary and of a "lower"[29] rank. For Aristotle, on the contrary, the being of beings is essentially a concrete presence, for example, 'this man, this horse here'. Alain even wrote in forcing the matter slightly: "The idea does not exist. What exists is the individual." Doubtless, but why? Is this a simple affair of taste? One opinion rather than another? This is the solution that one is generally happy to adopt. Aristotle, as Gilson says, was "a very different metaphysician to Plato." By what? "By his curiosity concerning the concrete, the real and by the gifts of the observer that he manifests in studying it."[30] Doubtless, this is a "tendency" (*sic*) that was lacking in Plato and that, in time, ends up in triumphing over Aristotle's "friendship" with Plato. "*Amicus Plato sed magis amica veritas*"—Plato is a friend but truth is a greater friend. Curiosity? Tendency? Here we find the vocabulary of psychology. It would be psychology, then, that would have decided concerning the relation of Aristotle to Plato. Consequently, philosophy, whose task as Nietzsche says is to "maintain the spiritual lineage of thought through the centuries," could be reduced in the end to a spectrum of psychological differences between philosophers. Will not the last word in this domain come back to this *ipsissimum* of psychology that is psychoanalysis, the only discourse to 'explain' rationally this collection of oddities that is the history of philosophy, and that made Cicero say, applauded by Montaigne: "Nihil tam absurdum dici potest quod non dicatur ab aliquo philosophum"—It is impossible to invent anything so absurd that it would not have been said by one philosopher arguing against another?[31]

Is it a question here, however, of a subjective divergence of 'tendencies', polarized by the objective opposition of certain qualities, such as general and individual, abstract and concrete, the one and the multiple, reason and experience?

In order to understand Aristotle's opposition to Plato, it is necessary to understand first of all what is common to them both. There can be an opposition only at the heart of one and the same question, which is here the unique question of being. But it is not only this unique question that is common to Plato and Aristotle but also the guiding thread in the elaboration of the question that is the λόγος: it is by means of the λόγος that both are engaged in the question of being. But what is the λόγος?

In the *Sophist* Plato undertakes, for the first time, a detailed analysis of it. The λόγος, as he says, is above all συμπλοκή, intertwining.[32] It was in weaving nouns onto a chain of verbs that the λόγος "came into being for us." To this, he adds two 'mere nothings'. First of all, all λόγος is λόγος τίνος, that is to say, λόγος concerning something, in the sense that Husserl, much later and without thinking explicitly of Plato, will write that all consciousness is 'consciousness of something'. And next, that λόγος, insofar as it is 'of something', has the property of being true or false according to whether it agrees or does not agree with the thing of which it is the λόγος.

Aristotle maintains all that Plato has said. On one point alone, however, he adds a third 'mere nothing'. If the λόγος, as λόγος τίνος, is true or false, this is not simply as λόγος τίνος but only to the extent that it consists of λέγειν τι κατά τινος, of saying something of something, of coming to pose itself on something else in order to make the second τι appear, which is in reality primordial, since it has the determination that the first shows and says.

Casting aside psychology and its explanations,[33] let us be content simply with a little logic. It is only in listening to the λόγος and only in its company[34] that it is possible to get "in contact with being,"[35] and this corresponds to the desire in man by which he is man. But if, on the other hand, the λόγος is essentially λέγειν τι κατά τινος, then being in the most fundamental sense will be that *of which* or *on which* there is λόγος: τὸ καθ᾽ οὗ λέγεται. We have a magnificent οἷον, a magnificent example of this in 'this man here' or in 'this horse here'. For if the εἶδος such as 'horse' or 'man' is, in one sense, a καθ᾽ οὗ, in the sense that one can say, for example, "a horse is a mammal" or "man is a living being," then it is not the *first* καθ᾽ οὗ, given that it is only said κατά τινος. This is why Aristotle will say deliberately: "The being of beings as said in the most supreme, first and fullest sense is said neither of a certain subject, nor as being found only in it: for example, this man here or this horse here."[36]

Plato certainly saw something of the being of beings. He saw its τί, its *quid*. But fascinated, as it were, by his own discovery, he stopped there in his philosophy. He followed the λόγος, which he had taken as a guide in the examination of the question of being, only within the limits of this fascination. Aristotle has neither more nor less taste for the concrete or for the abstract than Plato. Between them, there is no opposition of 'tendencies'. Aristotle limited himself to following the λόγος more faithfully, scrupulously, and farther than Plato. Hence: "amicus Plato sed magis amica veritas."

We have just translated the word οὐσία, in the text wherein Aristotle seeks to characterize what the word says 'in the first, most supreme and fullest manner', by the locution *being of beings*. Would it not have been simpler to translate it by *a being*? Are not this particular man and this particular horse what one can name *beings*? Would Aristotle, turning up his nose at the *Difference* between being and beings, simply discover that the basis of being is beings? Such is the traditional interpretation. Gilson goes as far as to say that Aristotle, in contrast to Plato, "begins by accepting the *brute facts as such,* even at the price of sidelining his inquiry concerning their abstract conditions of intelligibility."[37] It could be that talking in this way is tantamount to dreaming with one's eyes wide open. The philosophy of Aristotle does not in any way consist in returning, against Plato, from being to beings: it locates in the 'this here' the highest manifestation of being such as it presences into the open in the clearing of beings. In other words, Aristotle, as much as Plato, is unaware of any 'brute facts' that one would first have to record. In their eyes no 'fact' is ever 'brute'. A fact is as metaphysical, although in another sense of the word, as a thinking of the divine as beyond movement. Heidegger says to us: "Fact, the word has a fine appearance, but it is a fallacious word" (*WD* 162). Aristotle's τόδε τι is in no way, whether Gilson likes it or not, a 'brute fact', but a *Greek thought,* and thus a thinking in which the difference of being from beings vibrates.[38] Against what Plato's determination of the λόγος 'wanted', Aristotle discovers only that being is more present to beings in the τόδε τι than in the εἶδος, in which it is present only secondarily. What for Plato was there only as χαλεπὸν ὄν,[39] as being merely an *inconvenient encounter,* becomes for Aristotle πρώτως ὄν, κυρίως ὄν, a principal and primary presence. Plato's question was: how can one relieve the εἶδος of its displeasing frequentative form: εἴδωλον? With Aristotle, on the contrary, this particular horse, odious to Plato, is installed in the foreground of being in relegating *horseness* to the background. If *horseness* continues to determine being at its highest level, namely that of οὐσία, then it determines the latter only secondarily. From Plato to Aristotle, the passage is not from one point of view to another that would be more respectful of the 'brute facts', but one of the major episodes of what Plato names in the *Sophist* γιγαντομαχία τις περὶ τῆς οὐσίας, which he knew was in full swing before him.

The distinction within οὐσία of a first and second level responds to another distinction that Aristotle ceaselessly recalls, but that is also foreign to Plato, namely the distinction between ὅτι ἔστι (that it is) and τί ἔστι (what it is). For Aristotle, *that it is* essentially means the possible appearance of the thing as τόδε τι, as that to which the words 'here it is' can directly point:

> Here are the fruits, flowers, leaves and branches
> And here also is my heart, which beats only for you.[40]

To this the question of the τί is bound, but only on the next level: *what is, then, this thing here?* Such a distinction of the ὅτι from the τί had no sense for Plato, since the eidetic appearance of the τί was, for him, a sufficient response to any possible question. For Plato, philosophy had to 'dismiss' the τόδε τι—which was only ever an annoying encounter, even in the case of a 'beautiful girl'[41]—to take into view the τί alone: what is, then, a girl and what is beauty? The distinction of the τί and the ὅτι responds to Aristotle's thought that we are never more in the presence of being than when we can say of a being: here it is! The two parts of this distinction are, thus, not at all on the same level. Ἀρχὴ γὰρ τὸ ὅτι:[42] the that-it-is comes first. It forms, with the τί, a single whole, but in this whole it is "more than half";[43] οὐσία as πρώτη is 'more than half' of the whole of οὐσία because it is the principal aspect of it. In the same way as the primacy of the τόδε τι in οὐσία, the distinction of the ὅτι and the τί in being refers back to the *gigantomachia* of which Plato speaks. When Gilson limits himself to saying, not without a certain condescendence, "Today we call this difference the distinction of essence and existence,"[44] he effaces any trace of the *gigantomachia* to the profit of a nomenclature, as if the distinction of essence and existence — wherein metaphysics sees, as Leibniz said, the "principles of being"[45] — responded to an eternal question of philosophy. In reality, Aristotle is in no way already *a* philosopher of existence, as Kierkegaard aspires to be against Hegel, but *the* philosopher of being as in the first instance τόδε τι. The Aristotelian distinction between the ὅτι and the τί has nothing to do with the distinction of existence and essence. It is much rather the latter that has a lot, and more than it thinks, to do with the properly Greek distinction between the ὅτι and the τί.

We have seen that if the τόδε τι is first or primary for Aristotle, it is initially this as τὸ καθ᾽ οὗ, as that of which whatever it is fitting to attribute to it will be attributively declared. Nevertheless, a surprise awaits us. All the determinations that occur in this way *on* (κατά) presence in the first sense are *general* and *common* determinations, which respond to questions that are posed in the same terms about anything. What? Which? How much? Where? When? How? as we ask. It is only by means of these questions — Aristotle's categories — that the thing lets itself be determined as what it is, in contrast to its first appearance that allows us to see and know it in its 'most supreme' presence. These two modes of being, the singularity of the τόδε τι and the generality of its categorical determinations, are so narrowly linked that they never go without each other, to the point, as Aristotle says, that even when one of the ἀδιάφορα — of what it is "impossible to differentiate further," since it is what there is ultimately in presence — stands before us, it is immediately (πρῶτον) that we have in thought a general determination, "for example, the man, the man whose name is Callias."[46] *Presence* (οὐσία) *is thus a sort of counterpoint, with its song and its counter-song, the one saying and showing only the singular, while the other determines it only by generalities.* Yet the first is ahead of the second, for, without it, generalities would no longer have anything to "go back"[47] to, and they would be reduced to floating in a vacuum. But if presence in the first sense, namely the *that* or the *here-it-is*, is ahead of the τί, it is nevertheless only in the shadow of the τί that it occurs, since it is only ever the carrier of the τί itself. The whole of Aristotle's philosophy is, thus, the return to the foreground of what was initially placed only in the background, in such a way that what he had given the higher rank remains, so to speak, behind—*zurückbleibt*, as Heidegger says (*N* II 407)—in the manifestation of what categorially falls on it. Even in Aristotle, although the τόδε τι is *earlier*, it is already supplanted by what in it is said "according to the figures of attribution."

The withdrawal that begins with Aristotle, namely the withdrawal of what is nevertheless posed as first in being, will subsequently only be accentuated, all the more so when philosophy presents itself as a philosophy of existence. The destiny of Aristotle's thinking will distance him from what he wanted to say to such an extent that Gilson presents what he names "Thomism" as the discovery of what The Philosopher had not attained. It is quite the opposite that happens. If the return to the first rank of the secondary presence of the εἶδος, with the categories which follow from it, relegates to its profit the presence that is nevertheless named as primary in Aristotle's philosophy, the scholastic amelioration of Greek thought is the total exclusion of what already escaped the latter. From the perspective of 'Thomism' there is nothing else in the world other than creatures—not for having phenomenologically encountered them as such, but *ex lumine divinae scientiae* (from the light of divine knowledge)—whose appearance as *this here*, instead of being an initial source of wonder for us, is added to their metaphysical status as creatures. One knows neither why nor how this happens, for it is a miracle. Before the verdant field Aristotle could still say: οὕτως ἔχει, "it is so." Enlightened by the Scriptures, Saint Thomas can only say: "This is the work of God the creator who, after having spoken to our fathers by the voice of the Prophets, came, in this end of time, to speak to us through his son, having established him as the inheritor of all things." Certainly, this is very well said, and Saint Thomas has every right to speak in this way following Saint Paul. What is peculiar, however, is that in doing this he turns to Aristotle for support. This, in addition, is not forbidden. But then it is no longer possible to shrink back from a debate with a more original interpretation of Aristotle's thinking than the one with which his apology for biblical creation could content itself.

If, therefore, the ontological difference in the philosophy of Aristotle constitutes the origin of a major perplexity that will be the perplexity of all future metaphysics, another difference, that of the two modes of being whose unity alone poses οὐσία as a whole, is already a no less decisive, though more secret, embarrassment for it. For what predominates in this whole is, in the end, the part that was originally said to be subordinate. Such is the shadow cast on Aristotle's philosophy by

Platonism, for which the essence of being is the communal generality of the εἶδος. One can have, as Plato had said, as many tables and beds as one wishes, but "there is nevertheless for all these pieces of furniture only two *ideas,* one for what is a bed, one for what is a table."[48] Henceforth, the whole of philosophy after Aristotle will be the nostalgia for what hides itself to the profit of what overtakes it. It is this sense that Schelling will be able legitimately to characterize it as *negative philosophy* throughout its history. From the beginning, as he says, it never stops denying us "that toward which everything has aimed, and for which everyone has waited,"[49] endlessly demoting the *Dass,* namely *that it is,* to the profit of the *Was* in being, namely *what it is.* Consequently, Schelling's enterprise will be to provoke in philosophy a turning from the negative to the positive, in opening in it a more essential 'crisis' than critical philosophy itself, not to mention Hegelian speculation, which is in his eyes only a 'simple episode' of negative philosophy. No one more than Schelling felt the anguish of the radical withdrawal in being that Parmenides' μὴ ἐόν originally announces, and that Aristotle illustrates unknowingly in declaring to be primary what nevertheless escapes him from the beginning to the end of his *Logic.* But idealism, which remains the ground of Schelling's doctrine, prevents him all the more from recognizing and greeting the *positive,* for which he is so passionately searching "in what is held to be the privative essence of ἀλήθεια" (*PL* 51). This is why we have to wonder whether positive philosophy in Schelling's sense, as an idealistic apology of Judeo-Christian conceptions, does not further distance itself from Aristotle's supposedly negative philosophy of presence. Presence was, for this philosophy, οὐσία πρώτη, the sobriety of the τόδε τι, and it still knew how to point to it in saying simply: *here it is!*

The *this-here* is, for Aristotle, so decisive for beings in their being that he ceaselessly returns to it in order to scrutinize further the enigma that it presents. The *this-here* is, first of all, and as we have seen, the subject or the subjacent: what is already there so that something can be said of it. But being a subject or subjacent is an ambiguous determination. In book Z of the *Metaphysics* we read: "Concerning the subject, of which we have said that it underlies in two senses, either being a this, which is the way an animal underlies its affections— or as the matter underlies the *entelechy.*"[50] Entelechy is here a quite different mode of the appearing of being than the category. If being shows itself "according to the figures of attribution," of which the first is the τόδε τι as the καθ' οὗ, then it shows itself yet more supremely as entelechy. Speaking in this way, Aristotle means to say that being does not show itself in any better way than in the *achievement* or *completion* of the *this-here*—the completion of the fully opened flower, of man in the flower of his youth, of the temple that crowns the hill, of the house once built, or of a piece of furniture, such as it completes the residence in which it stands once it has left the carpenter's workshop. As synonymous with entelechy, Aristotle speaks also of ἐνέργεια. It is customary to translate ἐνέργεια as *act*. In truth, ἐνέργεια is in no way act: it is a plenitude at rest in itself, the plenitude of the work, poem, or monument that lacks nothing. This is why ἐνέργεια, in which one hears ἔργον, and ἐντελέχεια, wherein one hears τέλος, are synonymous—τέλος being no more a goal than ἔργον is an action or an act. Both words say that something is achieved rather than merely 'in progress' or not-yet 'in progress' in the sense of the tree in the forest in relation to the work of carpentry.

Whence were these two terms able to come into being, terms that speak of the latter 'more supremely' than the 'category'? Aristotle tells us in book Θ of the *Metaphysics:* "The term ἐνέργεια, which always relates to ἐντελέχεια, has been extended from movements, from which it comes to other things; in truth even ἐνέργεια appears best as mobility."[51] Having first of all come 'from movements' ἐνέργεια is no less a determination of beings in their being, which is as full as the categorial determination of being. For it is not limited to determining only those beings that are in movement, even if ἐνέργεια and movement are identical in the first instance. We begin to understand here that the view of the physicist, attentive to the movement in things, is still more decisive than the view of the logician, mobility being the very essence of φύσις and thus the most proper way for all the φύσει ὄντα to be *fully* themselves. Such mobility, which is "akin to the life" of φύσις, does not exclude rest. Rest is, on the contrary, intimately present in it, for rest itself is a mode of mobility. The animal at rest continues no less to grow old, and at the most rapid moment of its course it nevertheless remains at rest, at least as long as it keeps the same skin, for example, or remains the same animal. As ἐνέργεια mobility is, thus, *at once* movement and rest. Consequently, its completion is to be incomplete. It is only on this condition that certain states can be said to be more complete than others. It is the same for works of art that 'imitate nature'. They remain essentially mobile in their rest, even if they happen to last longer than the rose in flower, which nevertheless ceaselessly flowers in itself beyond all possible completion. The temple falls into ruins. The wood of the chest becomes worn out and is attacked by worms. Something physical can only be τελείως ἐνεργεῖν, "incomplete with regards to its end," relatively to the ἐνέργεια ἀτελής, "the incomplete 'actuality'," that is the essence of φύσις. But this reserve implies that the state of ἐνέργεια is what it is in relation to another state that, with regard to the former, is δύναμις. The planks, for example, are 'dynamically' the chest. They are not the chest, certainly, but they are ready to become it. As ἐνέργεια ἀτελής, therefore, mobility derives from what the wood in relation to the chest is δύναμις. Yet the ἐνέργεια of the latter in turn remains δύναμις insofar as the completed chest can still burn or rot. Only the ἀκίνητα are purely ἐνέργεια in excluding all δύναμις. Thus named they are thought from the perspective of movement but as nevertheless escaping it. It is, therefore, from mobility and from mobility alone that ἐνέργεια comes to be extended to other things.

The interpretation of being 'supremely as ἐνέργεια' is, thus, an understanding of what being offers for thought that is quite different to its categorial interpretation. Of course, the two interpretations are not contradictory since movement itself is able to be determined 'according to the categories', and thus according to οὐσία as generation or corruption, according to quality as alteration, or quantity as augmentation or diminution, etc. But what does not allow itself to be determined categorially is mobility as mobility, and what is bound to it, namely ἐνέργεια and δύναμις. It is rather only on this basis that the properly categorical distance between primary and secondary οὐσία is clarified. In distinction to the definition of man in general that is present in permanence, the man named Callias is sometimes here, sometimes not. But why? The response to this question is not a logical *response,* but a *physical* response. If Callias who was here is here no longer, it is because he left and that he has not yet come back, which means that Callias, in distinction from what he is only in a secondary sense, namely man, has the property of movement. It is in the *Physics,* however, that Aristotle determines mobility as mobility. But here what he says seems to contain a logical error, for he determines mobility by means of what can only be thought in relation to it, in saying: "the *entelechy* of the δυνατόν as δυνατόν, this is *mobility.*"[52] If entelechy and δύναμις both issue from movement, then the definition goes round in a circle. It is not, however, a simple *petitio principii,* for the circle in which it turns is a *hermeneutic* and not a *vicious* circle. If the definition of mobility clarifies it from the perspective of what derives from it, then this is in such a way that the derived terms send us back to that from which they derive, namely mobility. Hegel will characterize this movement of thought as *speculative.* If one takes the first part of the 'definition'—the *entelechy* of the δυνατόν—in isolation, it evokes, relatively to the wood, the chest, or relatively to the grain, the plant. But if we add ἧ δυνατόν: as δυνατόν, we find ourselves immediately sent back in the opposite direction from the chest to the wood, and from the plant to the grain, in such a way that we have to think the one and the other at the same time, yet without fixing our vision on any of the two, but rather on what is *between them both*. In a similar style, Kant will think the *schema* as the *between* of concept and intuition. Nothing is more difficult than a thinking of the *between*. In this sense, just as Kant will say that schematism is a "hidden art,"[53] Aristotle says of mobility that it is χαλεπὴ ἰδεῖν,[54] difficult to see and thus to say. Hence Aristotle's telling words will be the laughing stock of Descartes and Pascal. But Descartes and Pascal understand only mathematical language. Aristotle does not speak mathematically. Thus what he says has no meaning.

The light in which all beings are illuminated from the fact of mobility as ἐνέργεια and δύναμις, mobility itself being illuminated from this perspective at the same time, is not an explanation of beings by beings. Like categorial light, it is born from being itself insofar as it presences into the open as a clearing in beings. It is, therefore, an ontological light for beings, although it in no way derives from the categorial interpretation of the latter. Perhaps this is a more essential light than categorial light. It is, in fact, Aristotle himself who leads us to think this, when he says to us that the ἐνέργεια of the τόδε τι is *ousia* and *parousia*, more 'supremely' than the categorial determination of being, in which it appears only as καθ' οὗ, as *that of which* something will be said. Consequently, to extend the list of categories, as Brentano proposed, in adding possibility (δύναμις) and existence (ἐνέργεια) under the heading of categories of modality, finally completing them with the addition of a third concept, namely necessity, is to misunderstand Aristotle. Quite regularly, Aristotle reminds us almost incidentally — as is always the way of great philosophers when it is a question of something essential — that beings in their being are said in multiple ways: τὸ ὂν λέγεται πολλαχῶς. We can understand this to mean: the word *ontology* is in no way univocal. There is certainly an ontology "in the narrow sense," as Heidegger names it, which is categorial ontology. But Aristotle's ontology cannot be reduced to the latter. This is why one has every right to be surprised that in his otherwise extremely attentive study of the *Problem of Being in Aristotle* Aubenque holds the doctrine of the categories to be the "the essential, if not the unique chapter of Aristotelian ontology."[55] It is necessary to say, on the contrary, that if the doctrine of the categories and the logic that it founds are *an essential* chapter in Aristotle's ontology, it is far from the case that this chapter is *unique*. It is not even the most *important*.

Aristotle's ontology has the essential characteristic of surpassing it-self, instead of being all in one piece like the ontology of Plato. Noth-ing is more arbitrary than centering it exclusively upon the categorial interpretation of being in holding the latter, with Brentano, to be "the most important of all."[56] Perhaps this is why Aristotle, who did not hesitate before the creation of terms, did not forge the term ontology to designate what does not come under theology in his 'metaphysics'. For how can one name univocally a form of knowing that lends itself diversely to what it attempts to examine? The veritable title of Aris-totle's ontology is not a name, it is much rather the aphorism: τὸ ὄν λέγεται πολλαχῶς. But let us read the *Letter on Humanism:* "if man is called once again to find a resting place in the closest proximity to be-ing, he will have to learn to inhabit the nameless" (*PL* 60). It is cer-tainly Aristotle that Heidegger thinks of here, for who better than Ar-istotle teaches us such endurance? Who better teaches us, otherwise expressed and in the words of Aeschylus, to become 'experts in the test'? It is well after Aristotle and only after the limitation of the expe-rience of being to its more restrained scope that the term ontology will be formed symmetrically to theology. Ontology is only the scholarly or, as it were, the scholastic denomination of what was, for Aristotle, the mobile horizon of a question that he ceaselessly advanced, at the price of which his theology is much poorer, notwithstanding the fact that theology, as he says, is the most proper name of 'first philosophy'. But theological knowledge itself does not refer to ontology 'in the re-stricted sense' alone, and it refers to it only as a mere minimum con-dition. If it belongs to this knowledge to be, as one likes to say today, a "coherent discourse,"[57] this necessary condition is far from being sufficient. It is not simply a discourse *on* God that would say without contradiction something of this thing, but it allows the divine as di-vine to be said and thus to be invoked into its apparition, which sup-poses a quite different relation to being than the categorial relation. In the theology of Aristotle there still resonates the call that Hölderlin heard in the chorus of Sophocles: προφάνηθι θεός — "Be manifest to us, O God!"[58] This is to say that theology is itself only possible if ontol-ogy is not reduced to the supposedly 'unique chapter' that is Logic. Not that the 'attributive discourse' that derives from the latter would be only the "substitute of an absent vision."[59] On this point also we are opposed no less diametrically to Aubenque. Aristotle's logic, as he himself says, is radically *apophantic.* But what is apophantic in the τι κατά τινος remains beneath the 'more supreme' manifestation of being as ἐνέργεια. The ontological horizon of 'coherent discourse', the one that the categories determine, lacks the opening for the bringing into view of the divine insofar as it is, and that is to say, as ἐνέργεια ἀεὶ οὖσα.

In the preceding pages we have attempted to liberate the interpretation of Aristotle from two tenacious prejudices. The first is that it would differ from the philosophy of Plato in having more of a 'taste' for the 'bare facts'—facts toward which Plato would not yet have discovered the art of being inclined. The other one is that the ontology developed in the philosophy of Aristotle would remain at bottom as monolithic as Platonic eideticism, having no other goal than to reduce everything to 'logic' and 'coherent discourse', which it falls to logic alone to ground. The truth is that Aristotle is separated from his master Plato in a much more subtle manner. He is separated from him in thinking differently than him the difference being-beings at the heart of beings. No longer in dislocating them to the point of repudiating as not-being (μὴ ὄν) what in beings is only *this-here,* but in thinking the light that transpires in the latter as supreme οὐσία. In his eyes, nothing is more in being than *this* rose that flowers amid the dark green of the foliage. It is not the 'obfuscation' of an 'idea', for this is only of a second rank in it. But what is exactly *this rose* wherein being manifests itself at the height of its presence? First of all, it is only the καθ' οὗ, that is to say, the subject of the categorical interpretation of beings in their being. The latter is, in turn, the lowest degree of ontology. For *this rose* is not only subject or complement in propositions of which the totality would form a 'coherent discourse'. It is the marvel of ἐνέργεια. Such an ἐνέργεια is, however, ἀτελής, for although it is flowering now, the flower will soon disappear. This is why it is there only in corresponding to a higher ἐνέργεια, which is nothing like a rose, but whose name is ἀκίνητον, beyond-movement. Before the same flowering rose, Plato and Aristotle do not think the same thing. Plato recollects the 'idea' of the rose itself, which as 'absent from all bouquets' is eternally elsewhere. With his eyes fixed on the mobile flowering, Aristotle, on the contrary, goes beyond this flowering to think what is in its essence beyond-movement. This is not an eternal rose, but something else of which he has almost nothing to say, except that it is eternal. This is why his theology is so minimal. To the point that Sir D. W. Ross will not hesitate to judge it, for an Englishman of the twentieth century, "insufficient."[60] So be it.

Rather than logic, what captivates Aristotle and frees his thought is the marvel of movement, which Plato on the contrary, while magnifying it, approaches only with reserve. Hence this ontology of movement that the *Physics* is from its beginning to its end, and that, much more than logic, is the 'essential chapter' of his ontology. This essential chapter, whether the pride of modern science likes it or not, is perhaps the most original chapter of Aristotelian ontology. Doubtless, one continues to respect in his metaphysics, even in criticizing it, the dependence of the physical on the divine that it institutes. But the interpretation of movement according to δύναμις and ἐνέργεια passes for the defunct part of his work. Koyré will go as far as to say that it is "irremediably defunct."[61] Even Leibniz, who is nevertheless so close to Aristotle, said in his *Nouveaux essais:* "He overuses his 'act', which means very little."[62] We should probably understand this to mean: "Which we no longer make very much of." For Leibniz, the 'act' that itself harbors movement remains to be thought in a different way than Aristotle ever could. Not as a simple *state* of movement in opposition to its pure *possibility,* but as 'embryonic' even in speed and as already at work in rest. Such a thinking is essential to the *Reform of First Philosophy* that Leibniz announces in 1694. For Leibniz, therefore, the grandeur of Aristotle remains that he is, above all, the inventor of Logic. It is a question only of promoting it to a "good Characteristic" which is "one of the greatest servants of the human spirit."[63] It will be the same not only for Kant, but also for Hegel and, beyond him, for Brentano and for all the others. We have to wait until Heidegger for ἐνέργεια to be understood as the master-word of a phenomenology, which beneath mathematical physics seeks to respond to a 'dictation' of being that is still more original than Logic, which itself is more profound than Mathematics. It is in this spirit that he characterized ἐνέργεια as "the highest nomination of being that the philosophy of the ancients ever attempted" during the conference at Cerisy (1955). It is in the same spirit, and as if in speaking to himself, that he finishes his study on the first chapter of book II of Aristotle's *Physics* thus:

> Because φύσις in the sense of the "Physics" is one kind of οὐσία and because οὐσία itself stems in its essence from φύσις as projected in the beginning, therefore ἀλήθεια belongs to being, and *therefore presencing* into the open of the ἰδέα (Plato) and into the open of the εἶδος κατὰ τὸν λόγον (Aristotle) is revealed as one characteristic of οὐσία; *therefore* for Aristotle the essence of κίνησις becomes *visible* as ἐντελέχεια and ἐνέργεια.

Nothing is lacking from this meditative phrase that recalls the very procedure of Aristotle's thinking: ἀπόφανσις, ἐνέργεια, ἀλήθεια.

If the thinking of being as ἐνέργεια establishes a more essential chapter in Aristotle's ontology than the chapter of Logic, which is certainly essential, then is this more essential chapter the ultimate chapter? In no way if, still more than *mobility,* the being of beings is ἀληθὲς ἤ ψεῦδος: *present and unhidden* or *under the veil of another* aspect.[64] Was this ultimate chapter of ontology ever written by the Philosopher? Nobody will ever know. We have, however, at least a sketch of it on the last page of book Θ of the *Metaphysics,* which, without any transition, enigmatically examines the relation to the *simple,* of which the λόγος is no longer κατάφασις (proposition) but only φάσις (speech). Any proposition is speech, but all speech is not necessarily a proposition. When speech is a proposition, it falls to it to be sometimes true, sometimes false if that of which it speaks can become other than it is. It is, on the contrary, forever either true or false if what it says is beyond change. But when speech is only speech in responding to the call of being itself (τὸ ὂν ᾗ ὄν), there now is only possible for it is this θίγειν καὶ φάναι, "being in contact and speaking." *Die Pracht des Schlichten,* the "wonder of the simple," is opened in this, and nothing can be hidden from it, although it can remain unknown to many. Thus we can only see or not see that Cézanne's *Card Players* have the simplicity of, in the words of Braque, "constituting a pictorial fact." For "the regard of thought before what in itself is fully illuminated is like the eyes of nocturnal creatures before the light of day."[65]

Book III of *De Anima* responds to the final chapter of *Metaphysics* Θ, as does, in its own way, *Peri Hermeneias,* which is no way what one often makes of it, namely a simple link internal to *Logic* between the *Categories* and the *Analytics,* but rather a later meditation in which the last of the Greek philosophers supremely masters his own knowing. The fact that in these few pages Aristotle only treats the λόγος as ἀποφαντικος, and thus as κατάφασις (or ἀπόφασις), in other words as the *proposition,* reserves all the better the possibility of a φάσις, of a still more essential speech. Such a speech constitutes from one end to the other the very philosophy of Aristotle in the 'desire' that leads it to break through to being. We could say: even the interpretation of the λόγος as apophantic contains nothing of the apophantic in the categorial sense. The task that it takes up consists much rather in what Aristotle names: περι τὰς ἀρχὰς ἀληθεύειν[66]—to enter into the Open to the point where that from which all things issue and that never ceases to reign over them becomes visible. In this sense it commits itself to the supreme risk of a relation to what is simple. In this way Cézanne will work 'on the motif'. In this way Aristotle worked even in those texts wherein the tradition persists in seeing only a logician. For even the discovery of Logic is nothing logical. It is a more radical breakthrough in awe and wonder before the fact that: *it is so.*

Aristotle, about whom so many books have been written during two millennia, is still and all the more obscure for us. But it is Aristotle himself who gives us the word for the enigma that he is when he occasionally recalls the source of his wonder, which was for him, perhaps, no less an enigma that it is for us: τὸ ὄν λέγεται πολλαχῶς.

6

Energeia *and* Actus

Being, for Aristotle, in the 'most magisterial' sense is ἐνεργεῖν. Our word energy derives from this, which signifies the deployment of force or of an action, except if the energy remains potential, like that of the water that a dam restrains before it activates a turbine by its fall. Such would also seem to be, at least in appearance, the marvel of ἐνέργεια. It is, says Aristotle, ὅθεν ἡ κίνησις, that from which movement begins. In this way the fire that burns in the hearth lights the room in which it glows. But it also procures the cooking of food and heats the whole house, lending its well-being to those sitting at the fireside. It does not, however, carry out an action, for nothing leaves the fire, there is no 'influx' that would invade everything else in acting upon the latter to the point of transforming it into what it is not. It is rather against the ἐνέργεια of the fire that everything else measures itself in turning itself toward another measure of its own being. While energy evokes the uncoiling of a spring or the action of a force that pushes something into becoming something else, ἐνέργεια, far from pressing upon anything, awakens in what is other to it a latent aptitude that requires nothing else in order to bring itself to the fore, responding in this way to whatever awakens it. In the *Republic* Plato wonders how it would be possible for someone who lives in the company of the divine to respond to it without in some way being in harmony with it. Yet nothing emanates from the divine. It suffices that it be for movement to begin around it. Aristotle says of the divine: κινεῖ ὡς ἐρώμενον; it moves by its own grace, giving to what lives with it the grace to reveal itself otherwise

97

than it would without it. Such is the marvel of ἐνέργεια, which has always 'something of the divine'.

As Sophocles said, χάρις χάριν γὰρ ἐστιν ἡ τίκτουσ᾽ ἀεί — "Grace is that which always gives birth to grace."[1] Of course, this birth of grace from grace never goes without violence, if it is true, according to the word of the young Nietzsche, that "all birth is painful and takes place in violence." Aeschylus knew this, who tells us in *Agamemnon* (verse 182f.):

> Violence is the grace of gods
> All at their post on the bench of the sacred ship.

And Pindar:

> Destiny is master to them all,
> Mortals or immortals
> It guides high-handedly
> The most violent equity.

But here violence is not the only word for the enigma. More essential is the δίκαιον, the flawless adjoining where everything is in its own place. It is in this way that according to Hippocrates the doctor — procuring what he soberly names τὰ δέοντα — disturbs his patient and thus does violence to him. Yet the doctor needs the help not only of his patient but also of "those who assist the patient," and even of everything that surrounds him.[2] Only thus does the marvel of healing occur. In the same way, the sculptor attacks the marble in using his tools. But he needs the marble to follow him. And it is the τέχνη residing in him which "moves his hands"[3] without any violence. When violence gains the upper hand the tragedy of Prometheus occurs. But even the primacy of constraint guards a secret of which κράτος and βία, Force and Violence, are only the ὑποκριταί. We say the 'actors', but the Greeks called them 'hypocrites' — in other words, those from below.[4] It is from there that they act, the essential thing being not the constraint of which they are the instruments, but something more secret which is left for us to divine.

As soon as it appears, therefore, the 'classical' translation of ἐνέργεια by the Latin *actus* could not be more anti-Greek. It covers over the passage from one world to another, that is, the passage from the Greek to the Roman world, to which action is as essential as χάρις is to the former, such as it is harbored in the ἐνέργεια of Aristotle. But in the Roman climate, what is *is* only what *acts*, thus invading everything else in order to force it to become what it is not. The Romans named the thing *efficiency*. Hence the Ciceronian definition of causality as "id quod cuique . . . efficienter antecedit."[5] In this way a wound is the cause of death to the extent that by its efficiency it pushes to its death the living being in which it is present. For the Greeks, on the contrary, the wound causes death less than it prevents living, in undermining the movement of ζωή of which the living being is the highest modality; consequently, the wonder that is life is held in check. But now it is force against force, winner takes all. For *efficiency* has always more or less force. The word *force, vis* in Latin, is often used to translate the Greek δύναμις which is, with ἐνέργεια, one of the fundamental terms of Aristotle's *Physics*. In this way Leibniz will be content, in supposedly going back to the Greek from the Latin, to situate in what he names τὸ δυναμικόν the very essence of what is with the argument that nothing *is* unless it is able to deploy force (*vis*). But *vis* is not the Greek δύναμις but rather βία, which is only, for Aristotle, one of the essential traits of φύσις as κίνησις insofar as βία κινεῖσθαι, "to be moved by force," is παρὰ φύσιν κινεῖσθαι, "to be moved from nature." This is not the case for the Romans, who make of force, *vis*—itself understood as *potestas*, 'power over'—the very essence of what Lucretius named *natura rerum* in translating the Greek φύσις. From such a perspective what we have to know about things is above all the "force and powers," *vis atque potestates*,[6] by which they act upon each other. We are at the antipodes here of any knowledge of φύσις according to ἐνέργεια and δύναμις—according to the achieved presence and the aptitude that secretly pre-exists the former and that is bound to it. Such is, perhaps, the secret relation of the statue to the marble, but also of the grain to the plant or of the earth to the harvests that it bears.

From the perspective of the Greeks, force and efficiency are never primary. Certainly, the Greeks are not unaware of them, but they only ever attribute an intermediary and subordinate role to them. The vector that they compose is determined by Aristotle as ὑπηρετικόν, which we can translate as 'working in the background'. What counts here, first of all, is not the 'play of forces' but the domain in which such a play is itself only something secondary. This domain is that of the birth of the work, which is a quite different marvel than anything a mastery of the play of forces could ever assure us. The birth of the work is not for the Greeks a matter of force, but rather of what they named knowing; and knowing in the Greek sense is a quite different relation to things than that which they have to someone who sees only relations of force. For in the latter case it would be necessary to interpret the work of carpentry as extorted from the wood ἐμπεσόντος τοῦ ὀργάνου, "the tools falling upon it."[7] The blows of the hammer and the marks of the plane or the saw are, however, only the superficial aspect of a phenomenon whose ground consists in the artisan's being oriented πρὸς τῷ ξύλῳ, "toward the wood,"[8] by means of carpentry and its knowing. Not in order to mistreat it in untold ways, but in order to discover or clear in it the passage from the wood to the emergence of the work. If he does not first of all have the sense of such a passage, the carpenter is only a *hack*. The carpenter is in no way, therefore, an 'efficient cause'. But what is he then? He is, as Aristotle said, τὸ ποιοῦν. Doubtless, it is common to translate τὸ ποιοῦν by: the efficient cause. The Romanization of the Greek world is henceforth a fait accompli, and the Greek world has, as Nietzsche says, withdrawn to the profit of a quite other world that only obstructs our access to the former. But does not ποιεῖν signify a *making*, which is a way of *acting*? Not at all if, as Heidegger says, the Greeks understood ποιεῖν as a *letting appear*.[9]

If one translates ποιεῖν by *making*, itself understood as the action of an efficient cause, then, and it is worth repeating, Greek speaks Latin and everything is said. The question remains, however, of knowing if such is the secret of the work. It is quite natural to employ the word *making* (*faire*) without thinking too much about what it says, to the point of saying that Mallarmé was occupied with making poems. Maritain even writes: "The domain of making is the domain of art, in the most universal sense of the word." In truth, Mallarmé does not make anything at all, but he has a poetic relation with the language that he speaks. It is from this relation to language that the poem finally emerges for him, poetry existing in order to clear our path to what ordinary language never stops naming without making it appear. Mallarmé gives the title 'Apparition' to one of his poems. All of his poems merit the same title. The very sense of poetry, as another poet tells us, is to 'make us see'. In this way, Eluard and Mallarmé speak like Aristotle. By his relation to language, as Aristotle teaches us, the poet awakens in it a secret aptitude to *say*—the word meaning *to show*—what it has never said before, but that it says when it becomes a poem of Mallarmé, for example. This becoming is an achievement that belongs to the same secret as that of the completion of the work of carpentry in the wood. To be the man of such a secret is to be a poet instead of someone who is often much busier and who is only ever a maker, although, to be sure, there are more makers than poets in the world. Such was for the Greeks the essence of what they named ποίησις, and not what Valéry, fascinated by etymology, explained one day at the Collège de France in order to thank a minister who had made space for him. Valéry is not a simple maker. But the ποιοῦν, here the ποιητής, gathers to himself that from which something is born, namely language, and the figure according to which it happens to appear to him, namely that of a poem rather than that of a discourse or of a piece of furniture, in such a way that is from him, the poet, or rather from his τέχνη, poetry, that the poem is led to its resplendent completion.

> Perfect face and complete diadem.[10]

Ποίησις responds here only to φύσις which still more originally gathers in itself the ἐξ οὗ and the εἶδος so that it is from φύσις, and from it alone, that one of the φύσει ὄντα attains its ἐνέργεια, as when the tree, in the middle of the moor, finally stands in its 'pure elevation'.

> Da stieg ein Baum. O reine Übersteigung.
> There stands a tree. O pure Elevation.[11]

Aristotle even employs here and there the verb ποιεῖν with the noun φύσις as its subject. In this way he says all the more acutely that φύσις does not proceed by force, but rather insofar as "it contains, originating in it, the emergence of another figure."[12] The *epiphanic* depth of such an emergence is what predominates here, rather than the *dynamic* of an impulsion that would be its *efficient cause*. So the Greeks, then, would interpret φύσις *poetically*? Not at all. But they think both φύσις and ποίησις on the basis of a more fundamental characteristic, which is expressed by the verb φαίνεσθαι. So they interpret them *fantastically*? Perhaps. But only if one understands as they do the word φαντασία, which expresses, as Aristotle says, τὸ φῶς, the light in which the aspect of things appears. Hence he named φαντασία τῶν ἄστρων what the stars allow us to see throughout the night sky, being what they are, as Sappho said, by their φαεννὸν εἶδος. To this belong the phases of the moon, which are not lunar fantasies, but its modes of appearing, whether it shows itself as full, waxing, or on the wane. The Greeks are not, therefore, zealots of the fantastic, but those to which everything, including the gods, has the nature of being manifest. In this way they are men of manifestation or appearing, which they think in its plenitude. They experienced such a plenitude in naming it *limit:* τὸ πέρας. To see something in its limits — as, in other words, πεπερασμένον — was not in their eyes to see it only where it ends, but first of all to be able to grasp it in itself and as a whole. Limit was not for them, as it will be for Spinoza, negation, but a first and essential position. This is why for Aristotle the question of being is above all one of that by which ὥρισται τὸ ὄν — that by which beings as beings have a limit. First of all, this concerns only the categories. But the categorial delimitation does not suffice for the question of being. Aristotle will say, therefore, that it is also from δύναμις and ἐνέργεια that everything 'has its limit'. For being is not a monolithic block: it manifests itself in diverse ways. And from this trans-categorial delimitation there emerges yet another delimitation of being: that of beings as manifest in unhiddenness or as producing in the foreground an aspect other than its own which fools us at our own expense. Such is the country of being, the one where we speak and work, but also, as Pindar says in the seventh *Olympiad* (line 45 f.), the one where we are menaced by

> The cloud of λήθη, coming upon us without warning,
> That robs mortals of the straight path of endeavor.

Discovering the limit is consequently something more than human. This is why a relief in the Acropolis Museum makes it surge from a divine meditation, that of a *pensive Athena* "pricking the Greek soil with her lance."[13] But for us men, as Protagoras knew, things are never so clear. This is why Thucydides has Alcibiades say to the Athenians: "For our part, it does not belong to us to measure in advance, as does an intendant, the extension of our enterprise."[14] This is not, as Nietzsche will believe, a premonitory figure of his interpretation of being as will to power, but an essentially Greek characteristic of being, which is a question, above all, of limit. To the inhabitants of the country of being, limit was the question of questions. Such was even for them the essence of what they named tragedy, at least if, as Karl Reinhardt says, the real theme of Sophoclean tragedy is "the enigma of the limit between the human and the divine."[15]

The Greek world, including the philosophy of this world that was the very birth of philosophy, irremediably escapes anyone who does not think this secret relation of appearance (φαντασία) and limit (πέρας) in φύσις and ποίησις from the perspective of the ἐνέργεια in which they both culminate. This is why we cannot follow Aubenque when, in an otherwise solidly documented book on Aristotle, he reproaches Heidegger for holding the Latin *actus* to be something other than a faithful translation of the Greek ἐνέργεια.[16] This is to read Aristotle not from the perspective of the Greek that he spoke, but from that of the Romanization of Greek. What the Greeks always think in its limit and from the perspective of the grace that was for them the gift of presence, the Romans think from the perspective of action and its empire:

Tu regere imperio populos, Romane, memento,
Hae tibi erunt artes, pacisque imponere morem,
Parcere subjectis et debellare superbos.

Romans, be this thy care—these thine arts—to bear dominion over the nations and to impose the regime of peace to spare the humbled and to wear down the proud.[17]

Thus speaks Virgil. Tacitus echoes this: "Ubi Romani solitudinem fecerunt, pacem appellant," Wherever the Romans created desolation, they call it peace. It is, of course, a 'superb' person who is speaking. But the essence of Roman action is precisely to have done with what is superb in reducing it so that everything can be arranged in order. Thus it will reduce what is superb in the marble to the statue. But in this way the statue speaks in a quite different way than that of Polycletus. It is reduced to searching in the realism of resemblance a compensation for the coldness that is born from the desolation of the marble. The Romans may well have studied the Greeks, adding peristyles to their houses, decorating their interiors with paintings, constructing temples with columns, populating and surrounding them with statues, but it is not with them that Victor Hugo would have been able to feel, without having seen it, what he called in the *Voix intérieures:*

Something beautiful like the smile of a man
On the profile of the Propylees.[18]

Medieval philosophy binds itself deliberately to Greek philosophy, but through a Roman filter that is invisible to it. It is only in this way that we can understand the translation of ἐνέργεια by *actus* and the Thomistic interpretation of the God of the Bible as *actus purus essendi*— the pure 'act' of being. Such an interpretation of God supposes an interpretation of being which is, so to speak, on a par with it. This is the properly Aristotelian trait in scholasticism. Heidegger notes in his *Satz vom Grund* (p. 136):

What in Aristotle's sense determines beings with regard to their being and how such a determination happens is experienced differently than in the medieval doctrine of *ens qua ens*. Yet it would be senseless to say that the medieval theologians misunderstood Aristotle; rather, they understood him differently, responding to the different manner in which being offered itself to them.

Differently here supposes a more secret relation, without which it would only signify a pure and simple substitution in the sense that one nail drives out another. Without such a relation, the guarantor of an essential continuity, the reference to Aristotle would be not the spirit of Scholasticism but merely external to it. The *different* destiny of being, which differentiates medieval philosophy from Greek philosophy, remains in essence the guardian of a properly Greek destiny of being: that being, already in Aristotle's *Metaphysics,* is posed according to a characteristic doubling. From *Kant and the Problem of Metaphysics* (1929) Heidegger qualifies such a doubling as *merkwürdig,* remarkable. Later (1943) he will call it *onto-theological,* but it is only in 1957 that he will explicitly formulate the question as a question, in interrogating the provenance of onto-theology understood as the fundamental structure of metaphysics *as such.* In the interval he writes:

> The theological character of ontology is not merely due to the fact that Greek metaphysics was later taken up and transformed by the ecclesiastical theology of Christianity. Rather it is due to the way in which beings as beings have revealed themselves from early on. It was only this manifestation of beings that first provided the possibility for Christian theology to take possession of Greek philosophy—whether for better or for worse may be decided by the theologians on the basis of their experience of what is Christian, in pondering what is written in Paul the Apostle's First Letter to the Corinthians: "Has not God let the wisdom of this world become foolishness?" (*WM* 18)

When Gilson characterizes "Christian philosophy as Christian" by the affirmation of an "identity of God with being,"[19] therefore, he resolutely paganizes. Master Eckhart was much more essentially Christian when he dared to say: "Deo non competit esse"—it is not fitting for God to be—which Heidegger echoes in saying: "Sein und Gott ist nicht identisch"—being and God are not the same. The identity of God and being determines the philosophy of Aristotle as much as supposedly "Christian philosophy as Christian," since both come under the same representation of being, namely the metaphysical representation of the unity in it of a peculiar doubling. In *metaphysics* the prefix *meta* is profoundly ambiguous, no less than its Latin interpretation *trans. Meta* or *trans* speak, in fact, as much of the surpassing of beings toward their being as of the surpassing of beings toward the supremely Being. In the Middle Ages, the unitary difference of the transcendent and the transcendental—such as it will reappear in Kant's philosophy according to an inversion of its two terms—responds to this. But this difference is only the Aristotelian difference between the ὄν as κοινὸν πᾶσιν, "being as what is common to everything," and ὄν as τιμιώτατον γένος, "being as the highest genus." The first is a surpassing of beings toward what is more communal to it than the genus. The second surpasses beings in the direction of the supremely Being, which Aristotle names: the divine. The marvel here is that both constitute the essence of being, insofar as being is thought absolutely and without restriction, in other words, *fundamentally*. We can, in fact, translate thus the adverb καθόλου, which for Aristotle is fitting if we are concerned with the observations concerning beings insofar as they are beings, according to which the still anonymous science that will later receive the name of ontology proceeds, as much as it is for theology, which is also: καθόλου ὅτι πρώτη; it proceeds fundamentally because primary. Doubtless, from Aristotle to Saint Thomas the divine is reduced to one God, whereas Aristotle thinks it as a 'genus' of beings, the beings of such a genus being able, if one were ever to attempt to count them, to be greater or lesser in number. But this is still an external, incidental difference. A still more radical difference than monotheism separates Saint Thomas from Aristotle.

If, for both Aristotle and Saint Thomas, it belongs to being to have at once an *intimum* and a *summum,* the latter responding in all its purity to its *intimum,* then both are no longer thought by Saint Thomas on the basis of Greek experience, the experience of being as ἐνέργεια, but on the basis of a quite different domain, no longer Greek but Roman, where what is fundamental is determined as *virtus* and as *actus.* In this way everything is ready for the entrance in philosophy of a metaphysical equivalent of the God of the Bible, about whom the first verse of *Genesis* teaches us that he is a creative God. The Bible remains silent on the idea of creation itself. It is only on the details that it is prolix. It is the Greek translation of the Bible that will transform creation into a metaphysical question, in making the Greek ποιεῖν correspond to a Hebrew verb, the one that French and English, on the basis of Latin, will render as *créer* or *create*. This had been explained from Plato onwards in the language of being, which is Greek and not Hebrew or Latin. It is Plato and not the Bible that informs us: "Let us say that in all that is brought into being from a prior non-being, to bring is to produce (ποιεῖν) and to be brought into being is to be produced (ποιεῖσθαι)."[20] So the idea of creation out of nothing has a Greek and not a biblical origin? Certainly. And it is not at all by chance, if, in a book of the Bible which is originally Greek and not Hebraic, and which the Reformed hold to be apocryphal, it is said that God created everything "not from beings" (οὐκ ἐξ ὄντων). The Vulgate of Saint Jerome will say: *ex nihilo*. Doubtless, Christian theology understands the *nihil* in a different way than Greek philosophy, for which non-being is an ontological dimension rather than an ontic fact. The nothing of the theologians signifies, on the contrary, only a distance from beings that is measured from the perspective of the supremely Being. This is why in the eyes of Saint Augustine even the *informitas,* which is still in the closest proximity to nothingness, is already a first creature, being less far from God than absolute nothingness. But this naive return from the ontological to the ontic takes its measure from Greek language when it seeks to become thoughtful—and not on the biblical word, to which philosophy is as external, as Aristotle would say, as sound is to visibility. To suppose that such an exteriority will give birth in philosophy to a heretofore unknown depth could well be tantamount to what Kant, inspired by a Greek proverb, liked to formulate thus: "the ludicrous spectacle of one man milking a he-goat and the other holding a sieve underneath."[21]

The essential thing here is that although Saint Thomas follows in the footsteps of Aristotle, it is not from Greek but rather from the Romanization of Greek that he is able to characterize creation metaphysically as *unica actio solius Dei*—the unique action of God alone. By *actio* he imagines the exercise of a causality as *efficient,* and that is to say, a causality in which the supremely Being, which in its being has already held nothingness at a distance from itself, is going to come back to nothingness in order to force it, in a second anti-nihilist campaign, to be. In this way nothingness is not annihilated. It is only subjugated. Hence the infirmity of the creature into which nothingness always breaks through. It is in this way, as Valéry says, that Creation itself

> All the way up to Being, exalts the strange
> Omnipotence of nothingness.[22]

This representation of things supposes, as we have seen, a quite different interpretation of nothingness than that of Greek philosophy. For Plato, nothingness, rather than being the antithesis of God, was the screen of the εἶδος, such a screen announcing itself in the μὴ ὄν that was for him the immediate presence of beings, insofar as it gives us much less to see than the εἶδος, although, as εἴδωλον, it presupposes it. For Aristotle, the readiness of 'privation' (στέρησις) was more radical. Privation itself remains, however, as he said, "a sort of εἶδος."[23] But non-presence, which makes nothing manifest, and which Parmenides in his Poem thought strangely as on a par with presence itself, is still more radical than privation in Aristotle's sense. Consequently, non-being conforms no less than being to the initiality of the *destiny* (μοῖρα) that at once separates being, non-being, and beings. Non-being is thus a power of the highest order, as much as are being and beings, the latter signifying, correlatively to being, the appearance of the δοκοῦντα, whose power is also a power of the highest order.

The horizon of vision of Christian philosophy is quite different. Doubtless, in this horizon non-being remains a power, but it has less power than being, such as it is first of all supremely gathered in God, who only eternally distances nothingness from himself in order to come back to it so as to constrain it to carry the load of being. This is why all things cry at the top of their voice: *Ipse fecit nos*—He himself made us.[24] By this we are to understand: It is in triumphing once again over nothingness that He has made us, as He is, Him and Him alone, the Omnipotent. Thus nothingness is lowered, as if humiliated before being, which, stronger than the former, imposes on it its own law. This is why in the end nothingness is only the devil's portion:

Ich bin der Geist, der stets verneint,[25]

Goethe's Mephistopheles says to us, "I am the spirit that always says no." But this denigration is vanquished in advance, although it cannot be nullified, for the nullifying of nothingness would be at once the nullification of being. But having become a secondary power, nothingness remains a radical power that owes nothing to being. In one sense, God himself needs nothingness—in order to be, for he requires nothingness to be defeated, as a singular phrase of Bonaventure reminds us in evoking the metaphysical altercation of God and nothingness that is still more original than the creation of the world: "ipsum esse purissimum non occurrit nisi in plena fuga non esse sicut et nihil in plena fuga esse"—Being itself in its purity arrives only with the total rout of non-being, just as non-being in the total rout of being.[26]

Hence the necessity for theology to go back from Creation as an exercise of divine causality on non-being to the still more original altercation of being and non-being from which emerges even the existence of God, who is another and the most proper name for being. This time we find ourselves, as Saint John said and as Hegel will say, with what already existed "before the creation of the world." From the perspective of Christian theology such a *before* remains essentially relative to what it precedes and prepares, namely creation itself, which is the first truth that the Bible reveals to us. But it is exactly the same for Aristotle. In the guise of a theologian, Aristotle asks himself *from what* beings can first of all originate. Yet it is from the perspective of ἐνέργεια that he asks this, and his response is thoroughly consistent with it: from the being that, by itself, is 'already ἐνέργεια', the latter understood as deploying itself eternally (ἀεί) as such, and not only here and there (ἐνίοτε). It is from the being of such an ἐνέργεια, but without what is 'already ἐνέργεια' having to produce anything, that everything is moved around him by his grace, and which he moves in 'being loved': first of all the sky with the stars, then, by the intermediary of the sky, the whole of nature right down to the vicinity of nonbeing. But for Saint Thomas what is not God can only be created by it, in the sense of Creation as *ex ratione causae efficientis*. Correlatively to the Aristotelian interpretation of being as ἐνέργεια, the transformation of ἐνέργεια into *actualitas*, which is thought from the perspective of *agere* and not *esse*, responds to this.

But how are we to understand this term *actualitas* that aims to say in Latin what was said by the Greek ἐνέργεια? The actuality of a thing signifies in the first instance that it has been effectively posed in being by the action of an efficient cause, thanks to which—as Suarez will say later in responding to the scholasticism that preceded him—"it ceases being nothing in order to begin to be something" (*N* II 418). Actuality is thus thought as the result of a causality from which it is posed: *extra causas suas*. But in this way it is determined all the more by causality as efficiency. Only thus does the word 'exist' have its meaning: *ek-sister*, such a *sistere*, thought from the perspective of *extra*, being essentially *ex* and having a sense only on the basis of that from which it emerges. It is thus that "the thought of being as actuality gave to beings, for whoever takes them as a whole, the fundamental trait which the representation of things that constitutes the foundation of Judeo-Christian belief in creation is going to be able to take over in order to gain a metaphysical justification for itself" (*N* II 414)—the one according to which, as Saint Thomas holds, God "adest omnibus ut causa essendi," is present in all things as the cause of being. Determined in this manner, the concept of actuality is systematically lacking in Saint Augustine, who rather thinks the relation of the creature to nothingness, by which it is contrasted with God, than philosophically representing it as acted upon or actualized by him. Hence the marvel for him of what he strangely names: *ictus condendi*,[27] the 'blow' or event of creation in which

> God himself has overcome the obstacle
> Of his perfect eternity

to adopt "the low and, so to speak, humiliating condition of the Creator." Thus speaks Malebranche in the *Christian Meditations*, in all fidelity to Augustine.[28] But the concept of *actualitas* was elaborated much later than in the philosophy of the one whom Malebranche honored as his master. It is only with Saint Thomas that it gains the foreground to become the definition of being itself: "Esse est actualitas omnis formae" — being is the actuality of all forms.[29] Doubtless, philosophically it is perfectly acceptable to speak in this way. What remains surprising, however, is that Saint Thomas understands in what he terms *actualitas* what Aristotle had named ἐνέργεια. But here the question returns. If *actualitas* is the most general definition of being, then it must be able to be said, as Aristotle intended with his concept of ἐνέργεια, of God himself. Yet God is nevertheless not posed in being by the action of an efficient cause. If, as Descartes will write to Arnauld in proposing to characterize God as *causa sui,* it is legitimate to recognize in him the "dignity of a cause," one cannot attribute to him without blasphemy the "indignity of an effect."[30] This is why actuality in Saint Thomas's sense supposes causality only in order to transcend it by recourse to an activity superior to causality itself. Hence if each and every being, as created by God, is *actus essendi,* God himself is *actus purus essendi.* The *actus essendi* that is the *actualitas* of the creature remains, in fact, *permixtus potentiae.* Divine actuality, on the contrary, is without any admixture of possibility, and thus it is, as one will say later, *aseitas,* existing of and from itself.

In this way the *ictus condendi* that was, for Saint Augustine, the spectacular event of creation is now clarified as *actus,* namely *actus secundus* in relation to the *actus primus,* which precedes the former in God as the pure actuality of God himself. It is in this way that following much secular work the first verse of Genesis is finally provided with a metaphysical justification. But at what cost? At the cost of the 'translation' of the Greek ἐνέργεια by the Latin *actus.* Such a 'translation' has in no way, as Saint Thomas thought, the sense of a return to Aristotle, but constitutes, although Saint Thomas is unaware of it, a decisive distancing in relation to him. It is in such a divergence, which is much more essential than the question of monotheism, that the difference separating Saint Thomas from Aristotle resides. We could formulate it as follows: Saint Thomas, who thinks at once on the basis of the biblical narrative that he has *visibly* before his eyes and on the basis of the Romanization of Greek that is, on the contrary, invisible to him, lifts the Latin *agere* and its *actus* up into the essence of being, to the extent that for him the most proper name of the latter is *actualitas.* Aristotle, on the contrary, purified his representation of the cause from all reference to an action. One cannot imagine, beneath the appearance of a supposed identity, a more complete transformation. This is the passage from one world to another. Before being the Creator of all things, as *actus purus essendi* or *plena virtus essendi* God is the Virtuoso of Being, in the sense that Nietzsche will speak of the 'great virtuosos of life'. Being exalts itself in God right up to the virtuosity or actuosity in which he actively distances all non-being from himself, in being from the beginning: the one that is.

The distance that separates Saint Thomas from Aristotle is characterized by Gilson as a 'progress' of the former in relation to the later, which amounts to interpreting the Romanization of Greek as shedding light on Greek itself. The Romanization of Greek is much rather the edification of a wall between the Greeks and us that blocks our access all the more to the origin of philosophy, even if this wall has the 'greatness of Roman walls' as is the case with Thomism. Not that the wall in question allows nothing to pass from what it separates from us. Its other name is, in fact, *translation*. But nothing is more likely to lead us astray than translation. Its most extreme danger is to withhold what it aims to transmit. This is why Cicero hardly sees anything other than morality in Greek philosophy, the rest—and that is to say what is essential—remaining, as it would seem, invisible for him. It is only with Seneca that a scruple begins to arise that will permit him to go slightly farther in his reading than Cicero. This happens when Seneca, in order to render in Latin the Greek οὐσία, forges a new word that will have a long career: *essentia*.[31] According to him, this word is related to *esse* as οὐσία is to εἶναι. But it is still much later, perhaps even in the Middle Ages, that ἐνέργεια will be Latinized as *actus*. It seems that Saint Augustine is still unaware of this translation, which will appear thematically only in the thirteenth century. Would it suppose, as the eminent grammatologist Johannes Lohmann suggested, Aristotle's quite secular journey through the Arab world? Everything here is still obscure. This shows all the more to what extent the Romanization of Greek is still invisible, the translation of ἐνέργεια by *actus* appearing as little as a question as that of πρᾶγμα by *res* or of ἐνάργεια by *evidentia*. But in the first case it is even the date that is uncertain, whereas one can say that *res* has always responded to πρᾶγμα and *evidentia* to ἐνάργεια since Cicero, just as *essentia* has responded to οὐσία since Seneca. *Actus*, however, more than *actio*, and in opposition to *evidentia* and *essentia*, speaks, like *res*, a classical Latin. But it speaks in a completely different way than ἐνέργεια, in which the word ἔργον can be heard, in which, in turn, Aristotle 'understands' τέλος. Hence the synonymy for him of ἐνέργεια and ἐντελέχεια. In *actus*, on the contrary, it is the verb *agere* that is to be heard, which is the most 'active' of all verbs, since it speaks of activity itself, namely that which moves something else in pushing it. From there it adopts a sense that is almost as common as that of the French *agir* (to act), which is a calque of it. But is it cut off from its own origin? When Descartes writes in the seventeenth century that it is in a certain "pushing in a straight line" that "all the action of light"[32] consists, the word action returns to its source, the one on the basis of which the Romans were, as one knows, men of action. They imperiously acted upon the ancient world in imposing on it a peace, a *pax*, in which resonates the verb *pangere:* to drive a stake into the ground from high to low as a symbol, itself an imperative, of Roman action and its *imperium.*

In translating ἐνέργεια as *actus* Saint Thomas does not think all of this. It is much rather the language that he speaks which thinks for him, and well beyond what he himself thinks. At no point does he justify the peculiar amalgam of *agere* and *esse* in the locution *actus essendi,* although the latter passes for his 'original' interpretation of being. The verb 'being', as Gilson says, had for the thinkers of the Middle Ages "an essentially active sense."[33] Not that it would have needed, as the grammarians say, a 'regime' that would bear its action. It is to itself its own regime. It is active intrinsically. Gilson interprets *esse* in an active sense by the reflective *se poser* — 'to pose' — which is not yet to be found in Saint Thomas. In the most common sense 'to pose' is to place oneself in view: "he is posing as a victim," as one might say. But 'to pose' is much more. For a being insofar as it is, it is to have no need of anything other than itself in order to occupy a position, and in this way, and in this way only, to repel by force whatever would aim to occupy it in posing itself there also. In this manner the emperor maintained the barbarians at the frontiers of the empire by force. But God does more than the emperor. He alone poses himself absolutely, *nullum habens aliunde principium* — having no principle from another source. It is this privilege that he subsequently delegates to his creatures, according to which each one of them is posed — on his basis, analogously to him and within the limits of the relative rights that he confers to them in their creation — by the order of efficient causes. The latter, in acting on it or in activating it, finally give a being the possibility of acting in its own right, which constitutes its being. Consequently Gilson can write: "Of everything that beings *do,* the most marvelous is that they *are.*"[34] *Being* is thus thought with reference to *doing (faire),* which itself has its summit in *being* as the most exquisite possibility of the activity of *doing.* Not that *being* is only a *doing.* It is much rather the transcending of any and all *doing* by a still higher activity that is *actus essendi.* It is in this higher activity that it transcends the causality that remains at the level of *doing.* But it is from what it goes beyond that such transcendence draws what enables it to deploy itself at a higher level.

Doubtless, one can object that Saint Thomas, in contrast to what Suarez will say, thinks causality as the result of actuality rather than the latter as the result of the former. For, as Gilson says, causality "is only one aspect of the actuality of being."[35] But this is only insofar as actuality, according to Saint Thomas, is still more *powerful* than any causality. It thus translates all the better what constitutes the very Roman essence of causality. Even if one adds to causality, which only poses an effect in being, a self-posing of being—as does Suarez when he conceives *existentia* not only as *ex causis* but as *extra causis*—*actualitas* is still, as Heidegger says, thought "im Hinblick auf die *causalitas*," from the perspective of causality. This is indeed why, four centuries after Saint Thomas, Descartes could somewhat casually characterize the *aseitas* that is the eternal actuality of God as *causa sui*. In this way, as Gilson says, he "compromises by forcing" the truth of Thomism. Perhaps, on the contrary, this supposed 'forcing' is the bringing to light of what remains the *un-said* of Thomistic truth itself, whose reserve on this point is more the manifestation of timidity than of lucidity.

In his magisterial exposition of Saint Thomas's 'thesis of being' does not Gilson make the former say a little more than he actually says? Possibly. He speaks nonetheless in the same sense as him, and that is to say, in a properly Roman sense, which amounts to turning one's back on Greek thought. For Aristotle's ἐνέργεια has strictly nothing to do with an activity, and that is to say, with anything Roman. Not that it is purely passive. It is a sense of the word 'being' that is completely other to what the words 'active' and 'passive' say. The Greek εῖναι, taken in itself, is certainly no more loquacious than the Latin *esse*. But it speaks to us more distinctly if, instead of facing it head on, we approach it via the prefixes that often accompany it. "In the Greek εῖναι," as Heidegger says, "there is always to be thought conjointly what is often said thus: παρεῖναι and ἀπεῖναι. The παρά means coming closer; the ἀπό, going away" (*WD* 143). But the range of the former, as he says elsewhere, is so ample that "even and precisely absence remains determined by a presence that occasionally comes forth in an uncanny fashion" (*ZSD* 7). We should say, then, in weighing our words: being, for the Greeks, is essentially *presence*. But the presence of what is, which even transpires within absence 'in an uncanny fashion', is nothing simple. It says, on the one hand, that it is present to us and thus speaks to us from the perspective of time. On the other hand, it says that it is offered to us in its presence and thus that it opens itself to us to appear in unhiddenness. The Greeks did not explicitly formulate this. Perhaps they did not even explicitly think it. But this un-said and this un-thought could well be what secretly carries everything that they said and thought. Otherwise we would have to hold the Greek word ἀλήθεια for a term that designates in Greek something more generally named truth, and to consider as simply folkloric or picturesque the fact that the word οὐσία says at once property under the sun, to which the peasant in the course of the *Days* dedicates his *Works*, and beings thought insofar as they are, and thus as the stakes of an original *gigantomachia*. The taste for general ideas, just as much as that for a picturesque regionalism, which characterizes, as one says today, 'intellectuals', is certainly what is the most lacking in Heidegger. There is nothing of the intellectual about him. This is why, instead of saying with Gilson, the zealot of Thomism: "of everything that beings do, the most marvelous is that they are," he would say as an interpreter of the Greeks and at the risk of sounding slightly strange: "of everything that a being as such can be, the most marvelous thing is that it offers itself presently in unhiddenness." This is why to the Greeks the ὄντα were essentially, in their παρουσία, φαινόμενα, and as Heraclitus said, ἀληθέα.

For Aristotle, ἐνέργεια is the highest modality in which a being, as a φαινόμενον, manifests itself fully in unhiddenness. It manifests itself as a temple on the hill, thanks to which both attain the full measure of their presence. One could even say that it is by the fullness of such a measure that presence is truly presence. Neither active nor passive, ἐνέργεια is nonetheless the most proper name of being, which for the Greeks does not at all name *actum quemdam* given that such a locution speaks only on the basis of the interpretation of ἐνέργεια as *actus*, that is, from the Romanization of ἐνέργεια. The Thomistic interpretation of beings in their being as *actus essendi* or as *actualitas* responds in no way to the phenomenological sobriety of the experience of being as presence. It responds much rather to a metaphysical attempt to speak of beings as creatures, homologously to their Creator, whose *esse* is itself *actus* and even *actus purus*, creation being in its turn *unica action solius Dei*, the unique action of God alone. The distance from *actus* to *actio* can easily be traversed, since the latter is, so to speak, prefigured in the former, while what begins with ἐνέργεια is not an action but only a κινεῖν. This only ever expressly adopts the form of a ποιεῖν in the particular case of man. This is why Aristotle separates any πράττειν or, and more decisively, any ποιεῖν from God. But not the marvel that is κινεῖν. Quite to the contrary, Aristotle could have written without any hesitation: ἐν ἀρχῇ ἐκίνησεν ὁ θεὸς τὸν οὐρανὸν καὶ τὴν γῆν, in the beginning God set in motion the heavens and the earth. For him it is ποιεῖν that presupposes κινεῖν and not the inverse.[36] Ποίησις is only a properly human modality of κίνησις, and the latter is far from being only the consequence of a more original ποίησις. According to Saint Thomas, and to Gilson after him, this is a weakness of Aristotle. But this supposed weakness supposes in reality the phenomenological regard which is the very ground of Aristotle's 'metaphysical' enterprise. "This metaphysics is not at all a metaphysics, but a phenomenology of presence." Thus spoke Heidegger one day.

If the essence of the Greek enterprise is to "save appearances phenomenologically," then the essence of scholastic metaphysics is much rather to save Creation philosophically, about which it is instructed otherwise than by ἀλήθεια. It is to this end that Saint Thomas, with as much resolution as candor, Romanizes, whereas Aristotle Hellenizes, that is, remains a phenomenologist. Phenomenology was not, as Heidegger will say, instituted by Husserl. It has a Greek foundation. The sole criticism that Heidegger makes of Husserl is to not have been a phenomenologist with sufficient resolution, but to have limited himself to describing his own 'constructions'. It is quite likely that the phenomenology that is Greek philosophy is unable to attain the truth of Christianity. This would simply signify, in opposition to what Saint Thomas thought, that philosophy and Christianity brought back to their own sources are two different things. In order to install itself philosophically Christianity requires, according to a phrase of Cournot, "other preceptors than the Greeks."[37] But what need did it have to install itself philosophically? Philosophical theology, as Heidegger says, is different from true theology, the one that Luther defined as a "grammar of the word of the Holy Spirit." *Theologia est grammatica in Spiritus Sancti verbis occupata.*

Considering himself able to read the Bible and Aristotle from the same perspective, Saint Thomas is somewhere other than Aristotle, whom he does not see where he is. He is elsewhere as a result of the Latin translations that he offers of the Greek: that of οὐσία by *substantia,* of ἀλήθεια by *veritas,* and of ἐνέργεια by *actus,* with which he aims to follow Aristotle to the letter, and even, as Gouhier would say, to read him "with a magnifying glass." Philosophy, however, if it did not emerge from the Bible, does not have a Roman but a Greek origin, and it is only by the Greeks that the Romans are philosophers. *Graecia capta ferum victorem cepit*—Greece though conquered took her fierce conqueror captive.[38] Doubtless, the reading of ἀλήθεια as *veritas* and of ἐνέργεια as *actus* are not at all arbitrary, responding as they do to what was the *Ipsissimum* of the Romans. But recourse to the *Ipsissimum,* whether or not it is that of the Romans, does not suffice to found philosophy as such if the latter is not already, as philosophy, the *Ipsissimum* itself. It is to the Greeks and to them alone that it was this, in order to remain for those who still live from the Greek source, and not for others. There is, as Heidegger says in passing, no more Chinese philosophy than there is Hindu philosophy. Not that the Chinese and the Hindus would have abstained from thinking. But they did not think in a philosophical mode, that is, on the basis of the Greeks. We could say in the same sense: there is no Roman philosophy. The point is still more evident here. For the Romans only ever philosophized by imitation. This does not mean that there would not be a Latin depth or originality, and thus that the Latins would have lacked a ground. Simply stated, their ground leads them elsewhere than to philosophy. For depth and philosophy are two different things. Philosophizing, the Latins limited themselves to transporting into the Latin translations of Greek their own commonplaces that were invisible to them, without in any way seeking to explore them in themselves, as did the Greeks. The examination of Roman commonplaces, transposed by scholasticism in its interpretation of Greek philosophy, will be much rather the business of modern philosophy when it decides with Leibniz, on the basis of Aristotle but against him nonetheless, that the δυναμικόν is the essence of ἐνέργεια. An *Emendatio philosophiae* will well and truly result from this, a Reform in philosophy, itself understood as ontology, which is not the project of Saint Thomas since he only ever sought to 'recruit' philosophy in the service of faith in composing a *Summa theologica*. It is exclusively from there that what is ontological in his thought comes to him, whereas what is theological in it emerges from Revelation and remains in its service. Henceforth everything is linked together and coherence reigns. But it reigns to the profit of a gap—*Seitensprung,* as Nietzsche would say—and not, as Heidegger says, from a reprise of what is original, which he names thus: *Ursprung.*

It can be said, however, that Thomistic scholasticism is, unbeknownst to itself, the first philosophical reception of the fundamental trait that was, in the thinking of being, the Roman contribution, such as it came to cover over Greek phenomenology. Thus even Thomism has a *historical* significance. Yet this can be reduced to its sheltering an essential characteristic, wherein the latter remains static and as if still inert, that will only be explicitly thematized in modern philosophy. From Descartes to Nietzsche the business of the latter is, as Gilson says, to "compromise in forcing" the truth of Thomism. For if Saint Thomas is already *on the way* he is not yet *advancing along the way,* leaving to others the peril of going ahead. But perhaps the scandal that Gilson denounces here is elsewhere than where he actually sees it. What is scandalous could well be to interpret—as he does—the Thomistic

amelioration of ἐνέργεια by *actus* as the finally conquered unity of
what he names, on the one hand, the "the most intense contemporary
dynamism" and, on the other hand, the "most fully realized formal
immobilism."[39] In his eyes only the fanatics of dynamism or timorous
immobilists could remain unsatisfied with such a unity. At a distance
from the former as much as the latter, however, is Heidegger, for
whom the fundamental question of philosophy is in no way the quarrel of dynamism and immobilism, and that is to say, as under Louis-
Philippe, of the *Movement* and of the *Resistance*. It is rather, beneath
both, a quite different question, the one that Plato had experienced as
a 'battle of giants about being' and that he knew to have begun with
him. The heroes of this *gigantomachia* are the great philosophers. It is
possible to doubt that Saint Thomas, despite his worldwide
significance, is one of the greatest of them. Perhaps the same applies to
Karl Marx, regardless of the fact that he prevails over Saint Thomas in
terms of worldwide importance. Marx is certainly a propagator of
ideas, and the ideas that he propagated have in turn, as Alain said,
"worked over the earth." Yet not in plowing the furrows of language
that are less apparent than those that the peasant, advancing step by
step, forms in plowing his field. An obsession of our time is to confuse
philosophical revolution with political revolution. It is supposed that
the proper vocation of thought is to be 'in power'. Marxism in
power—or Christ in power, as is thought by those who seek only to
enable the triumph of a true politics drawn from the Holy Scriptures,
whether or not this is by Marxist means. Saint Augustine was in
power as a bishop and showed himself to be gifted for the role. But if
he occasionally happens to be a philosopher, this is less for having had
the office of governing at once a diocese and a doctrine than for having
explored, like Nietzsche, alone and to the point of desperation, a
thinking that does not make too much noise in the world, that of *being*
in its relation to *nothingness*. In this way he is, although unwittingly, in
an immediate dialogue with a few others who, from Parmenides to
Aristotle, preceded him. Saint Augustine's question is much less
pointed to Saint Thomas. The sign of this is the almost invisible mutation of the *de nihilo*, which for Saint Augustine was essential in an *ex nihilo*, where *ex* in the end has only the sense of *post*, which conforms
perfectly well to one of the possible uses of the preposition as Aristotle
underlines in book Δ of the *Metaphysics*. This is why Heidegger says exactly the contrary to Gilson, for whom the philosopher Saint Augustine hardly exists in relation to Saint Thomas. In Heidegger's eyes it is
the first who has a 'speculative mind'.

These remarks are in no way presented as so many articles of faith, and it is certainly permitted for any one of us to think differently. For that, it is enough to hold oneself at a sufficient distance from the texts in order to read them, as it seems, all the more closely. Anyone who would like to be more or less Thomist or Marxist, and even both at the same time, is at liberty to be so. But not without also having to meditate the definition that Kant gives of eclecticism, which consists, as he says, in "finding everywhere one's own obsessions."[40] In the same sense, Baudelaire will say concerning the Salon of 1846: "An eclectic is a ship that would like to sail with the four winds." Perhaps it is philosophy as such that refuses the 'four winds' of eclecticism. It is, in fact, in the wind of being, such as it arose with the Greeks and with them alone, that "this empty and mysterious verb, this verb BEING, which has had such a long career in the void"[41] was set on its course. When, in the wind of being, the breeze of power and action which comes from Rome suddenly begins to blow, something new happens in the history of the world, at a point where there "occurs in its time the meeting of languages that carry history."[42] This is already, as Heidegger tells us, the prodrome of modern philosophy, which it falls to Nietzsche to think to its end. The Nietzschean interpretation of being as will to power, however strange it may be, has nothing to do with a simple ontic discovery that would be found directly among things like the philosopher's stone. The will to power that according to Nietzsche is the *actus essendi* of being does not hide itself in any of the regions of beings of which it would be an observable property. It is everywhere and nowhere. This is indeed why Nietzsche so resolutely attacks the concept of will as a supposed psychological reality. It is no act of will. When one attempts to find it here or there with the hope of saying "here it is," one never finds anything, and everything disintegrates before our eyes. And yet nothing is more essential than the concept of the will to power, which as the 'most intimate essence of being' singularly allows us to foil, as Hegel would say, "the multi-colored brilliance of the sensible here-below just as much as the vacant night of the supra-sensible beyond," in order to enter with our eyes wide open into the "spiritual day of the present."[43]

It is the same with the *actus essendi* of Saint Thomas, which is no less for him 'the most intimate essence of being'. One cannot find it anywhere although it reigns everywhere *ut aliquid fixum et quietum in ente*,[44] as something fixed and stationary in being. It is not a being but rather the opening of the clearing of being in beings. Certainly, in relation to the God announced by the Bible Saint Thomas also says to us: the *actus essendi*, as *purus*, here it is! But does Nietzsche himself say anything different? Does not the will to power also have a highest point in view of which there only remains for us to say: here it is?[45] And is this not what Nietzsche finally reveals to us when he interprets the eternal return of the same as 'the highest will to power', adding that it is the 'summit of meditation'? Thus if, like the *actus essendi* of Saint Thomas, the will to power as the 'most intimate essence of being' is in no way a being, then it is nevertheless what in beings responds the most entirely to the nature of being. Henceforth it becomes the supreme Being that Nietzsche once again conceives in the figure of the eternal return of the same. It is in this way that Saint Thomas conceived the *actus essendi* as culminating in the *actus purus essendi*. In every metaphysics two thoughts appear as essentially undivided. Such an intertwining is itself what determines metaphysics, an advanced thinking, as such, although the summit that is the supreme Being can sometimes make its *ground,* beings insofar as they are beings, disappear from view. For such a ground is only ever sought and found in view of the summit, as Goethe seems to say to us in a distich of the *Divan:*

> If the country I'm to show
> Thou must on the housetop go.[46]

From where, then, does such a strange bifurcation that is no less obscure to Saint Thomas than it is to Nietzsche come to philosophy, a thinking that echoes itself? But from where did it come to Aristotle that οὐσία was for him 'principally' ἐνέργεια only to culminate in an ἐνέργεια that is μάλιστα οὐσία? Would philosophizing in a metaphysical mode be to enter into a circle wherein each of two equally fundamental thoughts can say to the other, as, in the Grimms' tale, the tortoise does to the hare: "I am already here"? On this point philosophy is not transparent to itself. Does it need a higher, more superior source of light? Or does it need to open itself finally and more soberly, in taking a step back from itself, to a still earlier thinking than philosophy? It is up to us, perhaps, to learn this in learning to meditate what, at the dawn of time, one of the thinkers before Socrates, the one that posterity has named the *Obscure,* says to us in words that he does not explain and that are still too far in advance of us. But what, then, does Heraclitus say, when, resuming everything in advance, he evokes the enigma that philosophy will never cease to be for itself? Let us listen to his words as words of a dawning of thought: "The One, the Wise, it alone, is little pleased although it is pleased to be said by the name of Zeus" (fragment 32).

7

The Enigma of Z

Among the texts which together constitute what we call Aristotle's *Metaphysics*, Book Z is the one in which we find for the first time an explicit articulation of the guiding question that animates the collection in its entirety, namely the question of being (τί τὸ ὄν).

It all begins with a brief recall of the *Categories* (chap. 1), as if the categorial meaning of being was going to be determinative in what follows, and this is succeeded by a no less brief discussion concerning *beings. Which* are they? Are there any beyond sensible things? Does there or does there not exist anything that might be separated from the latter? But before responding to these questions we have to characterize in its type what being itself properly is (chap. II). Such will be the subject of chapter III.

In this way the question *ti to on*, drawn back to this other question, namely *tis he ousia*, will become in the end: how are we to give the *hypotyposis*, which means the typical presentation, of *ousia* itself?

Two remarks on the above:

1. We refrain from translating οὐσία, which is already the Platonic name for being, by 'substance', as one commonly does. For to adopt this translation is from the very beginning to reduce *ousia* to one of its possible meanings, that is, substance, or in other words to the *subject*, such as it is going to be named in the lines that follow.

2. Similarly, we avoid considering the *hypotyposis* of which Aristotle speaks as a sketch, one that would be merely global or schematic, of *ousia*. It is rather a question of impressing on being a stamp that typically characterizes it.

In turning to chapter III we discover that a surprise awaits us. From the first lines of this chapter Aristotle characteristically begins by gathering diverse opinions on the question. *Ousia,* he tells us, appears, if not in many ways, then at least according to the four following titles: *what was being (to ti en einai),* the *universal (to katholou),* the *genus (to genos),* and in fourth place, the *subject (to hypokeimenon).* Not without humor, as it would seem, the text places at the head of the enumeration the one that is the least expected, namely the *ti en einai,* and it ends with the *subject* in specifying that it is this that we ought to examine first with regard to its right to a typical determination of *ousia.*

This quadripartition is almost immediately followed by a tripartition that, in "such a one" (τοιοῦτον), brings to light the three moments of *matter (hyle),* *form (morphe),* and the *composition (synolon)* of the two. Aristotle adds three examples destined to clarify the terms and a remark that in this threefold the highest rank falls to *form.*

But how are we to understand 'such a one'? It is here that the enigma begins.

A tradition that is at least seven centuries old, since it dates at least from Saint Thomas, consists in interpreting 'such a one' as referring to the *subject,* the last named of the quadripartition. On this point Saint Thomas gives us the following commentary: "Subdivit [Aristoteles] quartum modum praemissae divisionis; hoc scilicet quo dixerat subjectum . . . Dicit ergo primo, quod subjectum, quod est prima substantia particularis, in tria dividitur; scilicet in materiam, et formam, et compositum ex eis" — [Aristotle] subdivides the fourth moment of the division mentioned before; it is clear that this was said as the subject. He says, therefore, first, that the subject, the first particular substance is divided in three; in truth, into matter, form and what is composed from them.[1] One can say that since Saint Thomas every reader, without exception and up to our most recent contemporaries, will faithfully take up the Thomistic reading.

We have to wait until 1965 for this 'classical' reading to be examined for the first time with a critical eye. Such is the radical innovation of Rudolf Boehm's study *Das Grundlegende und das Wesentliche* (Martinus Nijhoff, Den Haag).[2] Τοιοῦτον, Boehme tells us, does not have the *hypokeimenon* as an antecedent but rather *ousia.* The neuter here, despite appearances, should not lead us astray: "Ein Beispiel dafür, dass das neutrum τοιοῦτον sich auf das femininum *ousia* beziehen kann, liefert in unmittelbarer Nähe schon eine Stelle in Z 2 (1028b 18–19)" — An example of the fact that the neuter τοιοῦτον can relate to the feminine *ousia* is furnished by another quotation that is to be found in immediate proximity in Z 2. Despite the tradition, therefore, the tripartition of Z 3 would in no way be the subdivision of the fourth term of the quadripartition that precedes it, but the resumption of the question of *ousia* itself. The reading proposed by Boehm leads us to the following translation of the whole of the beginning of Z 3:

> *Ousia* is said, if not in many ways, then at least principally under four headings; in truth 'what had to be', understood as the universal and, in this case, as the generic, seems to be the *ousia* of each thing and in fourth place the subject. The subject is that of which everything else is said, not being said, as for itself, of anything else; it is for this reason that we have to examine it first. Such a one (something such as *ousia*) is named, on the other hand, in one sense matter, in another form, and in a third sense what derives from both.

After having provided three examples of what it is fitting to understand by matter (bronze), by form (the configuration that it adopts), by 'deriving from both' (the statue), and after having underlined that if the figure presented (*eidos*) has precedence over matter—since it is more in being than the latter—it will also and for the same reason have precedence over the unity of both, Aristotle continues as follows:

> Our typical presentation of what *ousia* could be shows that it is not said of a subject, but that of which all the rest is said; we must not, however, stop there; in truth that is not enough; such a subject does not manifest itself in complete clarity and even matter (then) becomes *ousia*.

The text poses and justifies here the insufficiency of the subject for the determination of *ousia*. It poses it in saying: *ou gar hikanon*. It demonstrates it in saying: *auto gar touto adelon*. The reason for the *ouk hikanon* is: *adelon gar*. The demonstration adds to this that if *ousia* was simply the subject even matter would be *ousia*.

To begin at the end, if the subject was sufficient to determine *ousia* even matter would be the latter. Evidently, Aristotle does not want to say that the underlying matter is not at all *ousia*. In fact, there is no lack of texts that recognize the ontological right of the *hypokeimene physis* (*Phys.* I, 191a, 8). But the subjacent matter is the lowest degree of *ousia* as when one says, for example, that the fountain is 'wooden.' Defining *ousia* by the lying-beneath that the concept of the subject implies would be, thus, to privilege, from the point of view of being, what is merely subjacent in misunderstanding that such a lying-beneath is ultimately indeterminable. The final part of the demonstration does not, then, present any great difficulty.

It is not the same for what immediately precedes it, namely the *auto gar touto adelon*, which speaks of the subject's being unapparent as the first reason for its insufficiency. On page 86 of his so new and stimulating study, Rudolf Boehm interprets *adelon, unoffenbar,* as *grenzenlos,* limit-less. This is indeed what matter is in the end: totally and utterly indeterminate. Yet, in proceeding in this way does the author remain rigorously faithful to Aristotle's text, a text that he has just so fruitfully clarified by the interpretation of ὑποτυποῦσθαι as announcing not a 'schematic' or a 'global' interpretation but a typical presentation and, above all, by the interpretation of *toiouton* as referring to *ousia* and not to *hypokeimenon*? Does he not in fact clarify the very essence of *adelon* by that which is related to it in the dimension of the 'and what is more' (*kai eti*)? To say to someone: if you took up this profession you would find it boring and, what is more, you would lose money is not the same thing as to say that the profession in question would be experienced as boring and annoying in that it would occasion a loss of money. If such is the case, one must give to *adelon, unapparent,* a sense that is independent of what the words 'and what is more' add to it and not draw from what follows these words a retrospective clarification of unapparent. It is necessary, then, to draw from itself the sense of this term by interpreting *auto gar touto adelon* as, following Boehm, "dieses selbst (das erste Zugrundliegende) ist nämlich unoffenbar" — since this itself (the primary subject) is unapparent.

What exactly is the sense of the being unapparent of the subject when it is a question of the typical determination of *ousia*? In truth, the subject is unapparent in two ways.

First of all, it is unapparent as a properly metaphysical determination and not as an ontic property of beings. "It is one thing," as Heidegger says, "to give a simply narrative account of beings but another to grasp beings in their *being*" (*SZ* 39). Antisthenes said to Plato, as it seems at least, for this is what Simplicius relates to us: "O Plato, I can indeed see the horse, but I cannot bring horseness into view." He could have said to the latter's disciple: "O Aristotle, I can indeed see the particular thing, for example this red rose, but I cannot see it as a *subject* nor its hue as *categorial.*" In fact, neither the subject nor the category is an ontic property of beings, the only properties that Antisthenes was able to see. But if both escape our naive way of seeing, it is not at all the same upon the intervention of what Heidegger in *Phänomenologie und Theologie* (Klostermann, 1970, p. 14) names "die Umstellung auf das Seiende gerichteten Blickes: vom Seienden auf das Sein," the revolution of our regard that is primitively fixed upon beings when it turns from beings to being. Doubtless, this is, as Plato says, more difficult than "the whirling of the shell" (*Rep.,* 521c), but once this turning is accomplished everything changes. It is henceforth the subject with the other categories that become apparent as being the thing itself.

And yet Aristotle says of the subject: *auto gar touto adelon,* "in itself, it is unapparent." Formerly it could not have been more apparent, as least in the quadripartition of which it constitutes the fourth term, the one that, according to Aristotle, is the most decisive. How then can it be said to be unapparent? And where? There is, it seems, only one possible response to this question: in the space that is opened when we pass from the quadripartition to the tripartition that follows it. Now we cannot see at all the subject that just came at the head of the list. But what, then, do we see in its place? Something very different, namely, as Aristotle says, a *synolon* as *poioumenon.* In truth, one does not even see the latter, and Antisthenes could once again object: "O Aristotle, I can see this statue, but I cannot see the *synolon* of which you speak now, any more than I could see the *hypokeimenon* a moment ago." To see the *synolon* and to see in it the *eidos* as more in being than matter, whether the latter is marble or bronze, supposes once more what is proper to philosophy, namely the revolution of our regard that was primitively fixed upon beings and that is now turned toward beings in their being. But if we suppose this revolution accomplished, then the *synolon* is yet more present to us than the statue itself, which is only related to the former as an example.

The question is indeed, therefore, one of the exact relation of the tripartition to the quadripartition that precedes it, and Rudolf Boehm could not be more right to say that the former is in no way the subdivision of the fourth term of the latter, but rather that it is related, just as the quadripartite division, to *ousia* itself. The relation between the two is thus a relation between two relations, each one having to do with *ousia* in its own way, in the way that *medical* is the unique term to which the medical expert, the diet that he prescribes, and the sick person that he treats are equally yet disparately related. All of these, although diversely, look in the same direction, that is, toward health. Hence the alliance between them that is in no way synonymous, and it is in this sense that being is said in multiple modes. There is no reason, thus, to be surprised that what is apparent in one case should be unapparent in the other. From a certain perspective, that of the *kategoreisthai,* nothing is more phenomenologically apparent as a determination of *ousia* than the *hypokeimenon,* of which everything is said without it being able in turn to be said of anything else. But from the perspective of *poesis,* that of the ceramist, for example, there is no longer a *hypokeimenon* in this sense. What is subjacent is at the very most the clay, which indeed remains as underlying the vase understood according to the *eidos* that distinguishes it from a platter, for example, or from anything else able to emerge from the clay thanks to the marvel of movement. And it is in this way that the 'subject' is unapparent from the perspective of the ceramist, except if one were to reduce it to the clay in seeking to maintain its precedence; but the clay would then be a sufficient definition of the vase or the platter, which is quite absurd. Yet when one seeks to get to the bottom of the concept, the being-unapparent of the *hypokeimenon* does not result as much from the final indeterminacy of matter as it does from the fact that the *synolon* is not first of all a *hypokeimenon* that would become the *synolon* by the addition of a surplus, but rather something other that emerges from the clay which is apt in itself to 'adopt' a certain *eidos* (*Phys.*, I, 191a 11) if the movement and the origin of movement lend themselves to it. In other words, the ceramic production of a vase or of a platter, just as the production of a cask or of a rudder in carpentry, is irreducible to 'logic', which knows the predicative determination of being only with, at its head, that of which there is predicative determination, namely the subject.

But this irreducibility of the categorial and the poetical to each other, which leads to the essentially relative eclipse of the *hypokeimenon* in the poetic domain, does not, for all that, separate them crudely. This is why the same language can be appropriate for both. Within the perspective of production, the one that knows of the *hypokeimenon* only as the *hyle* that is quite far from being *ousia* in the full sense, one can very well continue to speak the language of the categorial. This is why Aristotle can say (*Met.*, B, I, 995b 35): λέγω δὲ τὸ σύνολον, ὅταν κατηγορηθῇ τι τῆς ὕλης, "I speak of *synolon* every time something is predicated of matter." Conversely, he readily assimilates to a *material cause* what the premises within reasoning are in relation to the conclusion. They are, as he says, ὡς τὸ ἐξ οὗ (*Phys.*, II, 3, 195a 19) in the sense that the rudder is made ἐκ τοῦ ξύλου, out of wood. Such a usage of terms in a domain where they did not originate is evidently not *synonymous* but is much more *metaphorical*. It manifests an essential belonging where things are nevertheless quite apparently different. This spacing that is not a rupture will disappear, however, to the profit of logic when the categorial determination has seized hold of the question of being that it will monopolize to its own ends. Concerning what Aristotle names the *possible* or of what exists *potentially*, Léon Robin writes (*Aristote*, Paris, 1954, p. 82) that he "struggled to define this 'possibility' otherwise than in relation to the 'works' in which it manifests itself effectively"—as if the possible was not, in the eyes of a more evolved philosopher, something much more elevated, namely a category of modality, due to which the advent of the work is only a grossly empirical phenomenon and, to say it all, anthropomorphic. Heidegger is rather held in wonder by what Robin holds to be something insufficient. The relation to the work seems to him, not as an easy way out, but what gives Greek thinking the superiority of its style. "This fundamental trait of man, no other people experienced it more openly than the Greeks," as he said in one of his lectures.

In September 1948, almost thirty years ago now, Heidegger led a seminar in Todtnauberg concerning Aristotle in which—sign of the times—I was the sole participant. Our question attempted to determine the sense of Greek philosophy in relation to Kant. The force of transcendental idealism, as we had established, consisted in not presupposing things but rather in experiencing their presence from the site in which they appear such as it is named by the word 'transcendental', from the "fertile *bathos* of experience" and not from the "proud towers of metaphysics standing in the wind that ordinarily blows about them abundantly" (*Prolegomena*, final appendix, Kant's note). It is customary today to consider Kant's transcendental philosophy as constituting a decisive progression beyond all that preceded it and to oppose it to Greek philosophy in particular, which would remain the refuge of a 'naive realism' content to think beings on the basis of the pressure that they exert on us from the outside, in forgetting transcendental truth. Heidegger said to me, on the contrary, and as still say the notes that I took while he was working out the question:[3] "If, for the Greeks, beings are in the beginning in no way related to man understood as the *Ego cogito,* that is to say, as Husserl would have it, to man thought 'von dem zentrierenden Ich dahin' and 'zum Ichzentrum hin' (cf. *Ideen* I, p. 160, and *Ideen* II, p. 105) [as emanating from or toward the Ego], it is far from the case that beings are not bound, in a critical mode, to a domain of manifestation inside which they deploy their presence." The whole question then is one of determining this domain that responds to the un-said of Greek thinking. Consequently, the question became: "If, on the one hand, Kant's transcendental question is fundamentally foreign to the Greeks, and if, on the other hand, a realism that distances itself from such a question is *unphilosophical,* then what for the Greeks takes the place of what constitutes, in Kant's eyes, the *a priori* dimension of the transcendental?" The rules of the game meant that it fell to me, not to him, to respond to the question thus posed. There then began an extraordinary exercise in phenomenology, phenomenology in Heidegger's sense, during which it was Aristotle—whose "*Metaphysics* is in no way what is commonly named metaphysics, but a phenomenology of what is present" — who himself was speaking.

Let us select an example, said Heidegger. What exactly is this fountain that we both see before us through the window? From one perspective it is merely wood.[4] Yet wood lying about here and there is not a fountain. For it to be a fountain, the wood must present a certain *eidos*, the *eidos* of a fountain and not of a table or of this cane, which are also wooden. If the *eidos* requires wood for there to be a fountain, then the latter is only what it is by the *eidos* that presents it as a fountain. In this sense, the *eidos* itself is more in being than the wood. But for the existent fountain, neither of the two alone provide the ἐξ ἀμφοῖν, as Aristotle says, or the *synolon* of both, inside of which the *eidos*, such as Plato named it, plays the role of *morphe*. Plato's *eidos* is in no way *morphe* if the latter refers essentially to *hyle*, that is, to something that Plato did not want to know anything about; "this wood bothers me," as he might have said before the fountain. For him this fountain is not yet the being of the fountain, since it is οἶον τὸ ὄν, ὄν δὲ οὐ (*Rep.*, X, 597a), which is to say: resembling being without truly being it. In this way, what comes to Kant from Aristotle suddenly became clear, namely the distinction of matter and form in beings in general, such as it intervenes from the beginning of the *Transcendental Aesthetic*. Only much farther on (A 266, B 322) will Kant say: "These two concepts underlie all other reflection, so inseparably are they bound up with all employment of the understanding." But it was, above all, the perspective within which the whole of Aristotle's interpretation moved that became clear. This perspective was that of the *production* of the fountain by the carpenter who, as he notes, "goes about his business before the wood" (*Generation of Animals*, I, 22, 730b 5), setting it in motion until it becomes a fountain. An other word than production or *poesis* is *techne*, such as it expresses, from before Plato and already in Aeschylus (*Prometheus*, v. 514), the highest point of knowledge:

> But knowledge is weaker than *ananke*, by far.

In the humble gesture of the carpenter, then, the highest knowing is held in reserve. Such is for us the lesson of the Greeks who are understood poorly as pure 'theoreticians', barely interested in anything that derives from praxis. If, in one sense, this is true for Plato, who accepted only geometers for interlocutors, it is not true for Aristotle, to whom carpentry is dearer than geometry. Not that he pretended to teach carpenters how better to do their work. He was much rather inspired by them in engaging in the philosophical question of beings in their being.

But, on the other hand, this fountain before us appears at the same time within another perspective. I can, in fact, speak of it, instead of delivering it from the wood and of meditating, on the basis of the wood, the marvel of its production. If *techne* for the Greeks is the most profound relation of man to beings, the *logos*, as *apophantikos* or indicative language, is for Aristotle a no less essential relation to the very same being, which is no longer a *poioumenon* but rather a *legomenon*. In this case it is encountered no less in its being. But now it appears in a quite different way. The *hypokeimenon* that from the perspective of the relation to the work could only be the *hypokeimene phusis*—the wood that the carpenter has at his disposal in order to produce a table or a cask—is now a quite different *lying-beneath,* namely the καθ' οὗ of the κᾰτηγορεῖσθᾱί, which is my essential relation to beings as the discourse that bears on them. Such a *hypokeimenon,* which was *unapparent* a moment ago, now becomes what *transpires* (*emphainetai*—*Met.* Z, I, 1028a 28) everywhere, toward which "all the other categories go back (*anapherontai*)" (*Met.*, Θ, I, 1045b 26). In other words, the whole landscape has changed, although it is still a question of the same thing. For Aristotle, this was not a matter of course but much sooner a source of wonder from which, as he tells us, "men now begin and originally began to philosophize" (*Met.*, A, 2, 982b 12f.). In this way they attempt to cease wondering, reserving the capacity to wonder for the possible appearance of something different from what exists. Thus "a geometrician would wonder at nothing so much as if the diagonal were to become measurable" (ibid., 983a 20f.). One can say, however, that Aristotle never ceased to marvel at the multiplicity of the 'meanings of being'. This is indeed why, meditatively, he repeats several times: *to on legetai pollachos.*

If a being in its being is indeed the *hypokeimenon* that *logic,* as the grammar of language bearing on it, knows categorially, it is something wholly different when it appears in the horizon of *techne.* And in 1948 Heidegger said: "In this way we see that for the ontological interpretation of beings which is Aristotle's metaphysics the two horizons characterized by *techne* and *kategoria* are equally determinative, the one never ceasing to refer 'analogically' to the other." Whereas Kant saw only *one*—considering himself to have reached the secret of the appearance of beings and thus confusing in his own way, as Aristotle said of Plato, "symphony and harmony, rhythm and the measured step" (*Pol.,* II, 5, 1263b 34)—Aristotle sees *at least two.* "With these two headings we have just named what we were looking for when we asked a moment ago: what is the unapparent dimension within the

Greek question of beings in their being which responds to what, for Kant, will be the transcendental problematic of the thing as an object of representation?"

Attentive to what is unsaid in Greek thinking, it is thus that Heidegger made manifest the enigma of Z 3 as one of the reflections of the multiplicity of the meanings of being in the philosophy of Aristotle, in teaching me to see that that the tripartition which follows the quadripartition is indeed a return to the source, but within another horizon than that in which the quadripartite division is deployed. If this change of horizon is not made explicit, this is because it is omnipresent. The whole beginning of Z 3 can be read only according to the following axiomatic presupposition: "Since beings in their being are manifest in multiple modes, *ousia* appears on the one hand, if not in several ways, then at least under four headings of which the fourth is the most important . . . and, on the other hand, is said as matter, as form, and as the compound of the two." In this reading, the *of* at 1029a 1 echoes the *of* at 1038b 33 on the basis of a clause that is presupposed here. But if this is the case, it is no longer even necessary to relate the neuter *toiouton* to the feminine *ousia*. It could just as well be related to *hypokeimenon*, which, furthermore, is a wonderfully polysemic word. If the *hypokeimenon*, understood within the quadripartition as κατθ' οὗ, becomes *ousia hypokeimene* in the tripartition, it has also another sense: stressing the radical *keisthai*, it bespeaks an entry into presence in the sense which "Ogygia, as one of the islands, appears (*keitai*) far from here" in the *Odyssey*.

Consequently, we would read the text of Z 3 in the following way: since beings in their being are said in multiple modes, *ousia* is, on the one hand, above all manifest as *hypokeimenon* understood in the sense of κατθ' οὗ, but the latter, on the other hand, is deployed before us not only in this sense, but also as the most proper presence of the thing itself in its matter and form, thanks to the composition of both. In other words: it is less essential here to relate *touiouton* to *ousia* than the whole of the text to the inexplicit axiom that beings in their being are said in multiple modes. If the *hypokeimenon* is insufficient for a complete determination of *ousia*, it could only be as κατθ' οὗ and as the *ousia* that is merely *hypokeimene* that it would become unapparent. This is perhaps what Heidegger has aimed at, when he interpreted in 1948, and still interprets today, *hypokeimenon* in another sense than κατθ' οὗ and *hyle*, the term itself expressing the return to the source that a comprehensive reading of Z 3 requires. One can, however, prefer Rudolf Boehm's reading as pedagogically more radical and philologically more elegant, insofar as it manifests a *tension* between *ousia* and the *hypokeimenon* in the logical or material sense. This is to say that it is difficult to decide. Heidegger writes in *Vorträge und Aufsätze* (p. 261): "Wanting to run after the objectively exact doctrine of Heraclitus is an enterprise which withholds itself from the salutary danger of ever being affected by the truth of a thought." One can say the same concerning Aristotle. Yet to understand a multiplicity of senses in the word *hypokeimenon* does not mean that Aristotle would have let himself off cheaply, but rather that he is above all responsive to the plurality and the richness of the meanings of words, while we, as Heidegger also said at Thor in 1966, "believe on the contrary, as logical *secateurs,* that a phrase is meaningful only if it has one meaning."[5] In other words, the sense that *hypokeimenon* has in the 'universe of discourse' is already perhaps merely the repercussion of a *hypokeimenon* understood in a more essential and more ample manner, from which derives, in addition, the quite legitimate sense that it has as *hypokeimene phusis.*

It remains for us to wonder, in returning to the first sentence of the text, why the first term of the quadripartition that Aristotle proposes—as we said, perhaps not without humor—is this remarkable τί ἦν εἶναι, which will return in Z 4 as the very subject of the inquiry and subsequently as the last word concerning *ousia* within another horizon than that of the universe of discourse. Without seeming to be at all surprised, Saint Thomas limits himself to rendering it by *quod quid erat esse,* as if it was quite natural that Aristotle should speak in this way. We have, as it seems, to wait until Schelling for a philosopher—if not a philologist—to concern himself with this question. Schelling does this in the seventeenth lecture of his *Introduction to the Philosophy of Mythology,* which is, as his son tells us, one of his final works. In his study of the *Problem of Being in Aristotle,* Aubenque tells us that "the expression, perhaps forged elsewhere . . . , must have been familiar to his readers."[6] It is possible to doubt this in holding, with Heidegger (*SZ* 39), that it relates rather to the "Unerhörtes an Formulierungen . . . die den Griechen von ihren Philosophen zugemutet wurden," to what was unheard of in the manner of speaking by which the Greeks were put to the test by their philosophers.

Τί ἦν εἶναι appears as an interpretation of *eidos,* as Aristotle specifies in the *Physics* II, (2, 194a 20–21), where it is stated that Empedocles and Democritus alone, although only marginally, τοῦ εἴδους καὶ τοῦ τί ἦν εἶναι ἥψαντο, had touched upon the *eidos,* and that is to say, the *ti en einai.* The two locutions are employed not only in the horizon of the *Physics* but also in that of the 'universe of discourse', as one sees in the *First Analytics* (if not in the *Categories* and *De Interpreta-*

tione). But there they are still related only to the *kategoroumena,* and this presupposes, as more essential, the categorial relation to the *hypokeimenon.* From this perspective, the *ti en einai* certainly appears with regard to *ousia,* but it is only of a second rank. The priority of the *ti en einai* intervenes only with the change of the perspective, which, in Z 3, poses the *eidos* as *more* in being than both matter and the *synolon,* the *hypokeimenon* in the sense of logic here having become 'unapparent'. This means that there is no "ambiguity" (Robin), and even less a "contradiction" (Brunschvicg), in posing the *eidos* as at once *ousia deutera* in the *Categories* and as *ousia prote* in the *Metaphysics* (Z7, 1032b 162). Pretending to unearth contradictions in a thinker of the rank of Aristotle is the most frivolous enterprise to which what Hegel calls "the delirium of presumption" — and Heidegger a "somnambulant security" — could possibly devote itself. It always leads the expeditious reader to pass over what is in question.

Aber das Imperfectum? (But the imperfect?) asked Schelling.[7] It shows us particularly well, as Heidegger said to me in 1962, the kinship of the *ti en einai* and the *eidos* insofar as the latter is essentially, as Plato says, an *anamneston.* Strictly speaking, I can remember only what, beforehand, *was* already, before having become unapparent for one reason or another. It is essentially Platonic *anamnesis* that resonates in the imperfect *en,* although even Schelling does not manage to say this precisely. If the being of beings is what is at stake here, the question is one of what *was* the being of a being so that we can recall it. One can only marvel here at the ingeniousness of the attempts of recent commentators to explain Aristotle's imperfect in neglecting its essential relation to Plato, to the point where Aubenque asks Solon for some light concerning Aristotle (p. 468f.).

Yet the question remains: why does Aristotle duplicate the *ti esti* of the thing, the one which made manifest the Platonic *eidos,* with a *ti en einai?* It is not only in order to recall that *anamnesis* is essential to the appearance of the *eidos,* for there would be in this case an identity between *ti esti* and *ti en einai,* whereas Aristotle distinguishes them in many texts, going as far as to play them off against each other. It is necessary, then, to explore more profoundly the distinction between the two.

An attempt of this sort demands that we go back, if not perhaps as far as to Solon, then at least to Socrates. Socrates, as is known, 'stung' or rather, dare I say, 'gadflyed' his contemporaries (*Apology* 30e) in pursuing them with questions which all came back to the unique question of *ti esti:* What is pity, beauty, wisdom, courage, virtue, etc.? It is in no way a question here of the question of being, such as Heraclitus and Parmenides had posed it and which Plato will take up again in the context of the Socratic problematic of "looking for the general in applying thought to definitions" (*Met.* A, 6, 987b 3–4). Yet if Socrates, as he himself says of Anaxagorus, quickly lost interest in proceeding *ta onta skopon*, in examining beings in their being (*Phaedo* 99d), occupying himself only with the *prakteon* — περὶ τὰ ἠθικὰ πραγματεύεσθαι (*Met.*, I, 29) — with him the verb is no less essentially determinative, determined as it is by the *ti* in the question: *ti esti*. Such is the Socratic moment which Plato, "having accepted Socrates as a teacher," makes his own. Not, however, to go no further with it. The Platonic view is not only the search for the *ti* of whatever is in question but the bringing into view of the *ti* as such and its interpretation as *eidos*, which is by no means a matter of course and should rather be for us a source of wonder. The path that leads to Plato consists thus of two stages. First of all, the Socratic reduction of the ζητητέον to the *ti* (*Philebus*, 58e), and then the *eidetic* interpretation of the *ti* itself. The latter is no longer Socratic, and it is the properly Platonic contribution, as Heidegger tried to show to a refractory audience during his paper at Cerisy. One can say that Aristotle, on the same path as Plato, attempts to follow it in the opposite direction. He asks: In what way does the *eidos* truly determine the *ti*? Here, again, a surprise awaits us. In the development of the question thus inverted the *ti* is in fact *doubled*, and to the one which Plato had known but which Aristotle now finds (as we read in the *Generation of Animals*, II, 8, 748a, 8) too general (*katholou lian*), there is opposed another *ti* which is determined not only as the *ti esti* but as that which is *proper* in it (*Posterior Analytics*, II, 6, 92a 7f.). This is what Aristotle calls in the *De Anima* envisaging the *ti esti: kata to ti en einai* (III, 6, 430b 28) or, as he had already expressed it: κατὰ τὸ οἰκεῖον καὶ ἄτομον εἶδος — "according to the particular or individual aspect" (III, 414b 27).

If the most intimate essence of *ousia* from the perspective of the relation to the work is the *eidos*, the latter in its turn is only fully itself as *ti en einai*. This is what Plato was not able to see as a thinker of the *eidos*, for faced with things "he treated them eidetically only to rest at a stage above" (*Prior Analytics*, I, 31, 46a 34). But in this case the question turns back on itself: if the most intimate essence of the *eidos* is the *ti en einai*, how far is it possible to push the research into the latter without confusing it with accidentality? It falls to Léon Robin to have tried to clarify this question for the first time in a note entitled "Sur la notion de l'individu chez Aristote," On the Notion of the Individual in Aristotle, published by the *Revue des sciences philosophiques et théologiques* (vol. XX, 1931) and reprinted in *La pensée hellénique des origines à Epicure* (P.U.F. 1942, pp. 486–490). If, says Robin, the *ti en einai* is more often than not limited to determining the lowest species, as when, before a bird in flight, instead of saying narrowly, "it is not a butterfly, it is a bird," I go as far as to say, "it is not only a bird, but it is a lark," then in the *Parts of Animals* there is at least one text in which Aristotle seems to go as far as the individuals themselves, which means "to assimilate Socrates and Coriscos to the *eschata eide*" (I, 4, 644a 23–b 7). In the final analysis the *ti en einai* of Socrates would be the appearance (*eidos*) of Socrates himself. He is not only a man, not only a philosopher, etc. When he approaches, his disciples do not only say we are going to *humanize* or *philosophize* but well and truly *socratize*. Such will be the still quasi-'quidditative' question, as a question of haecceity, of Socrates *ut hic* in the scholasticism of the fourteenth century, in the sense that Valéry will also say:

> Where are the familiar phrases of the dead,
> The personal art, the singular souls.[8]

As Aristotle often says, this cannot be understood from *ousia* as *hypokeimene,* and, indeed, it rather derives from the *eidos* in the sense of the *ti en einai.*

Will we go as far as this, in supposing with Robin that the text of *Parts of Animals* "is not corrupted"? One can indeed say that it is the whole of Aristotle's thought that goes in this direction from the beginning. Is not the last word of his philosophy that *ousia* is the *tode ti,* the 'this here' which logic interprets ontologically as the subject of which everything will be said, without it being able to be said of anything else? In fact, in the universe of discourse there is a necessary overturning of the *kata tinos* by the καθ' οὗ which means that *of which* the *logos* is *logos,* for otherwise we would speak of nothing. But in the horizon within which the subject becomes, precisely, unapparent and within which it is the *eidos* that is manifest as *ousia prote,* everything becomes more problematic, and the overcoming of Platonism is less easy. For the *eidos,* even thought as *ti en einai,* still keeps the Socratic nature of the *ti.* The relation to the work, understood as the most proper trait of beings in their being, is no longer capable of ridding itself of the shadow cast over it by the *ti,* even if the latter is thought as *eidos,* and *eidos* as *ti en einai.* This is indeed why Nietzsche, who nevertheless aspired "to have remained a poet up to the outer limits of the term," will say: "Socrates, I have to admit, is so close to me that I am almost always struggling against him."[9]

This 'struggle with Socrates' that is demanded by the thinking of the relation to the work, and that was the most proper horizon of the appearing of beings as the *tode ti* for Aristotle, is what Heidegger makes manifest in posing the question of *The Origin of the Work of Art* in 1935. It was enough to recall a poem that was in the memory of his listeners at the time, for they had all learnt by heart at school, Conrad-Ferdinand Meyer's "The Roman Fountain":

> The jet ascends and falling fills
> The marble basin circling round;
> This, veiling itself over, spills
> Into a second basin's ground.
> The second in such plenty lives,
> Its bubbling flood a third invests,
> And each at once receives and gives
> And streams and rests.[10]

Heidegger limits himself to adding: "This is neither a poetic painting of a fountain actually present nor a reproduction of the general essence of a Roman fountain. Yet truth is set into work" (*HZW* 26–27).

Is Aristotle not the first to occupy himself with the setting into work of truth in the singularity of the poetic work, thus formally breaking from his master, according to whom the poets ought to be exiled from the city, from the domain which it falls to philosophy to rule? They will be exiled, as Plato specifies, with great honors and led not to the *Gulag Archipelago* but only εἰς ἄλλην πόλιν, to other peoples, for they are nonetheless harmful and superfluous for us. Aristotle, on the contrary, becomes the author of a *Poetics* wherein he praises poetry which is, as he says in a way that opposes his master, "more philosophical and worthy of being cultivated than that which is only information concerning beings" (IX, 1451b, 5f.). But this apology is no less addressed to us in the name of philosophy, for it is from this point of view that poetry is worth more than pure and simple information. What is proper to philosophy is essentially the bringing into view of the *katholou*, the *general*. Poetry, however, which brings "before our eyes" (*Rhet.*, III, 11, beginning) something individually unique, just like information—"the marquess went out at 5 o'clock"—is nevertheless a taking into view of the general. But what does Aristotle mean by this locution here? He explains it in the seventeenth chapter of the *Poetics* in relation to tragedy, which, as he says, and Nietzsche will develop this in his own way, originated from the dithyramb. Taking one of the last tragedies of Euripides, *Iphigenia among the Taurians,* for an example, he continues thus:

> This is what I mean by taking into view the general, concerning *Iphigenia* for example: a young girl who is to be sacrificed is taken from those that

were to sacrifice her, without them knowing, to another country, where the custom was to immolate strangers to the Goddess; she is invested with this ministry; some time later the brother of the priestess arrives, and this because the oracle of the God ordered him to go there and in view of a goal foreign to the plan of the play, thus *kata symbebekos;* having arrived there and being made a prisoner, on the point of being sacrificed, he reveals who he is . . . In which resides the cause of his salvation.

The point is clear: no longer Iphigenia nor Orestes, but a young girl and her brother, no longer Tauride, but a country. Apollo himself and Artemis are no longer named. All the proper names are effaced. There remains a general situation in which theoretically anybody, one day or another, could find themselves—and because of this poetry is "more philosophical" than the simple "history" of the Atrides. It is in this way that Euripedes' *Iphegenia theoretai to katholou* (1455b 2).

This text shows us to what extent Socratism, through Plato, holds Aristotle back from what he wants to say, from that which he says better than Plato with his interpretation of the *eidos* as *ti en einai,* but which nevertheless escapes him because of the attraction that the Platonic generality of the *eidos* exerts on him. Even the height of presence in the work of art remains ineluctably for him an eidetic presence. If Aristotle goes as far as to think being as the simple marvel of *energeia,* which he does not yet do in Z—a book which responds only to the preparation of the ground in view of the much more decisive breakthrough of book H and, in particular, of Θ—the Platonism from which it issues remains an 'atavism', as Nietzsche would say, from which he cannot free himself. Heidegger notes this in his *Nietzsche* (II, p. 409): "That Aristotle [as a thinker of *energeia*] thinks in a much more Greek way than does Plato does not mean, however, that he would come closer to the initial thinking of being. Between *energeia* and the initially secret essence of being (*aletheia-physis*) stands the *idea.*"

Doubtless, book Z, going where it goes, does not go any further. Not Aristotle's *Metaphysics,* however, of which the book is only a stage, even if an essential one, for as Tugendhat remarks justly (*Ti kata tinos,* Freiburg-Munich, 1958, p. 88), the thinker in this book "maintains a large reserve" in relation to the concepts which will lead the subsequent researches.[11] If one searches for its trace or echo, as it were, the marvel of marvels in Aristotle's thinking is much rather what Z does not explicitly say in reducing from the beginning the plurality of the meanings of being to the diversity of the categories: that "admitting the one and being are said in multiple ways, the principal sense is that of *entelechia*" (*De Anima,* II, 412b 8-9). From this point of view the *ti en einai* is only the most resolute interpretation of what maintains even this principal sense of being as dependent upon the Platonic eidetic. It is not, therefore, the *ti en einai* but rather the richness of being in its multiple meanings which points in Aristotle's thinking toward the marvel: *Dass* Seindes *ist,* that a being is.

In such a *Dass* there resounds in anticipation that for which we ourselves are still *allzu unangefangen* (*WD* 45), all too 'un-begun' or inexperienced, as Heidegger said one day, in order to be able to think it as "das noch unbegreifbare und schon als *physis* aufgegebene 'Dass' des Ereignisses," the still inconceivable 'Dass' of *Ereignis,* which as *physis* is nevertheless already proposed to us as a task. Even the *pollachos legesthai* of being in Aristotle's sense is only an 'immobilization' (*Stillstellung*) of it. It is according to the guiding thread of Aristotle's thought, however, in a meditation pursued over fifteen years, that Heidegger came to clear with *Sein und Zeit* the question of the *meaning* of being before exploring more profoundly this question itself in the course of a 'second navigation' that suspended the publication of a pure and simple continuation of *Sein und Zeit* itself.

The enigma of Z 3 is more than two thousand years old, and in this sense it is far behind us. But perhaps it is precisely for this reason that it withholds a more essential future for us than that which futurology pretends to grasp. *Das Älteste des Alten kommt in unserem Denken hinter uns her und doch auf uns zu.* The origin of the ages, when our thought opens itself to it, comes from behind us, and yet it nevertheless comes ahead of us.

8

Aristotle and Tragedy

The uncontested presence of a *Poetics* in the work of Aristotle attests to his relation to Plato. It attests to Aristotle's opposition to Plato and to the central point of his own philosophical position, insofar as Plato—doubtless despite himself given that citing Homer comes so naturally to him and that his prose is always artistic—found it right, at least in the *Republic,* to distance the poets from the domain controlled by philosophy. For Aristotle, on the contrary, poetry, as much as mathematics, is an echo of being. This manifests all the more acutely in what secret sense he understands the word *being,* about which he limits himself to announcing here and there, and often incidentally, that *to on legetai pollachos.*

For Aristotle poetry comprises different genres, at the head of which he places the one that was the most decried by Plato, namely the properly *Attic* genre of tragedy. Plato clarifies the adjective τραγικόν by τραχύ (*Cratylus,* 408c), which evokes an idea of that which has not been smoothed out and the roughly hewn, in the sense that we speak of *la trachée artère,* the windpipe, in opposition to more supple vessels. Aristotle, however, proclaims the superiority of tragedy as a genre over the epic itself, which does not mean that the tragic poets are above the incomparable Homer.

In his study of tragedy, Aristotle transmits to us a tradition that will constitute a ray of light for the young Nietzsche, namely that its origin is to be found in the ἐξάρχοντες τὸν διθύραμον. Would this not be a question, as Nietzsche wonders, of those who have to explain the

136

whole, as in one of Euripides' prologues? Or does it not rather concern the *chorus* itself? The latter, says Nietzsche. It is definitely a question, therefore, of those who *intone* the dithyramb, namely the chorus itself, without anything else being able to be apposed to it. Nietzsche receives his inspiration here from a verse of Archilochus: "In my case also, I mean to *intone* the dithyramb." It is only in this way and in a Dionysian climate that Apollo comes "to touch with his scepter those that he recognizes as his own." It is not Archilochus who says this, but Nietzsche, in the fifth chapter of his book. It is possible to contest Nietzsche's interpretation and even the tragic character of the dithyramb, but I will leave this for another occasion.[1]

The *Poetics* attests, above all, to the taste that Aristotle had for the tragic poets. In the course of his long Platonic schooling did he go as far as to watch representations of tragic plays behind his teacher's back? He does not say. I think that he rather read them, believing their representation not to be indispensable (1450b 19–20). Doubtless, he read aloud (we have not yet reached Ambroise, who, to the surprise of Augustine, read with his eyes but with *vox et lingua quiescebant*—in silence and with a still tongue)[2] or had the text read to him. In any event, the *Poetics* is concerned with Aeschylus, Sophocles, and Euripides.

What marvelous times that Aristotle did not experience! He arrives just afterwards. But Sophocles is barely thirty years younger than Aeschylus (less than Racine in relation to Corneille), and Euripides is barely fifteen years younger than Sophocles (less than Racine in relation to Molière). They are each, however, so different that it is easy to imagine that they are separated by a greater stretch of time. But in this epoch of Greece the *acceleration of history,* as is said today, is at its height. We who pretend to live it are stagnant in comparison to our forerunners who set us on the way. Schelling will be the first to marvel at this. With Heidegger, the wonder is at its height.

In a brief presentation it is impossible to enter into details. I will only suggest a thesis: *The definition that Aristotle proposes of tragedy is properly Euripidean. But, in developing this definition, he secretly goes back from Euripides to Sophocles and to Aeschylus.*

It is in fact quite Euripidean to say, with Aristotle, that tragic 'imitation' (a term that I will not comment on), which supposes actors and not, like the epic, the simple notification of a story, provokes pity and terror, in achieving the 'purging' (another term that I will not comment on) proper to such emotions (1499b 25–28). This is tragedy envisaged from the point of view of the spectator, which, as Nietzsche will underline, is a Euripidean creation par excellence. Is it not the role of tragic poetry, as Aristotle says crudely, καὶ φρίττειν καὶ ἐλεεῖν, to give him the shivers and to make him feel pity? On this point, with a word that is almost untranslatable, German says to procure *Erlebnisse,* which roughly means *sensations.* Nietzsche comments on this untranslatable term in saying that the characteristic of *Erlebnis* is, in the way of flies or mosquitoes, to "irritate the epidermis, but in leaving a vacant heart."[3] What could be more delectable for such a spectator, which Nietzsche compares to a "debonair and sly famulus," than the moment when Racine's Phaedrus says:

> It is no longer an ardor in my hidden veins
> It is Venus as a whole attached to his prey,

from hearing Hecubus, who speaks like Phaedrus, retorting to Helen in the *Daughters of Troy:*

> My boy, he was as beautiful as the day.
> It is from your lust that you made yourself Cypris
> For the delirium of mortals is ever Aphrodite
> It begins this divine name as Aphrosyne.

This demagogic complicity with the spectator is what is today called 'demystification'.

Yet before having proposed his definition of tragedy, Aristotle had situated himself at the level of Aeschylus and Sophocles, rather than that of Euripides, in declaring: Ἀρχὴ μὲν καὶ οἷον ψυχὴ ὁ μῦθος τῆς τραγῳδίας, "the principle and the soul, as it were, of tragedy is myth" (1050a 39f.). With Aeschylus and Sophocles, tragedy is essentially the poetic presentation of myth and not its dramatic exploitation in view of the spectator. As for the myth itself, there is very little, as Homer knew, that can be changed, for otherwise one says "what the poet, and not what the myth wants to say" (1454b 33q). On the contrary, Euripides does not forego changing the myth—the same applies to Labiche and Feydeau—as in *Helen.* "Heavens above, my husband!—What do I see? It is my wife!" The scene is set in Egypt, where a shipwrecked Menelaus finds Helen, who never did follow Paris to Troy. But what is the myth that leaves, according to Aristotle, the poet with "so little to say." The poet says, according to Heidegger, "the mutual belonging together of gods and men insofar as this alone comprises the separation of their distance and, consequently, the possibility of coming together, and thus the grace of their appearing."[4]

"We would very much like to know something about the origins of the term μῦθος, but unfortunately it has no certain etymology, which already seems to plead in favor of its antiquity."[5] Thus speaks Walter-Friedrich Otto. For want of an etymology we have to learn from the use of language.

One often finds μῦθος in Homer's texts, where it means speech, but two other terms also mean this, namely ἔπος and λόγος. In Parmenides' Poem, the three terms *epos, logos,* and *mythos* appear as often as each other, and they are virtually interchangeable. In Homer, however, differences do tend to appear. Quite often Homer speaks of the *pterounta epea,* the winged words, to which Plato will oppose the *fixation* of writing in the *Phaedrus.* Words as *epea* are thus of the order of the *phonai,* the voices that make themselves heard in traversing space. The term speaks of the *phonetic* aspect of language, and Homer compares the *epea* to "snowflakes in winter" (*Iliad,* III, 222). As for *logos,* and this time it is Plato who speaks to us, it has its own peculiar property: to be essentially διπλοῦς, ἀληθής τε καὶ ψευδής (*Cratylus,* 408c) — "of a double nature, as much true as false." But myth? It seems to remain at a certain distance from the Platonic distinction between the true and the false, as something more original than both. When Plato evokes the "myth" of Protagoras, namely that man is the measure of all things, it is in this sense that he understands the term (*Theaetetus,* 156 c–164 d). Myth is originally revelatory of the thing of which it is the myth.

But this is not all. Not only is myth enigmatically an original authority on the thing itself, but it is this in a quite particular manner. Myth is the revelation whose contrary is not *pseudos* but *lethe.* This is what we learn in reading the thirteenth song of the *Odyssey,* which recounts the apparition of Ithaca to Ulysses. Ulysses is already on his island, where the currents of the sea have led him while he was sleeping. But he does not yet know anything about it, not even when he wakes up, for Athena, present at his side "in the figure of a young man, a goatherd as free as the son of a lord," had spread a cloud over the whole country,

> So that everything is to him,
> Unrecognizable, and so that she would have to say each thing
>   to him one by one.

Homer says: ὄφρα . . . ἕκαστα μυθήσαιτο. The verb *mystheisthai* comes from *mythos:* so that she would have to *give him the myth* of each thing. The verb *mytheisthai* is, in addition, clarified by a verb that intervenes around fifty verses later in the text, at the moment when the god disperses the cloud:

Well, I am going to show you (*deizo*) the land of Ithaca.

Instead of *mythesaito*, Homer could have said: *deizato* or *apophenaito*. Myth, therefore, has the essential function of *showing* what is. It is by virtue of it that *the earth appears* (ἔισατο δὲ χθών). One can say that in the *Mémoires d'outre-tombe* or *Memoirs from beyond the Grave*, the brief and beautiful page that Chateaubriand entitles "Apparition de Combourg" is a sort of echo of the *myth* of Ithaca, such as it makes the earth appear in the eyes of Ulysses, not only as he habitually evoked it in the clear-obscure of memory but, to speak like Baudelaire, in "the brilliant truth of its native harmony."[6] It is *time found!* Here, the revelation that is myth, its *aletheia*, has for a contrary not *pseudos*, as is more often than not the case in Plato, but *lethe*. Whoever is foreign to myth is, in relation to *aletheia*, in the situation of those who escaped from the plague of Athens, of whom Thucydides says: τοὺς δὲ λήθη ἐλάμβανε τῶν πάντων ὁμοίως — "forgetting seized them in relation to every object alike."[7]

Thanks to Homer we can see clearly here the power of myth. It is not only a presentation of what it says, but it is comparable to something coming out of a cloud that previously had covered everything. In the Greek sense, therefore, myth is the beam of sunlight that shines through the fog, the first apparition in its lightness. To say it all, it is the birth of a world. This in the sense that the second Sallust said ταῦτα δὲ ἐγένετο μὲν οὐδέποτε, ἔστι δὲ αεί, "that has never happened anywhere, but it never stops being thus everywhere"[8] — *die Mitte* or the 'midst': "O divine ether, swift winged breezes, and you . . . multitudinous smiles of the waves of the sea . . . Earth, mother of the beings of . . ."[9] The décor is immobile. Not a theatrical décor, but first of all the secret hearth from which everything has emerged and irradiates. If one understands by paganism this power of reception, then yes, Heidegger is pagan.

But if myth is the birth of a world, then it would not be something specifically Greek. When it is said to us, in a quite different world than the Greek world, that "in the beginning God created the sky and the earth," such words would be at least *mythical*. For here also something comes out of a cloud, which the cloud itself conceals, while language evokes things one by one in the week of their creation. The question is, then, one of knowing if there is something *proper* to Greek myth, and what this is. It seems to me that in the horizon of this question it is necessary to isolate two characteristic traits.

1. First of all, with the Greeks myth is essentially the business of poets. To attempt to begin with Greek poetry in order to disengage

from it a doctrine of which it would only be the superficial document is to get everything in the wrong order from the start. Myth here is in no way doctrinal. What singularity, as W. F. Otto remarks, in the fact that in the Greek world the divine "nicht von Propheten und Bekennern verkundet wird, sondern von Dichtern und Kunstlern," is not announced by prophets and confessors but by poets and artists.[10] There is nothing like this in the Bible. Not that it completely lacks poetic character. But it demands first of all and above all, as Kant held in the *Critique of Pure Reason,* to be read *to the letter.* One rediscovers here the discomfort of the Greeks before writing, which fixes once and for all, as Socrates says to Phaedrus, "winged words" that are originally like "snowflakes in winter," making them similar to someone sulking (*Phaedrus* 275d).

2. On the other hand, if mythical presentation is essentially a presentation of the divine as one of the essential dimensions of the world, then in Greek myth the god is never the last word or what is absolute in the question. This is, rather, beyond the divine, the destiny to which the god himself is subjugated. There is, in other words, a higher enigma than the divine. It is in this sense that in the *Iliad* it is not Zeus but the balance that he holds in his hand that decides how *victory changes men* and on whom *the completion of death* will fall. This is a fundamental trait of myth that will remain even in philosophy, for which it is only ever in the name of being that one can speak of God. On the contrary, the bible, or, if you will, the biblical myth, is God first of all, who has, as one knows since Daniel (VII, 14), "the reign, the power and the glory" —a God, as Maritain will say much later, "who has dominion over himself."[11] With Greek myth, on the contrary, it is exactly the inverse. The enigma of being and of its movement (*SZ* 392) is more determinative in it than the enquiry of the theologian.

But enough on this point, Horatio! Let this salutation to Greece suffice here, a salutation, to say it all in one word, to the Greek 'miracle', which is for us at the very least an ἅπαξ, a once only event. It only remains to me to add, as is the tradition: *thank you.*

Notes

Translator's Introduction

1. In addition to the four volumes of the *Dialogue,* Beaufret wrote the following books: *Le poème de Parménide* (Paris: Presses Universitaires de France, 1955); *Notes sur la philosophie en France au XIXe siècle* (Paris: Vrin, 1984); *Entretiens avec F. de Towarnicki* (Paris: Presses Universitaires de France, 1984); *De l'existentialisme à Heidegger* (Paris: Vrin, 1986; 1st ed.: Paris: Denoël, 1971). The most complete bibliography of Beaufret's work, compiled by Guy Basset, is to be found in the last text.

2. *Lettre sur l'humanisme suivie d'une lettre à Jean Beaufret* (Paris: Aubier, 1957), pp. 67–68 (bilingual French-German edition).

3. First published in *Fontaine* no. 58 (Paris, 1947), but now available in *De l'existentialism à Heidegger.*

4. A record of Beaufret's teaching, compiled from his own notes and those of his students, is available in the two volumes of his *Leçons de philosophie* (Paris: Seuil, 1998).

5. *Heidegger and Nazism,* trans. P. Burrell and G. R. Ticci (Philadelphia: Temple University Press, 1989). The controversy has recently repeated itself in France, occurring this time more as farce than tragedy, with the publication of Emmanuel Faye's *Heidegger, l'introduction du nazisme dans la philosophie* (Paris: Albin Michel, 2005).

6. Now available in *Aus der Erfahrung des Denkens,* 2nd ed. (Frankfurt am Main: Klostermann, 2002).

7. *Wegmarken* (Frankfurt am Main: Vittorio Klostermann, 1976), p. 286; trans. W. McNeill as *Pathmarks* (Cambridge: Cambridge University Press, 1998), p. 218.

8. *Vorträge und Aufsätze* (Frankfurt am Main: Vittorio Klostermann, 2000), p. 11; trans. W. Lovitt as *The Question concerning Technology* (New York: Harper & Row, 1977), p. 8.

9. Boehm's text was translated into French by Emmanuel Martineau in 1976 (*La métaphysique d'Aristote: le fondamental et l'essentiel* [Paris: Gallimard]), and it deserves to be translated into English.

10. See D. Graham, *Aristotle's Two Systems* (Oxford: Clarendon Press, 1987).

Letter to Martin Heidegger for His Eightieth Birthday

1. "Wege zur Aussprache," in *Allemannenland: Ein Buch von Volkstum und Sendung* (Stuttgart: Engelhorns, 1937), pp. 137–139. See also William J. Richardson, *Through Phenomenology to Thought* (The Hague: Martinus Nijhoff, 1962), p. 676.

2. *Die philosophische Schriften von Gottfried Wilhelm Leibniz,* ed. C. J. Gerhardt (Berlin: Weidmann, 1875–1880), vol. VI, p. 342.

3. Ibid., pp. 286–287.

4. Ibid., p. 309.

5. See Martin Heidegger, *Erläuterungen zu Hölderlins Dichtung* (Frankfurt am Main: Klostermann, 1981), p. 14ff.

6. *Gesammelte Schriften, Herausgegeben von der Preussischen Akademie der Wissenschaften* (Berlin: George Reimer, 1905), vol. II, p. 238.

7. See *WD* 59 and *SZ* 259.

8. *Critique d'art* (Paris: Folio, 1992), p. 116.

9. *Philosophische Schriften,* vol. VII, p. 456.

10. T.N. Beaufret refers here to Parmenides' Poem. Throughout this volume I have used John Burnet's translation of the Poem (in *Early Greek Philosophy* [London: A. & C. Black, 1930]) when translating Beaufret's French rendition of it.

11. Hölderlin, *First Letter to Böhlendorf.*

12. Victor Hugo, "Booz endormi," in *Le légende des siècles* (Paris: Livre de Poche, 2000), p. 83.

13. *Werke* (Leipzig: Kröner, 1899–1912), vol. XIII, §401.

14. See *SZ* §37.

15. Karl Marx, *Das Kapital* (Berlin: Dietz, 1979), vol. III, p. 293.

16. The translation was supposed to appear in 1971.

17. *Werde wer du bist,* become who you are, as Nietzsche translates.

18. *Wissenschaft der Logik,* Jubilee Edition (1931), vol. I, p. 164.

19. T.N. This is Elizur Wright's unsurpassable translation from his complete English edition of La Fontaine's fables that was first published in Boston in 1841.

1. The Birth of Philosophy

1. *Aesthetics*, trans. T. M. Knox (Oxford: Oxford University Press, 1998), p. 362.
2. Charles Baudelaire, "Les bijoux," in *Les fleurs du mal* (Paris: Gallimard, 1972), p. 185.
3. "Bénédiction," in ibid., p. 35.
4. *Der cherubinische Wandersmann*, ed. Will-Erick Peudert (Leipzig: Dieterich'sche Verlagsbuchhandlung, Sammlung Dieterich, ca. 1935), vol. 64, p. 37, no. 289 (*The Cherubinic Wanderer*, trans. Maria Shrady [New York: Paulist Press, 1986], p. 54).
5. *Sophist*, 246a.
6. Aristotle, *On Interpretation*, 16b24–26.
7. *On the Parts of Animals*, 645a15–23.
8. *Gesammelte Werke* (Munich: Musarion Verlag, 1923), vol. 15, p. 97.

2. Heraclitus and Parmenides

1. *Cratylus*, 474c.
2. *De Divinatione*, II, 58.
3. *On the Parts of Animals*, 645a15–23.
4. *Sämtliche Werke* (Stuttgart: Kohlhammer Verlag, 1957), vol. 3, p. 81.
5. *Lectures on the History of Philosophy*, vol. 1, trans. E. S. Haldane (Lincoln: University of Nebraska Press, 1995), p. 278.
6. *Thus Spoke Zarathustra, III*, "Of Old and New Law Tables," 19.
7. See "Le cimetière marin," in *Œuvres* (Paris: Gallimard, Bibliothèque de la Pléiade, 1957), vol. 1, pp. 147–151. See also Plato, *Parmenide*, ed. and trans. August Diès (Paris: Belles Lettres, 1923), 127b.

3. Reading Parmenides

1. T.N. The 1897 edition has been reprinted with a new foreword and revised bibliography by Akademia Verlag (Sankt Augustin, 2003).
2. John Burnet, *L'aurore de la philosophie grecque* (Payot, 1919), p. 213. T.N. Beaufret refers to the French translation of *Early Greek Philosophy* (Lon-

don: A. & C. Black). In the third (1930) and subsequent editions of the text this argument is found on p. 184.

3. U. V. Wilamowitz-Moellendorf, "Lesefrüchte," *Hermes* 34 (1899): 203–206 (repr. in *Kleine Schriften* [Berlin, 1962], vol. IV, 45–48).

4. See *L'aurore de la philosophie grecque*, p. 211, n. 3. T.N. See n. 1 on p. 183 of *Early Greek Philosophy*.

5. *Parmenides und die Geschichte der griechischen Philosophie*, 2nd ed. (Frankfurt am Main: Klostermann, 1959), p. 26.

6. See Plato, *Parmenide* (Les Belles Lettres: Paris, 1923).

7. *Dichtung und Philosophie des frühen Griechentums* (Munich: C. H. Beck, 1962), p. 409.

8. *Parmenides und die Geschichte der greichischen Philosophie*, p. 80.

9. T.N. Beaufret translates ἀλήθεια as *Ouvert-sans-retrait*, which I have rendered as 'Open-without-hiddenness', according to the argument that the Greeks would have understood the particle ἀ in ἀλήθεια as privative, i.e., as a negation, and thus they are "*not yet* at the proper level of the question that they themselves raised in naming *aletheia* what we call truth" (*Dialogue* IV, p. 79). The argument is, of course, Heideggerian, and Beaufret translated Heidegger's own rendering of ἀλήθεια, namely *Unverborgenheit*, in this way. But is not *Ouvert-sans-retrait* too decisive a translation of both the Greek and German terms? Does it not obliterate the ambiguity present in the 'privative' particles of both? Alain Renaut's answer to these questions was affirmative, but for Beaufret's rebuttal of his criticisms, see "*A propos de* Questions IV" in *Dialogue* IV.

10. *L'évolution créatrice*, in *Œuvres* (Paris: Presses Universitaires de France, 1970), p. 728.

11. *Œuvres*, vol. 1, p. 995.

12. *Die Wirklichkeit des ego cogito* (*PL* 83).

13. *Critique of Pure Reason*, A158/B197.

14. See *WD* 148.

15. *Le jour et la nuit: Cahiers 1917–1952* (Paris: Gallimard, 1952), p. 30. T.N. In 1952 Braque published his notebooks with this title.

16. T.N. Beaufret is referring to the last lines of the section "Observing Reason" in the *Phenomenology of Spirit*, trans. A. V. Miller (Oxford: Oxford University Press, 1997), p. 211.

17. Pierre Aubenque, *Le problème de l'être chez Aristote* (Paris: Presses Universitaires de France, 1962).

18. See Martin Heidegger, *Einführung in die Metaphysik* (Tübingen: Max Niemeyer Verlag, 1953), p. 74.

19. *Le jour et la nuit*, p. 12.

20. *Contra Gentiles*, vol. I, p. 22.

21. *Gorgias*, 473b.

22. *Urausgabe,* 1897, p. 9.
23. "Die Philosophie im tragischen Zeitalter der Griechen," in *Gesammelte Werke* (Munich: Musarion Verlag, 1923), vol. 4, p. 199.
24. "Mauvaises pensées et autres," in *Œuvres complètes* (Paris: Collection de la Pléiade, Gallimard, 1962), vol. 2, p. 801.
25. "H. Fränkel does pure Greek semantics. If there were another interpretation, it would come from India. M. Heidegger uses Greek semantics. But the interpretation is romantic." C. Ramnoux, *La nuit et les enfants de la nuit dans la tradition grecque* (Paris, 1959), p. 87, note.
26. *Republic,* X, 621b.
27. *Critique de la raison pure,* trans. A. Tremesaygues and B. Pacaud (Paris: Presses Universitaires de France, 1944), p. 21. T.N. See *Critique of Pure Reason,* trans. N. Kemp-Smith (London: Macmillan, 1929), p. 30.
28. *Urausgabe,* p. 85.
29. Ibid., pp. 71–72.
30. *Signes* (Paris: Gallimard, 1960), p. 217.
31. *Zur Farbenlehre,* in *Sämtliche Werke* (Munich: Carl Hauser Verlag, 1989), vol. 10, p. 20.
32. *Politics,* II, 5, 1263b 35.

4. Zeno

1. *Critique of Pure Reason,* A756/B784 (trans. Norman Kemp Smith [London: Macmillan, 1929], p. 604).
2. Ibid., A502/B530.
3. Following Hermann Fränkel (*Wege und Formen frühgriechischen Denkens* [Munich, 1960], p. 223f.), we understand here the προέχον as that which advances from each thing and not as something else which would be in front of it. But is it necessarily only a question of the outer surface understood as a membrane? Is it not rather the thing itself that, as a whole, sticks out from its rear, in such a way that no division can exhaust anything of the phenomenon without at once annulling it? In any case, it is true (p. 224) that the argumentation could be developed in the opposite direction, i.e., from the front to the back, and that it is probably "in order to simplify" that Zeno develops it only in one direction, unless it is language which speaks more easily in this way than in the other.
4. T.N. Beaufret seems to be referring to *Parmenides,* 136b.
5. Gérard Legrand (*Pour connaître la pensée des présocratiques* [Bordas, 1970], p. 129) says, on the contrary, about this evocation of Zeno: "The decasyllables that Paul Valéry devotes to him are the weakest aspect of the Cimetière Marin."
6. See on this question the study of Lachelier (*Œuvres,* vol. II [Paris: Alcan,

1993], pp. 3-15), which does not cite Fränkel, who himself refers only to Brochard's *Les arguments de Zénon d'Elée contre le mouvement* (1888) in the French domain. The text of 1888 has been reproduced in *Etudes de philosophie ancienne et de philosophie moderne* (1926).

7. *Science of Logic,* trans. A. V. Miller (Atlantic Highlands, N.J.: Humanities Press International, 1993), pp. 190-199.

8. *Œuvre romanesque* (Paris: Grasset, 1955), vol. 1, p. 198.

9. *Le jour et la nuit,* p. 35.

5. A Note on Plato and Aristotle

1. See *KM,* §2.

2. See *HZW* 324.

3. *Metaphysics,* 1075a 18-19.

4. *Enneads,* III, 3, 2.

5. Ibid., III, 3, 3.

6. Ibid., III, 3, 6.

7. *Summa Theologica,* I, q. 105, art. 6, in *Respondeo.*

8. *Enneads,* III, 3, 1.

9. *Politics,* II, 5, 1263b 34-35.

10. *Le système d'Aristote* (Paris: Vrin, 1931), p. 405.

11. *L'esprit de la philosophie médiévale* (Paris: Vrin, 1932), vol. I, p. 53.

12. *Physics,* VIII, 258b 11.

13. *Metaphysics,* Λ, 1076a 4.

14. Beginning of *Nemean 6.*

15. *Oedipus at Colon,* v. 1627f. See Reinhardt, *Sophocle,* trans. E. Martineau (Paris: Editions de Minuit, 1971), pp. 285-286. T.N. See *Sophocles,* trans. H. & D. Harvey (Blackwell: Oxford, 1979), p. 221.

16. *Critique of Pure Reason,* A590/B618.

17. *Beyond Good and Evil,* §20.

18. Ibid., §224.

19. *Der Feldweg, in fine.*

20. *Gay Science,* §382.

21. *Sophist,* 259e.

22. *Cratylus,* 408c.

23. Lachelier, "Note sur le *Philèbe,*" *Œuvres,* vol. II, 17-27.

24. *Odyssey,* IX, 25.

25. *Poetics,* 1456b 7.

26. *Physics,* 193b 4-5.

27. *Index aristotelicus*, p. 33 b.
28. *Also sprach Zarathustra, IV,* "The Convalescent."
29. *Philebus*, 59c.
30. *L'être et l'essence* (Paris: Vrin, 1948), pp. 56–57.
31. *De divinatione*, II, 58.
32. *Sophist*, 262dff.
33. See Heidegger, *N* II, 485.
34. *Phaedo*, 107b.
35. *Republic*, 484b.
36. *Categories*, 2a 11ff.
37. *L'être et l'essence*, p. 52. Our emphasis.
38. Whether this difference maintains the depth that it had in the thinking of Parmenides or whether, as Heidegger holds (*N* II, 407), it is already a metaphysical restriction of the latter is a question that we leave in suspense.
39. *Republic*, 284a.
40. Paul Verlaine, "Green," in *Romances sans paroles, Œuvres poétiques* (Paris: Gallimard, Bibliothèque de la Pléiade, 1962), p. 205.
41. *Greater Hippias*, 287c.
42. *Nicomachean Ethics*, I, 1095b 6.
43. Ibid., 1098b 24.
44. *Le Thomisme*, 4th ed. (Paris: Vrin, 1942), p. 53.
45. *Nouveaux essais*, vol. IV, 8, §5.
46. *Posterior Analytics*, 100a 15ff.
47. *Metaphysics*, Θ, 1045b 27.
48. *Republic*, 596b.
49. *Introduction to the Philosophy of Mythology*, 14th lecture.
50. *Metaphysics*, Z, 1038b 5f.
51. Ibid., Θ, 1047a 30–32.
52. *Physics*, III, 201a 10–11.
53. *Critique of Pure Reason*, A141/B180.
54. *Physics*, III, 202a 2.
55. *Le problème de l'être chez Aristote*, p. 374.
56. *Vom der mannigfachen Bedeutung des Seienden nach Aristoteles* (Freiburg im Breisgau: Herder, 1862), p. 72.
57. *Le problème de l'être chez Aristote*, p. 206.
58. *Antigone*, v. 1149f. (in the way that Hölderlin reads it).
59. *Le problème de l'être chez Aristote*, p. 376.
60. *Aristote* (Paris: Payot, 1930), p. 257. T.N. See *Aristotle* (London: Methuen, 1923), p. 183.
61. *Etudes galiléennes* (Paris: Hermann et Cie, 1939), fasc. I, p. 11.

62. *Nouveaux Essais,* vol. III, 4, §10.

63. Ibid., IV, 7, §6.

64. *Metaphysics,* Θ, 1051b 1–2.

65. Ibid., α, 993b 9–11.

66. *Nicomachean Ethics,* VI, 1141a 17.

6. *Energeia* and *Actus*

1. *Ajax,* v. 522.

2. Hippocrates' first aphorism.

3. Aristotle, *Generation of Animals,* I, ch. 22.

4. We offer here, of course, a liberal interpretation.

5. *De fato,* XV.

6. Lucretius, *De rerum natura,* II, 586f.

7. *On the Parts of Animals,* I, 641 a 11.

8. *Generation of Animals,* I, ch. 22, beginning.

9. See *VA* 160.

10. "Le cimetière marin," p. 149.

11. Rainer Maria Rilke, *Die Sonette an Orpheus,* in *Sämtliche Werke* (Frankfurt am Main: Insel, 2003), p. 731.

12. *Physics,* II, 192 b 18f.

13. Jean Charbonneux, *La sculpture grecque archaïque* (Paris: Editions de Cluny), p. 84.

14. *The Peloponnesian Wars,* VI, 18.

15. *Sophocle,* p. 26. T.N. Cf. *Sophocles,* p. 14. See ch. 5, n. 15 above.

16. *Le problème de l'être chez Aristote,* p. 441, no. 1.

17. Virgil, *The Aeneid,* book VI, line 851.

18. "A l'Arc de triomphe," in *Les voix intérieures, Œuvres poétiques* (Paris: Gallimard, Bibliothèque de la Pléiade, 1964), vol. 1, p. 465.

19. *Le Thomisme,* 5th ed. (Paris: Vrin, 1945), p. 120.

20. *Sophist,* 219b.

21. *Critique of Pure Reason,* A58/B83.

22. "Ebauche d'un serpent," in *Œuvres,* vol. 1, p. 146.

23. *Physique,* II, 193 b 19–20.

24. Saint Augustine, *Confessions,* ed. Labriolle, vol. II, p. 246.

25. Johann Wolfgang von Goethe, *Faust,* in *Sämtliche Werke* (Frankfurt am Main: Deutscher Klassiker Verlag, 1994), vol. 7, I, 3, p. 65.

26. Cited by Gilson, *La philosophie de saint Bonaventure* (Paris: Vrin, 1953), p. 149, n. 2.

27. See Gilson, *Introduction à l'étude de saint Augustin* (Paris: Vrin, 1969), p. 254, n. 1.

28. *Méditations chrétiennes et métaphysiques,* in *Œuvres complètes,* ed. H. Gouhier and A. Robinet (Paris: Vrin, 1967), vol. 10, XIX, 5.

29. *Summa theologicum,* I, q. 3, art. 3, Resp.

30. *Œuvres,* ed. C. Adam and P. Tannery (Paris: Vrin, 1983), vol. VII, p. 242.

31. See "Letter to Lucilius," LVIII, in Seneca, *Epistles 1–65,* trans. R. M. Gummere (Cambridge, Mass.: Loeb, 1917).

32. *Œuvres,* vol. II, p. 469.

33. *L'esprit de la philosophie médiévale,* vol. I, p. 93.

34. *Le Thomisme,* p. 119.

35. *L'esprit de la philosophie médiévale,* vol. I, p. 93.

36. *Generation and Corruption,* 323 a 20.

37. Antoine Augustin Cournot, *Considérations sur la marche des idées et des événéments dans les temps modernes* (Paris: Hachette, 1872), vol. 1, p. 44.

38. Horace, *Epistles* 2.1.156.

39. *L'esprit de la philosophie médiévale,* vol. I, p. 61.

40. *Immanuel Kants Werke* (Berlin: Cassirer, 1913), vol. IV, p. 362.

41. Valéry, *Variété* (Paris: Gallimard, 1936), vol. III, p. 174.

42. *HZW,* p. 342.

43. *Phenomenology of Spirit* (French translation), vol. I, p. 154 T.N. See *Phenomenology of Spirit,* trans. A. V. Miller (Oxford: Oxford University Press, 1977), pp. 110–111.

44. *Contra Gentiles,* I, 20.

45. In St. Augustine's sense (*Confessions,* II, 370): *Ecce Trinitas!*

46. *West-östlicher Divan,* book VI: "Hikmet Nameh," in *Sämtliche Werke* (Frankfurt am Main: Deutscher Klassiker Verlag, 1994), vol. 11.1.2, p. 61.

7. The Enigma of Z

1. *In metaphysicam Aristotelis,* ed. M. R. Cathala (Taurini, 1926), p. 382.

2. E.N. The importance of Rudolf Boehm's book, translated in French by E. Martineau, was signaled for the first time by J.-F. Courtine in "Schelling et l'achèvement de la métaphysique de la subjectivité" (in *Etudes Philosophiques* no. 2 [April–June 1974], p. 149, n. I, and above all pp. 158–170).

3. The phrases in double quotation marks in what follows have been transcribed exactly.

4. The fountain in question has, as is quite usual in the Black Forest, a hollowed-out tree trunk for a basin, into which the water falls from a horizontal arm that is carried by a vertical support, both sheathed in wood.

5. See *Seminare* (Frankfurt am Main: Vittorio Klostermann, 1988), p. 282.
6. *Le problème de l'être chez Aristote*, p. 460.
7. *Introduction à la philosophie de la mythologie* (Paris: Aubier, Montaigne Bibliothèque Philosophique, 1946), vol. II, p. 171.
8. "Le cimetière marin," p. 150.
9. In the Kröner edition of his *Werke*, vol. X, p. 217.
10. T.N. This is the translation of the poem that Albert Hofstadter offers in his translation of *The Origin of the Work of Art*, which first appeared in *Poetry, Language, Thought* (New York: Harper & Row, 1971).
11. To my knowledge, in Z the words *energeia* and *entelecheia* appear only three times.

8. Aristotle and Tragedy

1. T.N. Beaufret is, of course, referring to Nietzsche's *The Birth of Tragedy*, ed. M. Tanner, trans. S. Whiteside (London: Penguin, 1993).
2. *Confessions*, ed. and trans. Pierre de Labriolle (Paris: Budé, 1925–1926), vol. I, p. 120.
3. T.N. See Nietzsche's Notebook of summer 1883, in *Sämtliche Werke*, ed. G. Colli and M. Montinari (Berlin: de Gruyter, 1988), vol. 10, p. 425. "Was ist ihnen noch 'Erleben'? Wie Mücken sitzen die Ereignisse auf ihnen, ihre Haut wird noch zerstochen, aber ihr Herz weiß nichts mehr davon."
4. T.N. Beaufret seems to be referring to Heidegger's formulations in "What Are Poets For?" in *Poetry, Language, Thought*, trans. A. Hofstadter (New York: Harper & Row, 1971).
5. *Die Gestalt und das Sein* (Düsseldorf: Diederich, 1955), p. 67.
6. See Chateaubriand, *Mémoires d'outre-tombe*, 2 vols. (Paris: Bibliothèque de la Pléiade, 1996), and Baudelaire, *Critique d'art*, p. 116.
7. E.N. Beaufret passes over two words in this passage from chapter 49 of book II of *The Peloponnesian Wars*. He retains the reading in the Oxford edition of ἐλάμβανε instead of the ἐλάβετο that one finds in the Budé edition (*Les belles lettres*).
8. See Otto, *Mythos und Welt* (Stuttgart: Klett, 1962), p. 257.
9. E.N. In Aeschylus's *Prometheus* this is the moment when Prometheus begins to speak after the dialogue of Power and Hephaistos (see v. 88f.).
10. *Die Gestalt und das Sein*, p. 127.
11. *Trois réformateurs: Luther—Descartes—Rousseau* (Paris: Plon-Nourrit et Cie, 1925), p. 69.

Index

About the Authors

Jean Beaufret (1907–1982) was an important reader and translator of Martin Heidegger's work. He played a key role in Heidegger's reception in France and posed the questions to which Heidegger responds in his 1946 *Letter on Humanism*. The four volumes of *Dialogue avec Heidegger* were published between 1974 and 1985.

Martin Heidegger (1889–1975), who became famous for his theories of being and human nature, is considered one of the most original and influential philosophers of the twentieth century.

Mark Sinclair teaches at Manchester Metropolitan University.